Governments, NGOs and

The purpose of this book is to understand the rise, future, and implications of two important new kinds of 'integrity warriors' – official anti-corruption agencies (ACAs) and anti-corruption NGOs – and to locate them in the wider context and history of anti-corruption activity.

Key issues of corruption and anti-corruption are discussed in an integrated and innovative way through a number of country studies including Taiwan and South Korea, South East Europe, Fiji, Russia and the Baltic States. Some of the questions used to examine the development of new anti-corruption actors include:

- In what context were these born?
- How do they operate in pursuing their mission and mandate?
- How successful have they been in relation to expected results?
- To what extent are governmental and non-governmental actors aware of each other and how far do they cooperate towards the common goal of fighting corruption?
- What explains the shift in emphasis after the end of the Cold War, from national to international action?

Governments, NGOs and Anti-Corruption will be of interest to students and scholars of corruption, public policy, political science, developmental studies, and law.

Luís de Sousa is research associate at CIES-ISCTE, Portugal, and currently Gulbenkian Fellow at the Robert Schuman Centre for Advanced Studies/ European University Institute, Florence, Italy.

Peter Larmour is a Reader in Public Policy and Governance at the Crawford School of Economics and Government, Australian National University, Australia.

Barry Hindess is Emeritus Professor of Political Science at the Australian National University, Australia.

Routledge/ECPR Studies in European Political Science

Edited by Thomas Poguntke, University of Birmingham, UK, on behalf of the European Consortium for Political Research

The Routledge/ECPR Studies in European Political Science series is published in association with the European Consortium for Political Research – the leading organization concerned with the growth and development of political science in Europe. The series presents high-quality edited volumes on topics at the leading edge of current interest in political science and related fields, with contributions from European scholars and others who have presented work at ECPR workshops or research groups.

Also available from Routledge in association with the ECPR:

Governments, NGOs and Anti-Corruption

The new integrity warriors

**Edited by
Luís de Sousa, Peter Larmour
and Barry Hindess**

Routledge
Taylor & Francis Group

LONDON AND NEW YORK

Transferred to digital printing 2010

First published 2009
by Routledge
2 Park Square, Milton Park, Abingdon, Oxon OX14 4RN

Simultaneously published in the USA and Canada
by Routledge
270 Madison Avenue, New York, NY 10016

Routledge is an imprint of the Taylor & Francis Group, an informa business

Typeset in Times New Roman by
Taylor & Francis Books

British Library Cataloguing in Publication Data
A catalogue record for this book is available from the British Library

Library of Congress Cataloging in Publication Data
Governments, NGOs and anti-corruption : the new integrity warriors /
edited by Luís de Sousa, Peter Larmour and Barry Hindess.
    p. cm. – (Routledge/ECPR studies in European political science ; 55)
    Includes bibliographical references and index.
    1. Political corruption–Prevention. 2. Non-governmental organizations.
I. Sousa, Luís de, 1973– II. Larmour, Peter. III. Hindess, Barry.
    JF1081.G694 2008
    364.1′323–dc22
                             2008010888

ISBN 10: 0-415-46695-4 (hbk)
ISBN 10: 0-415-59961-x (pbk)
ISBN 10: 0-203-89197-x (ebk)

ISBN 13: 978-0-415-46695-0 (hbk)
ISBN 13: 978-0-415-59961-0 (pbk)
ISBN 13: 978-0-203-89197-1 (ebk)

To the memory of Véronique, for her friendship and courage

Contents

Illustrations

Figure

Tables

Contributors

Staffan Andersson is senior lecturer in political science at Växjö University, Sweden. He has been studying corruption since 1996 and contributed to several studies of corruption in Sweden, the UK, and Vietnam.

Frank Anechiarico is Maynard-Knox Professor of Government and Law. He is co-author (with James Jacobs) of *The Pursuit of Absolute Integrity: How Corruption Control Makes Government Ineffective* (1996). His latest project is a book on the relationship between ethics and the quality of performance in public management.

Matilda Dahl is a researcher and lector at the University College of South Stockholm in Sweden working on the project 'Baltic Sea States in a New Europe' and has recently published her PhD dissertation 'States under scrutiny: international organizations, transformation and the construction of progress' (2007).

Luís de Sousa is research associate at CIES-ISCTE, Portugal, and currently Gulbenkian Fellow at the Robert Schuman Centre for Advanced Studies/ European University Institute, Florence, Italy. He has been conducting basic and applied research on corruption control since 1996 and he has coordinated and participated in various national and international projects in this field.

Alan Doig is currently Council of Europe Resident Advisor on a public ethics and corruption project. Previously he was Professor of Public Services Management at the Teesside Business School where he specialized in public services and fraud/corruption management.

Christian Göbel is a researcher at the Institute of East Asian Studies, University of Duisburg-Essen, where he also teaches Comparative Politics and International Relations. He has done extensive fieldwork in Taiwan and China and he is currently finishing his dissertation on recent local government reforms in China.

Paul M Heywood is Dean of the Graduate School at the University of Nottingham, UK. He has published extensively on European politics and on corruption, including *Political Corruption* (ed. 1997). He is also editor of the international journal of comparative politics, *Government and Opposition*.

Barry Hindess is Professor of Political Science, Research School of Social Sciences at the Australian National University. He has published extensively on democratic theory and co-directed with Peter Larmour a three-year research project on 'Transparency International and the Problem of Corruption' funded by the Australia Research Council.

Peter Larmour is a Reader in the Policy and Governance programme at the Australian National University. He teaches master and training courses on corruption control, and has edited (with Nick Wolanin) *Corruption and Anti-Corruption* (Asia Pacific Press 2002). He coordinated a study of national integrity systems in 12 Pacific Island states for Transparency International.

Steven Sampson is associate professor of social anthropology at Lund University, Sweden. He is currently completing a study of anti-corruption initiatives with a focus on Transparency International. He has also done extensive fieldwork and consulting on democracy, civil society, and governance in the countries of southeast Europe.

Diana Schmidt-Pfister is a research fellow at the Institute for Intercultural and International Studies (InIIS) at the University of Bremen, Germany. She has researched extensively on anti-corruption efforts in post-Soviet countries as evidenced in her forthcoming book *Transnational Networks on the Ground* (Manchester University Press, 2008).

Daniel Smilov is a Professor in the Political Science Department at the University of Sofia and the Central European University, Budapest. He is also Programme Director at the Centre for Liberal Strategies, Sofia. His latest book is Daniel Smilov and Jurij Toplak (eds), *Political Finance and Corruption in Eastern Europe: The Transition Period* (Ashgate, 2007).

Foreword

Yves Mény, President of the European University Institute

The volume edited by de Sousa, Larmour, and Hindess sheds fresh light on the field of corruption politics, or rather on the less-explored area of anti-corruption strategies, policies, and groups. The authors are very conscious of the universality of corruption both in terms of time and space, but at the same time are slightly puzzled by the outburst of corruption over the past 20 years or so. It is difficult to find a convincing explanation capable of covering the multifaceted dimensions of this worldwide phenomenon. I will try myself to offer a few hypotheses which need to be empirically checked.

First, most attention is focused on corruption between public authorities and private persons and companies, and much less between private actors only. Corruption is primarily perceived as the violation of the red line separating public and private interests. If we accept this observation, it might be possible to infer that corruption is offered new opportunities when the relationship between state and market changes (which has dramatically happened recently). The more drastic the crossing of the line, the more sensitive the corruption issue. The hollowing out of the state and the corresponding rise of market values have offered a splendid opportunity for corruption because of the uncertainty about the respective roles of state and market. This is furthermore accentuated when the redefinition of rules, roles, and practices occurs abruptly, as has happened in Russia and China and in many developing countries.

A second hypothesis might be linked to the growing gap between formal rules and institutions on the one hand and values and principles on the other hand. A kind of vicious circle is developing: more and more institutions and practices are imposed rather than chosen by interested parties. Democracy and good governance are desirable objectives but they are also straitjackets imposed from outside by powerful actors (the US, the European Union, the former colonial powers, the international organizations). In many cases, while paying lip service to these beautiful concepts, political regimes lack the substantive understanding or practices that are at the heart of democracy and good governance. Corruption runs parallel to the formal rules. The vicious circle starts when the external mentors require further checks, controls, and punishment which in their turn offer further opportunities for cheating and misbehaviour.

A third hypothesis is related to the ongoing globalization process. Globalization as such should not be a factor of corruption. On the contrary, it favours transactions, opens new opportunities, increases competition, etc. However, the actual situation is a bit different given the huge imbalances and differences between actors in terms of power, influence, wealth, regulatory or fiscal constraints, etc. Corrupted actors play on a larger field using the facilities created by fiscal paradises, the cynicism of some politicians, the weakness of bureaucratic ethics in many countries, etc. In such a context, there is a big risk that competition characterized by such differences in rules and values ends up in a 'race to the bottom'.

International bodies might bark a lot; but they do not bite much. Paradoxically they have contributed to making corruption practices more sophisticated and complex. Most governments and large corporations wish to present themselves with clean hands to avoid negative perceptions at the international level. In practice, the music is different. The dirty job is done by local companies, offshore accounts, consultants and intermediaries. Hypocrisy has reached a climax, as recent 'affaires' testify. How is it possible for a company such as Siemens to claim it knows nothing of the use of hundreds of millions of Euros? How is it possible that the British government refuses any investigation into the BAE dealings involving Saudi Arabian rulers? How is it possible that so many billionaires have popped up in Russia and in the Third World in so few years? But globalization has also brought to the fore social and political movements that act globally as anti-corruption fighters. In principle, we should rejoice that international mobilization combining powerful networks with the use of modern technology and the media is directed against corruption practices. However the results are more problematic.

On one side of the coin there is the relative impotence or incapacity of these movements to seriously reduce the level of corruption. On the other side, we have to acknowledge that the anti-corruption organizations are a mixed bag of activists propped up by very different motivations and objectives. There are pure idealists who combat corruption whatever the consequences might be. There are others who have less pure ideals and use the anti-corruption motto as a tool to push elites out of power. This can be observed in many European countries, for example, where the anti-corruption stance has been a favourite of extreme-right or populist parties. If there is any common denominator between the otherwise extremely heterogeneous protest parties, it is the denunciation of corrupted elites. Populism has flourished with these anti-corruption campaigns and can be considered as one of the collateral damages inflicted on Western democracies.

In the developing countries, the pressures of the anti-corruption groups have neglected not only the local cultures and traditions which might have different views about the distinction between private and public, conflict of interests, and corruption – all concepts born out of the Western culture over centuries – but they have also imposed rules and regulations not sufficiently backed by the interested parties. This does not mean that anti-corruption policies should not be put in place. In fact, when it comes to deficient implementation, anti-corruption policies are not an exception. There is no chance that a policy can be fully implemented if it is not understood, accepted, and made their own by those who are supposed to put it in force. Most of the time anti-corruption policies conceived without prior and careful consideration of these implementation requisites have not only resulted in total failure, they have contributed to further destabilize fragile administrative and political systems. As the French put it, *le mieux peut être parfois l'ennemi du bien.*

Series editor's preface

Being against corruption is a bit like favouring sunshine over rain. Most people agree that corruption is a bad thing and should be avoided. However, this does not necessarily mean that all anti-corruption measures and all anti-corruption activists are necessarily benign and pursue exclusively uncontroversial goals. What is more, there are always unintended side effects, and even the most good-willing campaigner may eventually realize that their well-minded campaign has led to rather undesirable outcomes. This is, in a nutshell, the theme of the present volume which takes a sceptical look at the politics of anti-corruption around the globe. It focuses on anti-corruption activities by NGOs, government agencies, and international organizations like the World Bank, the United Nations or the OECD.

As the editors rightly point out in their introduction, the frequently used terminology of a 'war on corruption' invokes a claim to moral superiority that may, in some cases, not be without dangers for liberal societies. Furthermore, there is a general problem with the legitimacy of self-appointed campaigners for the common good – but this is clearly an issue all NGOs and (new) social movements share. They tend to benefit from a high level of public support if they choose a generally accepted cause. As a matter of fact, they are often regarded as morally superior compared to governments or, even more so, industry. Yet, they frequently receive large donations from international organizations, corporate donors, and national governments which may (in some cases) raise questions concerning their independence.

This volume addresses those and other questions by focusing on the shift from national anti-corruption activities to an internationalization of anti-corruption efforts which can, to a degree, be regarded as the inevitable consequence of the growth of global governance structures. How do national anti-corruption agencies (ACAs) and NGOs work and how do they interact? How successful are their efforts? And, importantly, what are the unintended (or intended) side effects of their activities?

Naturally, any discussion of these questions requires a clear conceptualization of corruption, which is a complex and multi-faceted phenomenon with different shades of grey indicating (rather than clearly marking) the boundary to legal and legitimate exchanges like lobbying.

Intimately related to these conceptual problems is the simple question whether corruption has indeed become more widespread. Alternatively, our impression that there is more corruption out there may simply be the result of an issue attention cycle. Furthermore, it may also partially be due to the activities of an 'anti-corruption industry' which aims at ensuring its organizational survival by drawing public attention to its cause – or, indeed, inflating it.

Clearly, this is not to say that anti-corruption activities should be regarded with principled suspicion, and the contributors to this volume are far from doing so. Nevertheless, they draw our attention to a range of highly relevant problems, including the inherently ambivalent nature of anti-corruption efforts. This is shown, for example, by the fact that they are often linked to wider campaigns for economic liberalism and representative democracy while the Communist parties of Vietnam and China, on the other hand, instrumentalize anti-corruption campaigns as a means to secure the control over state, economy, and society.

In addition, there are a number of undesirable side effects of anti-corruption campaigns which deserve more attention. They are likely to lead to additional layers of supervision which may limit the effectiveness of public administration because they inevitably involve the introduction of additional paper trails and sometimes cumbersome checks and controls. Daniel Smilov argues that there is a danger that excessive emphasis on anti-corruption breeds cynicism with economic and political elites in transition countries in Eastern and Central Europe. These are but two examples that show that a differentiated account of the politics of anti-corruption is appropriate. This extends also to the actors themselves who frequently thrive on the moral superiority that flows from being regarded as challengers to the established political machinery. Yet, as Steven Sampson forcefully argues, Transparency International is not a movement but a professional agency depending on donors, and a considerable share of the money comes from within the established political and economic machinery.

To be sure, a volume such as this cannot provide conclusive answers to all the questions raised, but it certainly represents an important stepping stone to improving our understanding of the complex nature of the politics of anti-corruption.

Thomas Poguntke, Series Editor
Bochum, May 2008

Preface and acknowledgements

Like many edited books, this one has a diverse and complex origin. At one level, it results from a research project on 'Transparency International and the Problem of Corruption' funded by the Australian Research Council and coordinated by Barry Hindess and Peter Larmour (both of the Australian National University) with the collaboration of Luís de Sousa (currently at RSCAS/EUI, Italy) who was Research Associate on the project in Canberra during 2004–05. We are very grateful to Peter Rooke of Transparency International, to his colleagues in TI Berlin, particularly Robin Hodess, and to participants at a TI AGM in Nairobi, who agreed to be interviewed for the project.

However, most of the book's contents derive from papers presented by the stimulating group of younger scholars and established authorities in the field of anti-corruption studies who joined us at two scholarly gatherings in the first half of 2006: *The International Anti-Corruption Movement*, coordinated by Luís de Sousa and Barry Hindess, Workshop 2 at the ECPR Joint Sessions in Nicosia 25–29 April 2006; and second, the international workshop *European Anti-Corruption Agencies: protecting the Community's financial interests in a knowledge-based, innovative and integrated manner* organized by Luís de Sousa, in collaboration with Peter Larmour, with the support from the Hercule Grant Programme of the European Anti-Fraud Office (OLAF) in Lisbon, 17–19 May 2006.

We are grateful to the Australian Research Council, the European Anti-Fraud Office, the Portuguese Foundation for Science and Technology, the Calouste Gulbenkian Foundation, and the British Council for their financial support, and to Dr Thomas Poguntke, coordinator of this Routledge series, for his encouragement and to Amelia McLaurin, Editorial Assistant in Politics and International Studies, for their support, and to Janet MacMillan for her wonderful job in copy-editing this work.

An earlier version of Chapter 1 appeared in *Third World Quarterly* (26(8), 2005), and parts of Chapter 8 are drawn from a paper in the Pacific Islands Policy Series published by the Pacific Islands Development Program at the East-West Center in Hawaii <http://www.eastwestcenter.org/publications/series/>.

We are grateful to the Editors of *TWQ* and the Pacific Islands Policy Series for permission to reproduce their material here.

Last, but not least, a special thanks to all the contributors for their interest and effort in helping us to put together this book. Without their precious contributions this collective work would have not been possible.

Abbreviations

ABA	American Bar Association
ABC	Australian Broadcasting Corporation
ACA	anti-corruption agency/agencies
ACC	Anti-Corruption Commission
ACMG	Anti-Corruption Monitoring Group
AGM	annual general meeting
AICPA	American Institute of Certified Public Accountants
AMM	Annual Members' Meeting (of TI)
AusAID	Australian Agency for International Development
BPI	Bribe Payers' Index
CBO	community-based organization
CEE	Central and Eastern Europe
CEO	chief executive officer
CIDA	Canadian Internation Development Agency
CLD	*Corporación Latinoamericana para el Desarrollo*
CPI	Corruption Perceptions Index
CPIB	Corrupt Practices Investigation Bureau
CPV	Communist Party of Vietnam
CSO	civil society organization
DANIDA	Danish International Development Agency
DFID	Department for International Development (UK)
DMP	Democratic Progressive Party
DNA	National Anti-Corruption Department (Romania)
DPP	Democratic Progressive Party (Taiwan)
DPPT	*Dirección de Planificación de Políticas de Transparencia*
EBRD	European Bank for Reconstruction and Development
ECPR	European Consortium for Political Research
ESCAP	United Nations Economic and Social Commission for Asia and the Pacific
EU	European Union
FCPA	Foreign Corrupt Practices Act
FDI	foreign direct investment
FICAC	Fiji Independent Commission Against Corruption

G8	Group of Eight (the G8 is an annual summit meeting that brings together the leaders of Canada, France, Germany, Italy, Japan, Russia, the United Kingdom, and the United States. In addition, the European Union participates and is represented by the president of the European Council and the President of the European Commission, but it cannot host or chair the forum)
GCR	Global Corruption Report
GNP	gross national product
GRECO	Group of States Against Corruption
GTZ	*Deutsche Gesellschaft für Technische Zusammenarbeit*
IACC	International Anti Corruption Conference
ICAC	Independent Commission Against Corruption (in various countries)
IG	Inspector General
IGO	international government organization
IMF	International Monetary Fund
INDEM	Information Science for Democracy
INGO	international non-government organization
IPSIG	Independent Private Sector Inspector General
ISO	International Organization for Standardization
JTInstitute	Jon Tönisson Institute
KICAC	Korea Independent Commission Against Corruption
KMT	*Kuomintang*
LAC	Latin American countries
LAWASIA	The Law Association for Asia and the Pacific
LDC	Less/Least Developed Countries
MC	Multinational Corporation
MENA	Middle East and North Africa
MJIB	Ministry of Justice Investigation Bureau
MOJ	Ministry of Justice (Taiwan)
MP	Member of Parliament
MSI	Management Systems International
NAK	*Natsional'nyi Antikorruptsionnyi Komitet*
NATO	North Atlantic Treaty Organization
NC	National Chapter (of TI)
NGO	non-governmental organization
NHS	National Health Service (UK)
NIS	National Integrity System
NLTB	Native Land Trust Board
NMSII	National Movement Simeon II (Bulgaria)
NORAD	Norwegian Agency for Development Cooperation
OCMPIC	Organized Crime and Money Politics Investigation Center (Taiwan)
OCTF	Organized Crime Task Force

OECD	Organisation for Economic Co-operation and Development
OLAF	European Anti-Fraud Office
OSCE	Organization for Security and Co-operation in Europe
PACO	Programme against Corruption and Organised Crime in South-Eastern Europe
PAM	Permanent Active Member (of TI)
PCAC	Presidential Commission on Anti-Corruption (Korea)
PHARE	Poland and Hungary: Assistance for Restructuring their Economies
PMU	Project Management Unit
PWD	Public Works Department
SDL	*Soqosoqo Duavata ni Lewenivanua* (United Fijian Party)
SFO	Serious Fraud Office
SIDA	Swedish International Development Cooperation Agency
SIS	Special Investigation Service (Lithuania)
SME	small to medium enterprises
SPAI	Stability Pact Anti-corruption Initiative
SRV	Socialist Republic of Vietnam
TAN	Transnational Advocacy Network
TI	Transparency International
TILAC	TI Latin American and Caribbean group
TI-S	TI Secretariat (Berlin)
TVR	Television Romania
U4	Group Utstein-group (initially (1999) composed of four development agencies MinBuZa (the Netherlands), GTZ (Germany), Norad (Norway), and DFID (UK). CIDA (Canada) and Sida (Sweden) joined in 2005, BTC (Belgium) in 2008)
UK	United Kingdom
UN	United Nations
UNCAC	United Nations Convention Against Corruption
UNDP	United Nations Development Programme
US	United States of Amercia
USAID	United States Agency for International Development
VDR	Vietnam Development Report
WB	World Bank
WEF	World Economic Forum

1 Introduction

Luís de Sousa, Peter Larmour and Barry Hindess

Few people will admit to favouring corruption.[1] In Europe, most people, when asked if they would bribe, vigorously condemn such conduct,[2] even if, in practice, many play along with it. In other policy areas, such as environmental protection or the war in Iraq, there are groups who are for or against. The case of corruption, in contrast, only attracts opponents.[3]

Western Europe has witnessed several waves of corruption scandals since the rebirth of democracies at the end of World War II: from the US aid scams during the reconstruction phase in the 1950s, through the corruption associated with the expansion of suburbs and the development of coastal resorts in the 1960s, to the bribery of Western European governmental officials by US airplane and arms companies in the 1970s. However none were lasting or led to major anti-corruption reforms or the creation of specialized anti-corruption bodies. The explosion of corruption scandals and anti-corruption reforms in post-Cold War Europe is unprecedented both in terms of scope and nature. The Western European press, magistrates, opposition party leaders, disaffected party members, populist movements, and non-government organizations all stood up 'against the arrogance and corruption of the elites' (Della Porta and Mény 1997).

In Eastern Europe, and Russia itself, the collapse of communism was accompanied by another explosion of international concern with corruption. Party rule and central planning had provided one set of opportunities for corruption. Party political competition and wholesale privatization provided opportunities for new kinds of corruption. There was a corresponding rupture or reversal in the ethical climate – favouring individual enterprise that had earlier been condemned – that left many people breathless, cynical, or feeling left behind. It was suddenly less clear what counted as 'corruption' and how much of it was going on.

The end of the Cold War affected perceptions of corruption in the developing world. Western countries became less reluctant to interfere in the domestic politics of countries that depended on them. Leaders of those countries could no longer threaten to seek Eastern bloc support. The World Bank coined the term 'governance' in relation to authoritarian rule in Africa and, during the 1990s, aid donors increasingly insisted on 'good governance' as a condition for foreign aid, loans, and preferential market access. There was also a liberalization of politics in South Korea and Taiwan, which had been on the anti-communist side of Cold War partitions. With democratic forms of politics came new concerns with corruption. Countries like Vietnam, where the Party still ruled, looked for new supporters among Western countries and international organizations.

Interest in corruption gained an international dimension through the signing of various international conventions and the emergence of a series of transnational actors. At the forefront was Transparency International (TI), a non-governmental organization (NGO) founded in 1993 by a group of disaffected international civil servants concerned about corruption in international business and foreign aid. TI initially met resistance, but its ideas have since been embraced by international organizations and aid donors, particularly the World Bank and the Organisation for Economic Co-operation and Development (OECD). It has also franchised the growth of national anti-corruption NGOs. Another set of domestic actors, of a governmental nature, grew in numbers and expanded from developing to developed countries: the anti-corruption agencies (ACAs) typified by Hong Kong's Independent Commission Against Corruption (ICAC). By the end of the 1990s, anti-corruption was on the agenda not only of national governments, but also of world and regional governance institutions. The European Union expects countries aspiring to membership to establish anti-corruption measures. A small industry of training and technical assistance has grown up to ensure compliance.[4]

Since they are seen as committed to eradicating an obvious evil, anti-corruption agencies and campaigns generally get favourable coverage. Here we take a more sceptical stance. While not (of course) favouring corruption, we are interested in the ways anti-corruption campaigns can be abused (or corrupted) to serve the interests of powerful groups, or have unintended consequences of other kinds. Frank Anechiarico, a contributor to this volume, was a pioneer of this critical approach and argued (with James Jacobs 1996) that the layers of supervision introduced after each new corruption scandal in New York severely limited the effectiveness of the bureaucracy. More recently, scholars in Eastern Europe, particularly Andras Sajó, who gave an edited collection on corruption the revealing subtitle 'A Sceptic's Handbook' (Kotkin and Sajó 2002), Ivan Krastev (2004), and Daniel Smilov (Tisné and Smilov 2004), another contributor to this volume, have raised questions about the negative consequences of donor-sponsored anti-corruption campaigns in Eastern Europe. Barry Hindess (in this volume) questions the doctrines of Transparency International, the pioneering anti-corruption NGO.

Another of our contributors Steven Sampson (2005) coined the phrase 'integrity warriors' to describe the new anti-corruption actors – government and non-government – that are the focus of analysis in this book. The term is slightly ironic in two ways that are important to our argument. The word 'integrity' suggests a condition in which there would be no corruption, so the term integrity warriors identifies those who are fighting to end it. Yet, there is disagreement about what such a society should look like and uncertainty about whether we could ever attain such a condition. Meanwhile we are faced with two all-too-real possibilities which might well coincide in practice: a 'policed society' might be possible – but at a high social cost – based on clean-up campaigns and selective or exemplary repression. A 'hypocritical society' is also possible and less costly, and would be based on feeding a scandalized public opinion with constant cosmetic reforms.

Sampson's word 'warriors' points to both campaigns and institutions, but also to the very real personal dangers faced by whistle-blowers and opponents of the nexus between politics and crime. TI rightly celebrates these brave individuals in an annual awards ceremony. Yet a 'war' may also be invoked to silence dissent and paint critics as traitors; it does not have to compete with other priorities for public attention and expenditure. The term can be used to suggest that everything possible must be done to ensure victory. It leaves no room for grey areas, relativism, or the rights of those accused, perhaps wrongly, of consorting with the enemy – in our case, corruption. Historically the 'war on corruption' has followed the 'war on drugs' as an international projection of US domestic policy (Woodiwiss 2006). In campaigns against money laundering it now dovetails with the equally open-ended, dissent-intolerant, 'war on terror'.

The purpose of this book is to understand the rise, future, and implications of two important new kinds of 'integrity warriors' – official anti-corruption agencies and anti-corruption NGOs – and to locate them in a wider context and history of anti-corruption activity. In what context were they born? What are their constitutive characteristics? How do they operate in pursuing their mission and mandate? How successful have they been in relation to expected results? To what extent are they aware of each other and how far do they cooperate with each other towards the common goal of fighting corruption? What explains this shift in emphasis, from national to international action, and from government ACAs to NGOs?

These are factual and pragmatic questions. The word 'corruption' also implies strong moral condemnation (Jos 1993). In the 1970s and 1980s, policy-makers tended to talk about 'controlling corruption'. Today corruption-talk has a more open-ended and moralistic tone of the kind that is characteristic of many social movements. 'Anti-corruption' became the buzzword of the 1990s. We can also observe a shift in emphasis from prosecution of individuals or incremental managerial adjustments to a more thoroughgoing and holistic reform of structures and processes of government that will, it is hoped, prevent corruption from ever taking place. What explains this shift in attitudes towards the phenomenon? Have moral arguments become more salient in campaigns?

Changes in the nature of corruption

Could the new politics of anti-corruption simply be a response to changes in the phenomenon itself, and thus to the fact that old approaches to controlling it are no longer enough? Mény and de Sousa (1999) suggest corruption may be changing in at least five ways:

The intensity of corruption

It is commonplace to say that corruption has become more visible, more widespread, more threatening to the functioning of democracy and the State. But is this intensity of corruption real or the product of sharpened perceptions? These perceptions are strongly shaped by the media, which tends to focus on the misdemeanours of senior politicians rather than lowly clerks. Perceptions vary according to the type of corruption, the status of the actors involved or unveiled, but not necessarily its volume.

Crime statistics are not a good guide. Penal frameworks have evolved. Enforcement agencies have been given more means and training. New agencies have been created and control frameworks reassessed. So corruption statistics tell us more about the effectiveness of a judicial system in dealing with this sort of criminal conduct than about the underlying volume of the conduct. The cases that are detected and condemned may be the tip of the iceberg. Or a population suspicious of government may believe there is more corruption than ever before. Even if it is difficult to find reliable indicators of the intensity of corruption, the importance of corruption to public debate can hardly be denied. If we had to choose the most influential issue in public affairs in the 1990s, corruption is likely to be on everyone's list – *la décennie de la corruption* as Mény defined it (1993: 19). In the early twenty-first century the intensity of concern has risen and involved more countries.[5]

The cyclical nature of corruption

While concern may be rising it could yet be part of a cycle of repression and toleration. Corruption is a dramatic policy issue with strong carrying capacity, determined in part by 'repeated bombardment of the public with messages of new symbols or events about corruption' (Frederickson 1993: 6), but there is no guarantee that such a rise in condemnation will endure. 'In many countries, we have witnessed long periods of systemic corruption followed by "clean-ups" that are in turn followed by other periods of corruption' (Bicchieri and Duffy 1997: 62).

Domestically, corruption seems to suffer from the same cyclical issue-attention as many other social problems. Following periods of increased concern about corruption, which leads to the passing or revising of control mechanisms, the issue of corruption is destined to lose intensity and enter hibernation until social forces mobilize it again. It is difficult, however, to determine what conditions lead citizens to become tolerant and lax about corruption. Some people may think that the most scandalous manifestations have been solved. Others may think that the issues at stake were after all not so problematic. Others again may become disillusioned or exhausted with campaigning. Once the issue drops from the public debate, political leaders feel consequently less pressured to reform. Public disinterest about corruption can be bliss to wrongdoers.

At the international level, however, the intertwined action of various governmental and non-governmental players may help to keep the issue on the agenda. This may have less to do with the strong carrying capacity of the issue itself, than with the fact that there is now a market for anti-corruption which needs constant feeding and care. What would happen to those UN, OECD, and World Bank (WB) anti-corruption departments and resource centres, and TI itself as the world's leading anti-corruption NGO should corruption cease to be a visible issue and a priority for state and market reforms? Merton (1940) alerted us to the tendency of organizations set up for particular purposes to suffer 'goal displacement' towards their own survival. There is an industry of anti-corruption which is conscious that its work and existence is contingent on the preservation of corruption as a priority issue.

The growing complexity of corruption

Today's corruption cannot be interpreted solely in terms of national criminal laws and penal codes. Heidenheimer (1989) distinguished *black* corruption – clearly defined, widely condemned, and prohibited by law – from those more *grey* transactions which have surfaced in many democracies in recent years, and whose definition tends to leave room for ambiguity, argument, and double standards. The complexity of today's corruption involves:

- *diverse actors*: multifaceted relations between active/passive, individual/collective actors of a different size and nature (such as municipal mayors, parties, companies, foundations, businessmen, magistrates, etc.). Moreover, it often involves what Thompson (1995: 7) calls 'institutional corruption' where the gain sought is political rather than personal. As an example, we might think of the dishonest American and British case for invading Iraq. Thompson notes that institutional corruption is often hard to distinguish from conventional political conduct;
- *complex exchanges*: the dyadic exchange of a bribe is typically the pinnacle of a long process of socialization and construction of social networks which serve as camouflage for the illicit pact. Support and complicity reduce the costs of the transaction and the need for explicit language (the players involved know their role, what is at stake, and play along) (Della Porta and Vannucci 1999: 78–92). Corrupt exchanges are not simply about the payment of money in exchange for favourable decisions, but a complex set of relations that help constructing a climate of opacity and *omertà*.

- *sophisticated mechanisms*: lobbying a local councillor for future public works contracts does not require the same degree of sophistication as lobbying a minister for the adoption of a particular market regulation. Whereas the former is still based on familiar and personal relations, the latter is impersonal and often done through multi-client networks of influence. The creation of phantom centres of study or foundations to process false accounting in order to launder political financing operations or the commissions paid to brokers in arms deals, require a greater sophistication than the petty bribe paid to a traffic police officer to avoid having a driving licence suspended. Some of these mechanisms, such as the use of slush funds, false invoicing, and offshore accounts, have contributed to the efficacy of corrupt transactions by making them more invisible than before.

The high profile and systemic nature of corruption

Recent decades show that there is more to corruption than sporadic and wrongdoing on the part of public officials: the so called 'rotten apples' theory. Corruption has a more systemic and organized nature and involves collective political actors – such as companies and parties – hitherto excluded from the penal interpretations of the phenomenon. Before, corruption might have resulted from undue pressure or the manipulation of bureaucratic instruments, policies, or procedures to the advantage of unscrupulous individuals. Today's corruption is characterized by a series of practices or behaviours that have become a way of life, a systematic and organized violation of the standards governing public as well as corporate life. It is about corrupt organizational cultures and organized (transnational) schemes to extract illicit rents.

The reported cases that cause considerable uproar in public opinion often involve prominent figures, such as leading politicians, senior officials, businessmen, magistrates, etc. It is no longer the petty bribe, but complex exchanges, involving a variety of single and collective actors, nationally and abroad, and large sums of money and other types of rewards that affect the mechanisms and distort the principles underpinning democracy and the rule of law. Practices such as illicit lobbying, political financing, insider trading, traffic of influence, etc., fall under this category.

The transnational nature of corruption

Governments have resorted to international initiatives as they attempt to overcome the insufficiency of traditional State sovereignty in confronting the complex and cross-border mechanisms of corruption. This 'shift in obsessions', as Krastev put it bluntly, 'has started to resemble the anti-slavery rhetoric' (2004: 1) to the extent that we can now ponder whether it is legitimate to talk about the emergence of a global anti-corruption movement.

However, this *prise de conscience* by national governments has not always resulted in effective action. At their core, anti-corruption campaigns are still nationally-oriented policies geared to safeguarding and enhancing the principles underpinning democracy and the rule of law, and which remain largely territorial or nation-based concepts. In practice, international instruments are but empty shells: beautiful declarations of principles and intentions that have to be implemented by potentially corrupt, indifferent, or incapable national agencies. The increased condemnation of corruption at the international level is mainly elite-based and shaped by contradictions (Larmour 2006). For the majority of citizens, especially in Europe, corruption as a transnational malaise still raises only minimal and ephemeral indignation.

These five transformations in the nature of corruption have pushed governments and societies in different countries to go beyond traditional institutional frameworks and strategies to combat it. Governments feel a growing need to pass a clear message to public opinion and world financial institutions about their intentions to boost detection and sanctioning mechanisms or, at least, to give the impression that they are doing so.

The politics of anti-corruption

Anti-corruption activity is not simply an ensemble of actors, initiatives, measures, and instruments. It is also a process of value change through which standards defining what is and what is not acceptable are continuously being challenged and revisited (de Sousa 2002). A number of different actors take part in that normative process. The media looks for a scandal that will sell newspapers or attract listeners and viewers. The incumbent party turns to an anti-corruption campaign to refresh its image, while the opposition tries to use it against them. Populists seek to conquer the heart and soul of the disillusioned electorate. The magistracy are sometimes driven by the conviction of the need to guarantee the ethical standards governing public life, but at other times use their intervention as a means towards a successful political career. All actors seek to extract some advantage from that widening gap between values and actions. Anti-corruption is not a neutral technical activity (de Sousa 2002).

While everyone is against corruption, they do not necessarily agree on what they are for. Concepts like 'integrity' and 'good governance' are frustratingly vague, but that vagueness serves to cover a profusion of political goals. Hence it permits unlikely alliances in the war on corruption. International organizations and NGOs are impatient with unfruitful 'theoretical debates' on what corruption amounts to. However, their pragmatism seems less secure when it comes to describing what a condition of non-corruption would look like. As Mark Philp (1997: 29) put it succinctly:

the term 'corruption' is not in itself problematic: it is rooted in the sense of a thing being changed from its naturally sound condition, into something unsound, impure, debased, infected, tainted, adulterated, depraved, perverted, etcetera. The problem arises in the application of this to politics. Definitional problems are legion because there is hardly a general consensus on the 'naturally sound condition of politics'.

For example, the World Bank and other donors explicitly link anti-corruption to other agendas of public-sector reform, privatization, and deregulation. Yet, many opponents of corruption, for example, among politcial leaders and NGO activists of developing countries, or in the transitional economies of Eastern Europe suspect the World Bank's version of a minimal state pro-viding the conditions for a free market. Hindess' chapter in this volume (Chapter 2), for example, links TI's campaigns to a broader 'neo-liberal' project of which he disapproves, without thereby condoning corruption.

What are they? Defining ACAs and NGOs

The distinction between an ACA and an NGO is partly a constitutional one. ACAs are set up under acts of a legislature or executive decree and staffed by public or civil servants. While typically many parts of the government have responsibility for dealing with corruption – managers of departments, a public service commission, or the police – a single agency focuses and dra-matizes a government's or society's concerns. There are arguments for and against a single agency approach, particularly in developing and transitional economies – arguments rehearsed in Doig's contribution to this book (Chapter 5). Constitutionally they are arms of the State.

NGOs are defined by what they are not: neither governmental nor profit-making, they are typically set up under legislation dealing with associations or companies. National traditions differ, and may even fail to recognize the possibility of an NGO. TI's founders affected not to know what an NGO was, and its secretariat is constituted under German law as an association while its national chapters constitute themselves under the legislation that happens to prevail in their country. National chapters are staffed by volunteers or staff on short-term contracts. Constitutionally, they locate themselves in 'civil society', a world of associations outside the State (on the one hand) and the bonds of family and tribe (on the other). This may be a small ground to stand on. And many NGOs, including TI, depend on government funding, perhaps indirectly through the foreign aid budget, or tax-exempt foundations.

When we look at functions, however, there is more overlap between ACAs and NGOs. Meagher (2004: 2) identifies six distinct functions carried out by the ACAs:

1. receive and respond to complaints;
2. intelligence-monitoring and investigation;
3. prosecution and administrative codes;
4. prevention research, analysis, and technical assistance;

5. ethics policy guidance, compliance review, and scrutiny of assets documentation;
6. public information education and outreach.

Several of these functions can and have been carried out by NGOs: receiving complaints, monitoring government activity, research analysis and technical assistance, public information education and outreach. Thus the distinctiveness of ACAs often lies in their access to the harder powers of the State – the right to conduct surveillance, interrogate suspects, make arrests, and mount prosecutions – which anti-corruption NGOs cannot aspire to. However, this does not imply that ACAs are more successful in reducing opportunity structures for corruption than their civil society counterparts. Their efficacy is often curtailed by lack of collaboration from conventional enforcement agencies which often do not welcome the creation of such distinctive institutional creature with special powers.

Table 1.1 identifies some similarities and differences between ACAs and NGOs in the field of anti-corruption.

The governance of anti-corruption

The distinction between 'governmental' and 'non-governmental' actors – ACAs and NGOs – is part of a broader distinction made in liberal societies between 'public' and 'private' concerns. It makes little sense in authoritarian political systems, though they may nevertheless be committed to reducing corruption among their officials – an extreme case being the SS's campaigns against corruption among its officers in the Nazi death camps. Thus in China or Vietnam, for example, the Communist Party rather than NGOs has sometimes taken up the role of public campaigner against official corruption.

Following this liberal distinction the World Bank defines corruption as 'the use of public office for private gain'. The boundary between the two sectors has shifted in processes of privatization during the downsizing of the welfare state in the West and transition to democracy in formerly socialist countries. A consequence of redrawing the boundary has been the increased visibility and self-organization of a third sector of non-government organizations, neither wholly public nor wholly private, with an ideology of the third way to justify it. A three-sector model distinguishes non-profit government and non-government organizations from a profit-motivated private sector, each embodying a set of fundamental principles of social organization identified by economic historians like Karl Polanyi (1944) as hierarchies, markets and communities.

Theorists of 'governance' noticed the interdependence of these three sectors and the increasing difficulty, in complex liberal societies, of deciding who is in charge. There used to be talk of 'iron triangles' in which legislators, bureaucrats, and private contractors were locked into a system of mutual backscratching and revolving-door careers. Now the links in what Rod Rhodes (1997) characterized as 'network governance' are made through

Table 1.1 The role of ACAs and NGOs in the fight against corruption: differences and similarities

	ACAs	NGOs
Context of formation	Post-World War II Although embryos of these institutional units can be traced back in time, in the form of parliamentary committees, inquiry committees, special police branches, anti-corruption leagues, the first anti-corruption agencies (ACAs) date from the postcolonial period in the aftermath of World War II: 1952, Singapore, Corrupt Practices Investigation Bureau; 1967, Malaysia, Anticorruption Agency; 1974, Hong Kong SAR, Independent Commission Against Corruption.	Post-Cold War
Scope	Domestic	Global and domestic
Functions	Investigation Prevention Education	Lobbying Awareness raising Reporting Education
Focus	Cases/targeted	Causes/diffused
Goals	Development, legitimacy, and modernization of the state	Development and quality of society, economy, democracy

Table 1.1 (continued)

	ACAs	NGOs
Driving standards	Legality Impartiality	Legitimacy Transparency
Professional skills	Law, public administration	Law, lobbying, media
Funding	State budgets, foreign aid budgets	Foreign aid budgets Foundations Subscriptions Fee for consultancy
Accountability	To executive or legislature or both	To members, potential members, sponsors, and potential sponsors
Performance criteria	Efficiency Effectiveness Probity Avoidance of scandal	Media hits Access to decision-makers Growth in funding and membership Avoidance of scandal

shared ideologies and there is a movement of personnel from NGOs into government, and back again. ACAs and NGOs may become linked in policy communities – or the advocacy coalitions invoked in Diana Schmidt-Pfister's chapter (Chapter 9) – serviced by academics (like ourselves) and supported by the private suppliers of training, trips, and equipment to both. The 'omnibus' anti-corruption programmes promoted by donors in Eastern Europe, and described in Daniel Smilov's chapter (Chapter 6), combine state and non-state officials, ACAs and NGOs. And Steven Sampson's theoretical approach in this volume (in Chapter 11) gives no particular privilege to sectoral affiliations of the actors playing various roles in the anti-corruption landscape: everyone plays their part.

TI talks in a 'governance' way of coalitions between public, private, and not-for-profit sectors and is funded by governments, foundations, and private companies (mostly governments). Its founders came from large international bureaucracies and were reluctant to see themselves as an NGO, with its connotations of noisy activism, unkempt appearance, and left-wing views. Its spirit is intergovernmental, particularly in its annual meetings with folkloric entertainments, lobbying for positions, and squabbles between national delegations. This sectoral ambiguity and coalitional ideology often distinguishes TI from more statist colleagues in ACAs who like to believe that the state is still in charge of society, and can regulate itself, and regulate the private sector, in accordance with some overarching view of national security or the public interest.

The focus of this collection is ACAs and NGOs – Sampson's new integrity warriors – and the relations between them. A 'governance' approach, however, also draws attention to a repressed third term, the private sector, which has corruption problems of its own (cf. Enron), as well as acting as a source of temptation for public officials and as an object of suspicion for many activist members of NGOs. Here, TI is particularly interesting in recasting the private sector as victim as much as perpetrator of corruption. Before TI's existence, Klitgaard's (1988) anti-corruption doctrine invoked the private sector as a potential partner for reforming officials, such as the controller of customs who seeks the support of shipping agents against the petty corruption of customs officers. Anti-corruption's valuation of the private sector is part of a broader neo-liberal suspicion of state activity in general, and suspicion of the motivations of state officials in particular. But in valuing interactions and interdependence between sectors it downplays the classical liberal concern with drawing the line between public and private, and nineteenth century concerns to separate politics from administration.

The comparative approach/transfer/lesson-drawing

The main focus of the collection is Europe, though chapters range to include the US, several African countries (in Doig's chapter, Chapter 5), Vietnam, Fiji, Taiwan, and South Korea.

The collection is comparative in several senses. First, comparison draws attention to what otherwise may be taken for granted. In country A it may be taken for granted that police will be corrupt. Comparison with country B, where police corruption is rare, shows that reform may be possible.

Second, comparison suggests alternatives. Hong Kong and Singapore are often taken as examples of success in anti-corruption measures. Hong Kong's ICAC model is often copied, but Singapore's CPIB (Corrupt Practices Investigation Bureau) may provide an alternative model. The practical consequence of this kind of comparison is lesson-drawing and policy transfer, such as in the donor-sponsored anti-corruption campaigns in Eastern Europe, Africa, and the Pacific Islands (Michael 2004b, Larmour 2005).

Third, comparison may be a substitute for experiment. Natural scientists can carry out experiments to identify the effect of different factors on a particular outcome. Social scientists have to make do with what they find, but the variety of actual countries provides them with a sort of natural experiment. However the small number of countries compared in the following chapters is not enough to draw statistically significant conclusions about cause and effect.

Nor are the countries sufficiently independent of each other to act as experiments. They borrow from neighbours, and are equally affected by supranational organizations, like the EU, or supranational tendencies, like globalization. Most of the countries compared are in Europe, or its regions, like the Baltic or Eastern Europe. Background similarities can make comparison easier – the more similar cases are, the more their differences stand out. Why, for example, does Baltic state A have a lively NGO sector, and Baltic state B not? Might it be related to another obvious difference, such as religious affiliation or historical relationship with Russia? But comparison need not only be between similar systems. A relationship between religious affiliation and NGO activity in countries otherwise quite different may also be convincing. Hence the experience of Taiwan, Korea, and Vietnam is relevant to Europe, in spite of obvious 'cultural' differences, and particularly if we are interested in the effects of democratization (and democratic reversals, as in Fiji). The least comparative chapters are those on the US and Russia, but both countries have been influential models for other countries, often coercively. The US often defines itself by its exceptionalism. Russia has been a deliberate borrower of foreign ideas since Peter the Great. Both have been involved in exporting ideas about anti-corruption: the former was a pioneer in the criminalization of the bribery of foreign officials, while the latter was an exporter of a socialist model that gave the Communist Party a role in supervising the bureaucracy, as in Vietnam, and did not recognize much space for NGOs.

The chapters in this book are comparative in these several ways. They help the reader understand her own country more clearly, by showing how things can be done differently. They describe alternatives that may be adopted in other countries and also show the problems of borrowing, exporting, or insisting on anti-corruption reforms as a condition of membership of the EU. The chapters are also somewhat comparative in the third 'experimental' sense.

Comparison between similar and different countries may suggest hypotheses about the relationship between anti-corruption and democratization; about the transferability of anti-corruption; about the relationship between liberalism and anti-corruption; and about the relationship between government agencies and NGOs. The chapters also show the effect of overarching supranational institutions (the EU, the World Bank) and processes (transition, transfer, and globalization) in reducing variation between national cases.

The chapters

The chapters in this volume fall into three broad groups. The first three locate the global war against corruption in wider campaigns for economic liberalism and representative democracy. The campaign against corruption is also a campaign for a particular view of 'good governance'. All three take a critical perspective on this overlapping agenda. In Chapter 2, Hindess suspects that anti-corruption campaigns, like those promoted by the NGO Transparency International, serve the less obvious purpose of promoting neo-liberal values of competition and individual responsibility. Andersson and Heywood's chapter (Chapter 3) wonders when well-intentioned current approaches to understanding and fighting corruption can actually constitute a risk to democracy and democratic stability by displacing discussions of policy and creating cynicism and disillusionment among voters, or, in authoritarian settings, being used to cement non-democratic rule. Anechiarico's chapter (Chapter 4) unfolds the assumptions about ethics and official integrity that underlined the reforms prescribed and implemented by the American Progressives, and shows how ingrained in the American political culture were these beliefs about the distribution of power. His chapter also suggests how American progressivism has influenced the definition of the international anti-corruption agenda through various public administration reforms promoted and sponsored by the Bretton Woods institutions.

The next group of chapters looks comparatively at the structure and functioning of government anti-corruption agencies and the effects of international pressure and national democratization on them. Doig (in Chapter 5) reflects on the track record of anti-corruption agencies sponsored by international organizations in developing and transition economies, He identifies the conditions that have determined why some have succeeded and others have failed. Smilov (in Chapter 6) considers why government politicians in south-east Europe have – perhaps surprisingly – decided to embrace the model of an investigatory and prosecutorial anti-corruption agency in place of the 'toothless' programmes earlier promoted by donors. He notes the institutional interests behind different definitions of corruption, and shows how government politicians have an interest in creating and controlling what he calls 'discourse coalitions' that co-opt potential adversaries among the NGO community, the media, police, and prosecutors. An agency focusing on narrowly defined illegal acts of corruption satisfies these various interests. Göbel (in Chapter 7) offers another comparative perspective on anti-corruption activity, but in a different region. He is interested in the effects of democratization on anti-corruption campaigns and institutions, and the chapter looks at the different ways that Taiwan and South Korea tackled corruption as they became more democratic. Larmour's chapter (Chapter 8) looks at the role that anti-corruption has played in the reversal of democratization by *coup d'état* in Fiji. While invoking the donor rhetoric of 'good governance' a military clean-up showed many of the hallmarks of populist campaigns elsewhere, including purges of the civil service, public humiliations, bashing of civilians, semi-official tribunals, and appeals for Moral Rearmament. The clean-up also created dilemmas for the local branch of TI.

The last group of chapters turn away from governmental institutional approaches against corruption to look closely at the role of emerging anti-corruption NGOs, particularly TI. Each chapter puts the NGOs in a different theoretical framework. Schmidt-Pfister (in Chapter 9) investigates transnational advocacy networks in campaigns against corruption in post-Soviet Russia, and points to the variety of local actors and the complexity of relations between them and the national government. Dahl (in Chapter 10) examines the work of TI in the Baltic States. She sees external scrutiny and accounting as part of a process by which new states become institutionalized. Sampson (in Chapter 11) considers the motley combination of official and unofficial actors that constitute the anti-corruption movement in southeastern Europe. He uses the metaphor of an 'anti-corruption landscape' with its distinctive actors and scenery. De Sousa concludes by explaining how TI contributed to the spread of the anti-corruption doctrine through a process of franchising national chapters. It came to assume a central role in international as well as domestic anti-corruption initiatives, despite its own internal governance tensions.

Notes

1 In much of the world it is not hard to find people who defend conduct that outsiders, like TI and the World Bank, call corrupt, perhaps by insisting on cultural specificity and distinguishing, in Rose-Ackerman's terms (1999: 5), between a bribe and a gift, but few defend what they themselves see as corrupt.

2 Second round of the European Social Survey (ESS2–2004), Rotative Module on Economic Morality in Europe (coordinated by Susanne Karstedt), and International Social Survey Programme, Module on Citizenship 2004.

3 As Steven Sampson (2005: note 2) puts it 'there are no pro-corruption forces'. Corruption may be organized, but it has no spokesmen or lobby groups acting on its behalf.

4 Declaring an interest, one of us (Larmour) has been a member of TI since 1997 and coordinated its National Integrity Systems studies of the Pacific Islands (Larmour and Barcham 2006).

5 TI's 2003 corruption barometer shows that in three out of four countries surveyed, people overwhelmingly identify political parties as the area from which they would most like to see corruption removed (Transparency International 2003c: 13).

Part I

Theories and concepts

Corruption, anti-corruption, and democratic politics

2 International anti-corruption as a programme of normalization

Barry Hindess

On 13 January 2004, Transparency International's 'Daily Corruption News' carried an Associated Press report – 'Bush signs proclamation against corruption' – saying that the US was taking steps to prevent corrupt individuals from travelling in the United States. The previous day, the President had approved a decree barring public officials accused of corruption from entry into the US. The decree appeared to be aimed especially at public officials from Latin America. It was issued in the lead-up to the Summit of the Americas in Monterrey, Mexico, at which US proposals on corruption were denounced by several delegates who were unhappy at being told by the US about what to do about corruption. A few days later, the President's special envoy for Western Hemisphere affairs told a conference of Panamanian business leaders that Washington had 'declared a war on corruption, similar to the one being waged against terrorism' (*Agence France Presse*, 22 January 2004). The US Attorney General, John Ashcroft, said in Davos that 'we need to expand our efforts to fight corruption'. Ashcroft insisted that what particularly concerned him was not the kind of corporate malfeasance that had led to major scandals in American and European corporations like Enron, Tyco, and Parmalat; rather he urged that official corruption, a 'contagion that cannot be contained by borders', be combated through strong political leadership, cooperation and transparency (*International Herald Tribune*, 23 January 2004).

There is a display of arrogance here which is as monumental, in its way, as the Grand Canyon and other impressive natural phenomena that we have come to associate with the US. A campaign against official corruption in other independent states is mounted by officials of one of the most corrupt political systems in the Western world, and moreover by the administration of a President who came to power in the 2000 election only through what, on almost any definition, must be regarded as flagrant official corruption in Florida, a state governed by his brother. In practice, as we might expect, the rhetoric of these various pronouncements gives a misleading impression of the purpose of this US campaign. The detail of Bush's proclamation makes it clear that the campaign is directed less at combating corruption in general than at cases of corruption that have a 'serious adverse' effect on US business, US foreign aid programmes, the security of the US against trans-national crime and terrorism, or the political stability of democratic nations and institutions (*Associated Press*, op. cit.). If we place its specifically American characteristics to one side, however, the story also illustrates two central planks of the international anti-corruption movement: the claim that the problems posed by corruption are especially serious in developing rather than advanced countries, and the decision to focus primarily on corruption in the public rather than the private sector.

More importantly for our purposes, the selective focus of the US campaign strongly suggests that, like so many features of public life, international anti-corruption is not what it seems, and that behind its apparent objectives lies another, rather more complex, policy agenda. This chapter aims to support this perception and to consider how we might think about the international campaign against corruption. Much of my discussion focuses on the work of Transparency International (TI), an international non-government organization based in Berlin, which is now the major international agency concerned specifically with combating corruption. Like other international agencies, TI is an active sponsor of research on corruption. Yet, apart from a short account by one of its founders (Galtung 2001), it has yet to be studied in its own right – unlike the much larger World Bank (Caulfield 1997, Gilbert & Vines 2000) and the International Monetary Fund (IMF) (Blustein 2001, Harper 1998).

TI's situation in this respect reflects a more general pattern in the literature on corruption. If corruption is regarded as an urgent practical problem, then anti-corruption activities will tend to be seen as a matter of more or less successful responses to this problem. This perception suggests that the most important issues relating to corruption are the incidence of corruption itself and the effectiveness of various attempts to deal with it. In focusing on anti-corruption, our aim is not to deny the significance of these issues, but rather to suggest, along with a growing critical literature, that anti-corruption activity in the international arena has grown to such an extent that it has become an important object of study in its own right. This focus reinforces my initial suggestion that there may be more to international anti-corruption activity than a simple response to the problem of corruption.

This chapter begins with a brief discussion of TI and its place in the international anti-corruption movement. It then shows that TI's anti-corruption strategy cannot be understood simply in its own terms. While its commitment to combating corruption is undeniable, TI's preferred strategy reflects a more complex international agenda. My final section suggests that TI's activities and the wider anti-corruption movement can be seen as contributing to a broadly liberal programme of government aimed at regulating the conduct of states and actors within them, and that international anti-corruption bears a striking resemblance to an earlier programme of normalization which operated over independent states through the instrument of 'capitulations'.

TI and national integrity systems

The latter part of the twentieth century saw striking changes in governmental perspectives on corruption: *first*, a tendency to treat corruption and its consequences in economic terms; *second,* a shift in the perceived relationship between corruption and development; and *third*, the internationalization of the problem of corruption. TI can be seen both as symptom of this changing understanding of corruption and as influential in taking it further, complementing its international diplomatic activity with the activism of its national chapters. It was founded in 1993 specifically to campaign against corruption, which is understood as 'the misuse of entrusted power for private benefit' (TI 2000: 1). While TI has close links with major aid donors and international financial institutions, which locate their own anti-corruption efforts within a broader programme of 'good governance', it remains distinctive in presenting corruption as its primary focus. TI's role in the internationalization of the problem of corruption means that it is also an agent in the growth of what is sometimes called 'international civil society'. Its rise reflects an increasing willingness on the part of the international community – the major Western states and the agencies that they effectively control – to insist that concerns about national sovereignty or cultural difference should not excuse failure to adhere to universal standards of economic liberalization, human rights, and good governance.

TI originally defined corruption as the use of public office for private gain. It later adopted the more expansive definition noted above: 'the misuse of entrusted power for private benefit'. It explained this shift as taking account of privatization and the growth of private monopolies in the supply of formerly public services, such as water and electricity (TI 2000, Chapter 1). The initial definition certainly covers an important aspect of what is commonly regarded as corruption in the public sphere. Yet it is doubtful whether it is able to capture the range of corruptions involved in, for example, the practice of police brutality and its condoning by public authorities, the Singapore government's use of the courts to silence its political opponents, or dubious elections in, say, the US and Zimbabwe. TI's initial understanding of corruption thus involves a selective focus whose provenance needs to be investigated. The somewhat later definition cited here retains the earlier focus on the misuse of power for private gain but, following major business scandals in the US and elsewhere, TI now acknowledges that problematic conduct in the private sphere may sometimes have considerable public significance. Since this redefinition appears to open private sector activity to anti-corruption scrutiny, it also suggests issues for further investigation.

TI's perspective on the problem of corruption exhibits the two central planks noted earlier. First, like other international agencies, TI takes the view that corruption is everywhere. 'Yet', its Source Book tells us, 'if matters are serious in the industrialized countries, they are in crisis in much of the developing world and in countries in transition' (TI 2000: 1). Second, as we have seen, TI now recognizes that corruption may appear in the private sector as much as in the public sector. Corruption 'strikes at the heart of the market economy, distorting decision-making, and rewarding the corrupt and manipulative rather than the efficient and the productive' (TI 2000: 2). The Source Book nevertheless continues to treat 'corruption' as involving 'officials in the public sector [who] ... enrich themselves, or those close to them, by the misuse of the power entrusted to them' (TI 2000: 2). The Source Book appeared in 2000, before the most recent wave of corporate scandals in the US. TI has since acknowledged that there may be significant 'weaknesses in governance structures in the private sector' (TI 2002a: 1).

TI describes official corruption as having a range of damaging economic and social effects: raising the costs of goods and services, reducing productivity, contaminating the environment in which the private sector operates, increasing a country's debt-servicing costs, damaging public respect for constituted authority, and threatening 'the viability of democratic institutions' (TI 2000: 3). Corruption is thus presented as a major threat to both economic development and the legitimacy of government.

Finally, and again like other international agencies, TI regards legalistic and punitive approaches – such as those adopted by Hong Kong's Independent Commission Against Corruption (ICAC) and Malaysia's Anti-Corruption Agency or laid out at length in the recent UN Convention against Corruption – as of limited value in reducing corruption (Kaufmann 2003). First, such programmes often target corruption in areas that are politically unproblematic 'at the expense of addressing more difficult and challenging areas' (TI 2000: 34). We shall see that this charge might also be directed against TI's preferred strategy of building coalitions. Second, 'the broader societal context' conditions the impact of anti-corruption policies (TI 2000: 12). TI argues for reform of the societal context itself and 'a practical framework of checks and balances for averting the damage which corruption causes to the public interest, and for fostering an environment in which the quality of official decision-making is heightened' (TI 2000: 12). The reference to 'checks and balances' here invokes the classic liberal alternative to top-down or bottom-up systems of control. Such vertical systems, TI argues, should be complemented by 'horizontal accountability' 'in which power is dispersed, where none has a monopoly, and where each is separately accountable' (TI 2000: 33).

To be effective, in other words, anti-corruption agencies require a broader institutional framework for promoting and maintaining good government. TI's major contribution to the good governance agenda has been the idea of a National Integrity System (NIS) (TI 2000: 36):

> Picture, if you will, a 'National Integrity System' as being rather like a Greek Temple: a temple with a roof – the nation's integrity, supported at either end by a series of pillars, each being an individual element of the

National Integrity System. At one end … are the institutional pillars –
the Judiciary, the Parliament, the Auditor-General's Office, the
Ombudsman, free media, civil society and the like. At the other end …
[are] the core tools which the institutions must have at their disposal to
be effective … Resting on the roof are three round balls: 'quality of life',
'Rule of Law' and 'sustainable development'. … it is crucial that the
roof be kept level if these three round balls and the values they encompass are not to roll off. The 'temple' itself is built on and sustained by
foundations which comprise public awareness and society's values.

The metaphor is intended to reflect the interdependence of the various
components of the NIS. The Source Book elaborates the implications of this
view, noting, for example, that if one pillar weakens its load will fall on the
others. There will be trade-offs to accommodate the variation across societies
in the strength of individual pillars. In Singapore, the Source Book notes,
'comparative lack of press freedom is compensated for by an intrusive anti-
corruption bureau' (TI 2000: 36). However, if several pillars weaken, the roof
will tilt and '"sustainable development", "Rule of Law" and "quality of life"
will roll off, crash to the ground and the whole edifice collapse into chaos'
(TI 2000: 36).

I conclude this section by noting important features of the NIS framework
which are taken up in the remainder of the paper. *First*, the image of a
classical Greek temple with modern institutional pillars – judiciary, parliament, Auditor-General, etc. – to safeguard societal rectitude is a curious one
to use in this context: it appeals to both the traditional sources of a distinctly
Western culture and a modern Western institutional framework. This suggests that adoption of such a framework is the answer to the problem of
corruption (Brown 2003: 19). The related image of an edifice collapsing into
chaos carries this suggestion further, implying that without this framework a
society cannot hope to survive. Where the World Bank uses the problem of
poverty to legitimate its good governance initiatives (Rojas 2004), TI uses
the problem of corruption to promote a major programme of societal
reform. *Second*, alongside the institutional pillars listed above, the Source
Book identifies two further pillars: 'the private sector' and 'international
actors'. Both are interesting, although for rather different reasons. The location of the private sector as a pillar of NIS, not an area that should be subject to its oversight, reflects a presumption of many international agencies
that a properly organized private sector possesses its own capacity for self-
regulation (Brown 2003: 13, cf. Jayasuriya 2002). As for the place of international actors, we might note the negative reactions of Western states to
any suggestion that their own integrity required the intrusion of international
agencies in what amounts to a tutelary role.

Finally, TI's own anti-corruption activities eschew campaigns against
individuals suspected of corruption, in favour of building coalitions between
government agencies, NGOs, and the private sector designed to prevent such

cases of corruption from occurring. The political assumptions underlying this approach are certainly worth exploring. Consider, for example, the claim that the lack of press freedom in Singapore '*is compensated for* by an intrusive anti-corruption bureau' (TI 2000: 36, emphasis added). First, the restriction of press freedom might itself be seen as a clear case of what Dennis Thompson calls 'institutional corruption' in which the gain is political rather than personal (1995: 7). This kind of corruption is hardly something that can be compensated for by a crackdown on corruption in other areas. Second, the claim strongly suggests that this last issue is best avoided, that the NIS framework is designed to enable anti-corruption activities to develop and take root without needing to directly confront powerful individuals and political forces. We may recall that this is the charge that TI raises against the approach of official anti-corruption agencies. Precisely because it avoids dangerous targets, the NIS approach might also be seen as allowing corruptions of the well-connected to continue unchecked. It thus has distributional effects which need to be weighed against the anticipated benefits of reducing the incidence of (certain kinds of) corruption. We should also note that the building of such coalitions shifts the focus away from the issue of dealing with bad individuals and/or bad practices to the very different issue of societal reform – in this case of changing the social context in which such individuals and/or practices are able to flourish.

In the name of anti-corruption

TI's programme of building coalitions between government agencies, NGOs, and the private sector represents a project of large-scale social engineering (Lindsey & Dick 2002: vi). TI presents this as the only effective means of fighting corruption and achieving the broader societal outcomes that widespread corruption continues to undermine. Narrowly-focused anti-corruption drives may produce short-term gains, but, TI suggests, their impact is ultimately conditioned by the broader context in which they occur. This section presents a critical examination of TI's rationale for its anti-corruption drive. I argue that while there are cases in which corruption poses an urgent practical problem, it is not significant in the way TI suggests and, further, that its proposed remedy does not address the problem it describes.

The suggestion that anti-corruption practices are likely to have limited success is hardly new. David Kennedy (1999), for example, argues that the anti-corruption movement's moralizing stance stigmatizes much of the developing world (cf. Sajo 2002). This is an obstacle to effective anti-corruption practice because it provokes resistance far beyond the direct beneficiaries of corrupt practices. The implicit message of the examples used in the TI Source Book, that only countries that adopt a Western institutional framework have a hope against the destructive impact of corruption, is a striking example. TI's strategy of building coalitions goes only a small way towards overcoming the resistance that this is likely to provoke.

Or again, Tim Lindsey and Howard Dick argue, focusing on Indonesia and Vietnam, that 'good governance' reforms cannot succeed unless they also tackle the power of major vested interests – which is, of course, ruled out by the coalition-building strategy. The real puzzle, they suggest (Lindsey and Dick 2002: vi–vii), is: 'Why are international agencies, donors, and NGOs continuing so strongly to push a new reform agenda that cannot achieve its objectives?' After canvassing a range of motivations which might keep activists and agencies going in the face of disappointing results they conclude with the conventional call for further research: '… more might be achieved sooner by much better understanding of political, legal, commercial and social dynamics'.

There is much to be said for such critiques but they nevertheless offer a limited view of the anti-corruption movement itself. As noted in my opening discussion, the apparent urgency of the problem of corruption supports the view that the really important issues in this area concern the incidence of corruption and how best to combat it. This results, with few notable exceptions, in failure to take anti-corruption seriously as an object of study.

Our focus, in contrast, on anti-corruption itself suggests a different answer to Lindsey and Dick's question: why do the agencies support an 'agenda that cannot achieve its objectives?' Such phenomena are not uncommon in the public policy area. We need only think, for example, of the resources poured into Prohibition, and the US wars on drugs and terror. Such programmes clearly serve a range of symbolic purposes and the fact that they have little chance of achieving their headline objective is not the point. Part of the reason anti-corruption agencies keep going is that their activities are not focused only on combating corruption. In addition to their symbolic functions, they also reflect a broader programme of governmental reform.

Corruption as a threat to legitimacy

We begin our discussion of this last point by noting that TI and other international agencies involved in anti-corruption have focused on limited areas of corruption. In this respect, TI's 2004 Global Corruption Report, with its special focus on political corruption, marks an important shift. The Report defines political corruption as 'the abuse of entrusted power by political leaders for personal gain, with the objective of increasing power or wealth' (TI 2004b: 11). While the phrase, 'misuse of entrusted power' covers a range of concerns, the qualification 'for personal gain' narrows the field, leaving no room for the problem of 'institutional corruption' noted earlier in which the gain is 'political rather than personal'. We might think, for example, of the massaging of intelligence reports by the American, British, and Australian governments in the lead up to their invasion of Iraq in 2004. The abuse of entrusted power in this case was aimed not primarily at increasing the wealth of political leaders but at promoting a widely contested policy decision.

In his discussion of this issue, Thompson acknowledges that institutional corruption is 'closely related to conduct that is a perfectly acceptable part of political life' (Thompson 1995: 7). Yet there is a more important point to be noted here. If the line between corrupt and acceptable conduct is hard to discern, then its location will be contested. This is my second point: what counts as corruption on TI's definition depends on how 'misuse of entrusted power' is itself identified – in terms of administrative or legal norms, duties of public office, or broader public expectations. There are problems with each of these, as Mark Philp's careful analysis (1997) has shown, but all draw, implicitly or explicitly, on the notoriously contestable idea of the public interest. We might expect, for example, professional politicians, public servants, and those who have privileged access to them to take a more relaxed view of what is acceptable than the rest of the community.

In practice TI, and other international anti-corruption agencies, are likely to argue that it is more important to deal with the causes and consequences of corruption and work out how to bring it under control, and that we need a pragmatic definition which can be modified as circumstances develop. As noted earlier, this view draws on the perception that corruption is an urgent practical problem in many countries because of its consequences for economic growth and political legitimacy. The contestable character of the concept of corruption is particularly relevant to the second of these concerns.

This impatience with problems of definition reinforces my earlier point about TI's strategy of building coalitions between government agencies, NGOs, and the private sector. Failure to address the contested character of the public interest or the misuse of entrusted power enables TI to promote a range of anti-corruption activities without having to confront powerful individuals and political forces. We have seen that this strategy risks allowing corruptions of the well-connected to continue. It also allows ruling groups to determine what is to count as the misuse of entrusted power.

Legal and administrative definitions of appropriate conduct cannot resolve this issue since, if corruption is widely accepted as part of the way things are done, legal and administrative protocols will adapt accordingly. 'The law itself', Philp observes, 'can originate in corrupt practices: that an act is legal does not always mean that it is not corrupt' (1997: 25). TI's own Global Corruption Barometer shows that, in three countries out of four, political parties are the institution from which people would most like to have corruption removed. Since the rules under which parties operate are generally established by the major parties themselves they will normally take a more limited view of corruption in this area than many in the broader population (Hindess 2004a). If corruption is a threat to the popular legitimacy of government, then the strategy of building coalitions between government, NGOs, and the private sector is unlikely to address the problem.

Corruption and economic growth

However, TI's more important case for the urgency of tackling corruption concerns its consequences for economic growth: corruption 'strikes at the heart of the market economy, distorting decision-making, and rewarding the corrupt and manipulative rather than the efficient and the productive' (TI 2000: 2). That corruption distorts markets and rewards the unproductive is the common currency of neo-liberal discourse (e.g. Kaufmann 1997), and suggests that, other things being equal, corruption will lower the general welfare of the population. Yet such *a priori* accounts tell us nothing about the importance of corruption relative to other problems affecting the economy in particular national economies. The sense of urgency in the Source Book's discussion comes from neither these general propositions nor hard evidence about the relative impact of corruption; rather it reflects the claim that 'corruption is deepening already indefensible levels of extreme poverty' (TI 2000: 2), and especially the image of striking at the heart of the market economy. TI's Source Book supports this view with anecdotal evidence – a side bar on page 5 carries the heading 'Small bribes wreak major damage on Kenya's roading system' – and it is not difficult to think of other examples. We are all familiar with allegations that leaders of desperately poor countries are salting millions away in Swiss banks. Yet there are enough cases of economic growth under corrupt regimes – the US throughout its history, and Italy, Japan, and South Korea in the second half of the twentieth century – to show that the relation between corruption and economic growth is less straightforward than the rhetoric of TI and the World Bank suggests.

In addition to anecdotal evidence, the Source Book cites an influential statistical study, 'How Taxing is Corruption on International Investors?' (Wei 2000), which appears to support its claims concerning the economic effects of corruption. Wei explores the impact of corruption on foreign direct investment, and examines bilateral investment from 14 source countries into 45 host countries in 1990–91. He claims that, ranking corruption levels from zero to ten, a one point increase in corruption produces a 16 per cent reduction in the flow of foreign direct investment (FDI). Corruption, in effect, is a substantial cost for the private sector, and the reaction of foreign investors is very negative. 'For a country to attract optimum levels of FDI', the Source Book concludes, 'it must minimise corruption and its illicit tax on investors' (TI 2000: 5).

This analysis deserves careful examination since the conclusions that its evidence support are not those drawn by Wei and TI. I begin by noting that the precise incidence of corruption is always difficult to determine because many of those involved in corrupt conduct will have a clear interest in keeping it hidden. This is why indirect measures of the incidence of corruption, such as Transparency International's annual Corruption Perceptions Index (CPI) and its biannual Bribe Payers Index (BPI), have proved attractive to researchers, Wei included. The CPI is a composite index based on polls and surveys by institutions ranging from the World Bank and Columbia University to commercial enterprises like PricewaterhouseCoopers. The surveys themselves are mostly conducted among professional risk analysts and businesses, both resident and expatriate. Their results reflect the perceived impact of corruption on private business, not its impact in other areas of society. Wei uses the CPI together with an index derived from a similar Business International survey of business opinion.

Wei's study runs a composite measure of the opinions of businesses and risk analysts concerning the costs imposed on business by corruption in several countries against a measure of business investment in the same countries. Not surprisingly, it finds a strong correlation between foreign business opinion and foreign business investment: countries seen as bad places in which to do business find it difficult to attract FDI. Wei suggests not only that corruption acts as a tax on business, but also that it impacts severely on decisions about FDI. Yet, far from establishing this last claim, his study shows only that businesses are reluctant to invest in places where business observers believe corruption has a significant negative impact on business activity. The problem it addresses does not arise from the actual incidence of corruption in different countries – something that Wei makes no attempt to measure – but rather from the perceptions that professional risk analysts and business people have of these countries.

If TI's Source Book treats perceptions as standing for the actual incidence of public sector corruption, perhaps we should treat the problem of corruption that it seeks to address in similar terms: that is, as lying in the perceptions of international investors and international agencies, not in corruption's actual incidence and effects. The suggestion, in other words, is that TI aims to work on these perceptions by promoting within developing countries an institutional environment in which international investors can feel at home and in which they feel able to do business. This suggestion throws a different light on the character of the international anti-corruption movement.

NIS as the solution to the problem of corruption

We have already noted a discrepancy between the problem of corruption with which the Source Book begins and the NIS which it presents as the solution. Corruption, especially in the public sector, is said to undermine both economic growth and political legitimacy, and large-scale social reform – through the progressive establishment of an NIS with international agencies playing a tutelary role – is presented as the only realistic solution. Yet the links between the different steps in this argument simply do not hold. Not only is it misleading to suggest that public sector corruption will always have the dire consequences that the Source Book identifies, and thus that it calls for drastic remedies. Moreover, there is no reason to suppose that the development of an NIS will have much impact on the problem.

The strategy of building coalitions between government agencies, NGOs, and the private sector promises to allow anti-corruption measures to be put in place without directly confronting powerful individuals and political forces. The advantages of avoiding damaging political confrontation are clear, yet this strategy risks allowing the corrupt practices of the well connected to continue unchecked. This strategy should not be expected to impact much on economic growth and political legitimacy, at least in the short term. TI's claim that the effects of focused anti-corruption measures will always depend on 'the broader societal context' (TI 2000: 12) is beyond dispute. However, like the claim that corruption damages the efficient workings of the market, this functionalist perception gives no indication of the relative importance of the problem in any particular case. Analyses based on a combination of *a priori* argument and anecdotal evidence cannot establish that the broader societal context is in need of drastic reform, still less that contemporary international agencies should have a significant tutelary role in the process.

My final point about the NIS framework concerns its place in TI's activities. TI may be the major international agency concerned specifically with combating corruption, but it is a minor player on the international scene. It is not in a position, as the IMF and World Bank sometimes are, to impose its views on states in which it operates. TI combines different levels and styles of organization. Internationally, it is an organization of 'suits', discreetly lobbying international public servants in the World Bank, the Organisation for Economic Co-operation and Development (OECD), and the UN and suggesting how to tackle the scourge of corruption. At another level it is an organization of small national chapters relying on the work of a few local activists and engaging, like many NGOs, in projects funded by national and international agencies. Even if, as I suspect, it is an organization of 'suits' all the way down, the local suits will often be of a different cut from those of TI Berlin. At neither level, however, is TI really in the game of implementing the NIS design. Thus, while the Source Book describes the problem of corruption as matter of extreme urgency – suggesting, for example, that much of the developing and ex-socialist world is 'in crisis' (TI 2000: 1) – and the NIS plays an organizing role in the Source Book's discussion of solutions to the problem, it does not explain what one might do when confronting this urgent practical problem. Rather, the Source Book offers TI's national chapters and national and international agencies a framework (that is, the NIS) for addressing the issue of corruption and a checklist of items that they might like to include in their reports: recommendations that civil society and international agencies should be invited to play a greater role in the fight against corruption, that the state should not normally 'undertake tasks which the private sector can perform more efficiently' (TI 2000: 4), etc. It uses the concerns of activists and national and international agencies about corruption to promote its image of a long-term future for the developing and ex-socialist worlds to which both groups might aspire.

TI and international neo-liberalism

This last point brings us to a final question. If TI is less concerned with tackling the immediate problems of corruption than many of its public pronouncements might suggest, what should we think about its work? I noted earlier that TI's Source Book uses the metaphor of a Greek temple to support its argument that the NIS is the long term solution to the problem of corruption. Since the NIS is itself based on an idealized and distinctly neo-liberal image of a Western institutional framework, this suggests that the Source Book should be seen as promoting a broader neo-liberal programme of normalization. I use neo-liberal and related terms here to identify governmental projects concerned to corporatize or privatize public sector institutions, to expand the sphere of competition and market-like interaction, and to promote individual choice alongside or in place of public provision. What these projects have in common is a desire to govern activity indirectly through suitably organized fields of free interaction (Hindess 2004b, Rose 1999). Neo-liberalism differs from earlier forms of liberalism in taking this approach into areas of public life that had previously been organized in other ways. In the national economic arena it aims to regulate the conduct of individuals, private bodies, and many public agencies through the use of auditing and of market or market-like arrangements instead of direct control by the state. Like earlier forms of liberalism, it promotes international commerce and the associated disciplines of the market as indirect constraints on the conduct of states themselves, but it also makes use of well-developed financial markets and powerful international financial institutions for this purpose.

Where the World Bank uses concerns over poverty in the developing world to promote its 'good governance' version of the neo-liberal agenda (Rojas 2004), TI uses concerns over the problem of corruption to promote its NIS. The World Bank insists that poverty is a major problem in many developing states and that it would be best not to tackle the problem directly. What is needed, rather, is to set in place the political and economic conditions which, economic theory tells us, can be expected to lead to steady and reliable economic growth and thus to an all-round improvement in living conditions. TI takes a similar approach to the issue of corruption, suggesting that it is indeed a major problem that is best tackled through the establishment of a NIS. In both cases, the extent to which the programme advanced can effectively address the initial problem (poverty or corruption) remains, at best, open to question.

In the case of the World Bank it has also been suggested that this is not really the point, that the problem of poverty is used rather to legitimate its 'good governance' programme and that the programme itself has a different purpose. Anthony Pagden has noted, for example, that while the discourse of 'good governance' is most commonly associated with development in postcolonial states, it is more appropriately seen as promoting a way of thinking about international relations that involves not only states, but also 'non-statal and avowedly non-political bodies, particularly the international financial agencies and multinational corporations' (1998: 7). The aim here, we might say, is to secure the position of international financial agencies, multinational corporations, and credit-rating agencies in an international governmental regime. The discourse of good governance operates in a distinctly cosmopolitan idiom, acknowledging that states have an irreducible measure of cultural particularity. Yet it also promotes an agenda of neo-liberal reform, focusing on the conduct and the organization of states and asking them to accept a common set of governance values, institutions, and practices. A recent International Anti-Corruption Conference (Seoul 2003), at which TI provided the Secretariat, had the title 'Different Cultures, Common Values'. This suggests that the global anti-corruption movement is promoting a universalism of much the same kind. It plays a small, but nonetheless significant, part in the larger programme of neo-liberal reform.

Some commentators (e.g. Gill 1995) have described international neo-liberalism as a fundamentally disciplinary enterprise, but this is surely misleading. Programmes of social reform seldom operate solely through coercive means. Like older liberalisms (Hindess 2004b), contemporary neo-liberalism is by no means averse to the use of coercive measures when appropriate. Yet, it prefers to work through the freely chosen actions of the states and other agents with whose conduct it is concerned and it is promoted by a variety of state and non-state actors. The case of TI reminds us that, at the international level, the agenda of neo-liberal reform should not be seen simply as the province of the World Bank and other Western-dominated inter-governmental organizations. It also relies on agencies, such as TI, with no coercive powers of their own, and which operate through persuasion and example, suggesting to activists, states, and other agencies ways in which they might address their concerns and insisting, most particularly, on the role of civil society, the private sector, NGOs, and international agencies.

As for the issue of normalization, an example from another policy area suggests what is involved here. Commentators have noted the one-sided response of the IMF to the recent Asian crisis, imposing structural reform on less developed countries while refusing the option of managing international capital flows (Chang *et al.* 1998). But it has also been suggested that the structural reforms in question promote a broader programme of normalization, displacing Asian patterns of business organization and finance in favour of an Anglo-American model (Wade 1998, Vestergaard 2004). Both the World Bank's 'good governance' programme and TI's NIS address a similar task in the broader governmental arena: suggesting a Western institutional structure for the state, noting that such a state nevertheless has important limits, and insisting on the role of civil society and the private sector in the overall government of society. NIS also accords an important role to international agencies and places them in what amounts to a tutelary role.

Finally, TI uses business and risk analysts' perceptions as a surrogate for the actual incidence of corruption. I suggested that TI's activities might usefully be seen as working on these perceptions; that is, as seeking to foster an institutional environment within developing and ex-socialist countries in which international investors feel at home and in which they feel able to do business. In this respect, we might suggest that NIS and good governance represent an updated version of the older system of capitulations, which required independent states to acknowledge the extra-territorial jurisdiction of Western states (Fidler 2000). There is, however, one significant difference. As befits its post-colonial character, international neo-liberalism prefers to adopt a less intrusive approach. It places international agencies in a tutelary position – as there to advise and assist – while the promotion of good governance and NIS suggests that states should undertake for themselves the reforms required to satisfy international investors.

3 Anti-corruption as a risk to democracy

On the unintended consequences of international anti-corruption campaigns

Staffan Andersson and Paul M. Heywood

Introduction

Governments, international financial institutions, and non-governmental organizations are devoting ever more resources and attention to fighting corruption (see Krastev 2003, UK Government 2000, USAID 2003, World Bank 2006c). And indeed, few could seriously argue against combating corruption given the negative effects it is known to have on institutional performance, integrity, and political and economic development (see Tanzi 1998, Miller *et al.* 2001). However, the fact that corruption is harmful to society does not necessarily mean that the growing focus on anti-corruption strategies can only bring benefits. On the contrary, there may also be some serious drawbacks to such a focus (Heywood and Krastev 2006).

This chapter explores, in the context of transition countries and non-democracies, the relationship between corruption, anti-corruption, and democratic politics. In particular, we are interested in when and under what circumstances well-intentioned current approaches to understanding and fighting corruption can actually constitute a risk to democracy and democratic stability. What is the tipping point from good to bad? Amongst the risks of anti-corruption campaigns that we identify as being particularly important to investigate are:

- The generation of a sense that politicians and political institutions are irredeemably corrupt, which in turn promotes disaffection and disillusionment amongst citizens – an ideal breeding ground for the growth of populist protest.
- The potential distortion of political debate through a growing obsession with 'cleanliness' rather than policy issues, as has arguably happened in many of the former Communist countries of Eastern and east-central Europe – leading to a depoliticization of policy choices in favour of an emphasis on moral propriety.
- The development of scepticism towards democracy itself in transition countries, if anti-corruption initiatives are seen as being part and parcel of democratization and yet corruption continues to flourish.

- The use of anti-corruption by non-democratic regimes as a pretext to crack down repressively on opponents rather than supporting genuine transparency and accountability.

The chapter is structured in four sections. The first discusses the dominant anti-corruption approach, its development origins, and success, and in particular, the impact of the 'good governance' discourse. In the following section, we investigate the principal driving forces behind anti-corruption campaigns and in section three we look at how, in some cases, such campaigns can have unintended consequences for democratic stability and development. We use empirical examples drawn from transition countries in Europe and non-democracies in Asia (mainly Vietnam, but also China). The final section concludes.

Corruption, anti-corruption and 'good governance'

Since the increasing attention on corruption really began to take root in the 1990s, the issue of how best to combat it has become a core focus both of international organizations such as the UN, the World Bank, the International Monetary Fund (IMF), the Organisation for Economic Co-operation and Development (OECD), and various non-governmental organizations, notably Transparency International. Corruption is nowadays regarded as one of the key obstacles to political and economic progress in the developing countries. The World Bank has identified corruption as '[t]he single greatest obstacle to economic and social development' (World Bank 2006a). And in established democracies too, corruption has assumed an increasingly high position on the political agenda, not least in relation to concerns about political parties, lack of trust, and voters' increasing cynicism and apathy towards politics and politicians.

The increased attention paid to corruption is often seen as either a reflection of an increase in real levels of corruption, or else an increase in the visibility of corruption – itself the result of a host of changes, including the end of the Cold War, the rise of a new type of media, the spread of democracy, the rise of the global market, the mobilization of civil society, and the rise of organized crime. But as has been shown by Krastev (2003: 4), the increased attention being paid to corruption and the new anti-corruption rhetoric can alternatively be explained as a response to changes in the politics of international trade and financial institutions, which have provided the real stimulus to an increased focus on corruption and a new conceptualization of its role (see also Brown and Cloke 2004).

Although Hong Kong and Singapore are regarded as recent successful examples of countries combating corruption, overall the results of the major efforts to fight corruption over the last 20 years have yielded rather meagre results (see Bertucci and Armstrong 2000, DeWeaver 2005, Keuleers 2005, Cirtautas 2001, Doig and Marquette 2004). Naturally, fighting corruption when it has already become established at a high level and also embedded within society is not an easy mission to accomplish. Moreover, since many anti-corruption campaigns take place in tandem with efforts to fight poverty in countries where corruption is often very widespread, we should perhaps not be surprised by poor results. Put simply, it is a very difficult task to break the vicious circle of corruption since even if corruption is very obviously detrimental to economic and social development from a macro-perspective, from the micro-perspective of an individual facing a given situation it may still be the least bad alternative (Grødeland *et al.* 1998). One other significant problem in the fight against corruption is the still rather limited knowledge that we have of the causal mechanisms that lie behind various different forms of corruption and the continued heavy reliance on perception indices in many studies which seek to identify factors that are causally linked to corruption.

In general the focus of the anti-corruption approach of the World Bank, and also to a large extent that of other agencies and non-governmental organizations (NGOs), is to promote democracy and economic development, or the values of liberal democracy. Indeed, research has established a clear statistical relationship between democracy and economic development, but the direction of that relationship remains contested and it has been pointed out that the relationship exists only when democracy has been an established feature for a very long time, or that it even disappears when controlling for other factors (see Treisman 2000; Record 2005; Sandholtz and Koetzle 1998: 11; Lane and Ersson 2000: 110–13). In particular, programmes to fight corruption have often not been based on an identification of the types of corruption involved and their underlying situation-specific causes. This is a very important explanation of why 'one-size-fits-all' programmes have not worked effectively (Shah and Schacter 2004). We should note here, however, that the World Bank Institute has promoted an important development through its diagnostic studies of corruption and governance, which have generated much more multifaceted and experiential data on corruption.[1]

In the development of approaches to combat corruption, the World Bank (and the World Bank Institute[2]) as well as Transparency International, itself founded by former World Bank executives in 1993, have been very influential in formulating the dominant approaches. The prevailing view has been to focus on broad reforms, rather than to combat concrete cases of corruption and corrupt individuals (Krastev 2003: 5). The aim has been to limit opportunities for corruption and the incentives involved. In the words of the World Bank (2007): 'Corruption prevails where there is ample opportunity for corruption at little cost. Incentive structures encourage corrupt behavior. Anticorruption strategies therefore aim at reducing the opportunities for corruption while increasing the expected cost, i.e. the risk of being caught and severely punished.'

This has meant that, at least initially, when the World Bank started to deal with corruption in the mid-1990s there was a strong focus on state deregulation and on reducing the opportunities of corruption. However, this approach has met with much criticism. First, because of the impact that such an approach has on the quality of public service and social welfare in general. Second, because the state downsizing argument in general seems not to be supported by empirical success. Third, the World Bank was often criticized for not giving enough consideration to indirect means of reducing corruption, such as strengthening public institutions and improving public education and awareness. Moreover, the principal-agent framework that underpinned the approach hinged partly on the notion of the principal as always non-corrupt and committed to reform, which is obviously problematic in many countries. However, this factor has to some extent been taken into account by acknowledging the need for different policies in high-level and medium-level corrupt countries (Andvig and Fjeldstad 2001: 105–06; Schah and Schacter 2004). Fourth, the role of the private sector as a driver of corruption was insufficiently acknowledged, overlooking major forms of corruption such as the purchase of influence and state capture and their impact on reform measures (see Kaufmann 2003: 21–22; Hellman *et al.* 2000: 1; Hellman and Kaufmann 2001; see also Heywood and Krastev 2006: 19).

So, even if much of the fundamental understanding of what causes corruption and how to combat it remains in place, there have been changes and the dominant approaches to combating corruption are moving away from directly targeting corruption towards broader and more inclusive measures. Transparency International has developed the National Integrity System approach which takes a holistic view of fighting corruption, pinpointing the pillars of integrity – key institutions, laws, and practices that contribute to integrity, transparency, and accountability – to identify causes of corruption and the effectiveness of anti-corruption measures. It dismisses the idea that a single-ideal-type model can be implemented in any country, and it reflects a practitioner perspective on earlier failures (Transparency International 2007a; Doig and McIvor 2003: 318–19).

The emphasis of the World Bank is illustrated by Kaufmann (2005: 88) who states:

> A fallacy promoted by some in the field of anti-corruption, and at times also by the international community, is that the best way to fight corruption is by fighting corruption – that is, by means of yet another anti-corruption campaign, the creation of more anti-corruption commissions and ethics agencies, and the incessant drafting of new laws, decrees, and codes of conduct.

So anti-corruption programmes are now beginning to look beyond just public administration and financial management reform to broader structural relationships, for example the internal organization of the political system, state-firms relationship, and the relationship between the state and civil society (World Bank 2007).

More specifically, 'good governance' has become the keyword in fighting corruption and in development literature more generally, and reflects a high association between good governance and key development outcomes across countries (see Kaufmann 2003: 17), although the direction is not always clear-cut.[3] Moreover, 'bad governance' is increasingly seen as one of the root causes of nearly all evil within societies (see UN ESCAP 2006; UNDP 2005a; Jayawickrama 2006). International financial institutions and major donors are in turn increasingly making their aid and loans conditional on the undertaking of good governance reforms; recently, the World Bank has cancelled or suspended loans to India, Bangladesh, Argentina, and Kenya following evidence of corruption (*The Economist*, 2006).

This emphasis on good governance, which could be regarded as a result of a 'post-Washington consensus', suggests the need for states with a stronger regulatory capacity as a precondition for liberal markets since deregulation in the absence of frameworks like competition policy may risk power transfer from state to private-sector oligarchies. This approach is based on a particular understanding of politics that can serve to ground the economic reforms advocated by multilateral agencies such as the World Bank (Jayasuriya 2002: 26–29).

Governance, in general, is a broader concept than corruption, but the two are increasingly treated as being directly linked – that is, environments characterized by bad governance offer more opportunities and incentives for corruption (see IMF 2003; Kaufmann 2003: 5). Essentially, governance is about the process of decision-making and the process by which decisions are implemented. It can operate at various levels such as national, local, and international, and – depending on context and level – may include various actors such as the government, industry, associations, NGOs, religious leaders, finance institutions, political parties, and so forth. Good governance is described as participatory, accountable, transparent, responsive, consensus-orientated, effective and efficient, equitable and inclusive, and follows the rule of law (see UNDP 1997). In general, good governance has implied a very broad approach to tackling corruption, focusing on improving political accountability, strengthening civil society, competitiveness in the private sector, institutional restraints on power, and public sector management. In a speech delivered in 2001, the Vice-President of Europe and Central Asia Region at the World Bank stated that because of the power of vested interest to resist change, 'Promoting good governance therefore, tends to require fundamental changes in the nature of incentives that are closely intertwined with the existing structure of political and economic power' (Linn 2001: 1).

In Asia, the dominant governance approach has stressed the lack of democracy and reinforcement of the regulatory capacities of the state as one of the main explanations of the Asian crisis in 1997. Thus many multilateral and bilateral aid activities have been directed towards governance reforms, and development projects are justified in governance terms involving, for example, legal institutional reform, anti-corruption activities, and the strengthening of civil society (Lindsey and Dick 2002; Jayasuriya 2002: 26).

The results of efforts to improve governance are not conclusive, but overall it appears that there has been stagnation or deterioration in governance[4] (Kaufmann 2003: 10). However, the same research also shows that, between 1996 and 2004, some countries did succeed in improving governance in a rather short time, notably in some of the transition countries that were promised membership of the European Union, whilst governance stagnated or deteriorated in those that were not offered membership (Kaufmann 2005: 87–88).

So the contrast between the period before and after 1995 is stark. For example, the World Bank did not really engage in anti-corruption projects before 1995 as they were regarded as interfering in the politics of recipient countries, which according to the World Bank's articles of agreement is not allowed. This led to criticism of the Bank for lending to corrupt regimes and regimes that violated human rights (Marquette 2004: 413–14). The current approach, with involvement in far-reaching anti-corruption programmes in recipient countries to improve governance, is mainly defended against allegations of political interference by the claim that action is undertaken only at the request of the recipient country. However, help is only provided with the proviso that programmes address not just corruption, but broader governance issues as well; one-off activities are discouraged (World Bank 2006b). And earlier governance programmes did not pay as much attention to the regulatory capacity of the state and the creation of market order (Jayasuriya 2002: 29).

The current approach naturally raises other questions. What are the risks with anti-corruption strategies that so overtly champion Western democratic ideals or at least liberal democratic values (see Hindess 2005: 1396)? In relation to East European transitions countries, Cirtautas (2001: 1) argues: 'It is clear that the heavily promoted, supposedly universal standards, derived mainly from idealized Western standards, are meant to supersede completely local customs and practices.'

Even if good governance and anti-corruption are not the same, in practical terms anti-corruption programmes that fully address governance make the two look the same. Moreover, the broad approach and range of criteria might also undermine the credibility of sincere reformers if judged by standards that in many case took decades to achieve elsewhere (see Linn 2001). Credibility is further undermined if anti-corruption approaches seem to reflect a double standard, such as membership conditions imposed by EU, which the present members could probably not meet themselves judging by recent high profile corruption cases (see Cirtautas 2001: 3; EurActiv 2003). Another related concern is whether the disjuncture between the increased focus on the involvement of civil society at large in anti-corruption reforms and the continued emphasis on the role of elites might drive a further wedge between post-communist politicians/civil servants and their own populations. Breaking the vicious circle of corruption that reduces trust, lowers public revenues, and weakens the credibility of the state is seen as resting on decisive leadership, which in unreformed structures has not often been forthcoming (Cirtautas 2001: 3–4).

As we have seen, the World Bank has identified corruption in almost apocalyptic terms, and its former president, Paul Wolfowitz, has described corruption as the greatest evil facing the world since communism (*The Guardian*, 26 January 2006). Such rhetoric may underline the World Bank's senior management's determination to combat corruption, but it also carries significant dangers. One of the most significant is that it not only legitimizes the near obsession with corruption that has taken hold in some parts of the world, but that it may also compound the problem if it fails to offer effective countermeasures.

Put into the context of emerging democracies or non-democracies in Asia, could such good governance and anti-corruption rhetoric be used for other purposes than reducing corruption such as, in the case of China, helping the leaders to keep power or get rid of political opponents (DeWeaver 2005: 5), and legitimizing using very harsh combat measures? The following sections address these and other concerns by looking at the impact of anti-corruption campaigns in both the former-communist transition economies and in non-democracies in Asia. It is shown that the good governance model can have unintended consequences – in terms both of the model itself and also the broader focus on corruption.

Anti-corruption in European countries in transition

In regard to the notion of good governance, there are two issues that need to be highlighted. First, the very assumptions underpinning 'good governance' as understood by the World Bank, with their emphasis on private sector competitiveness and restraints on the role of the state, lend themselves easily to the promotion of what looks like a neo-liberal blueprint (see Linn 2001). Yet, it is now widely understood that some core elements of the neo-liberal model – such as a reduced role for the state in economic management to be achieved through extensive privatization and deregulation – have generated significant opportunities for corruption in the transition economies (Rose-Ackerman 1999). As Holmes (2003: 199) has argued: 'the neo-liberal model is conducive to corruption, and ... it had become dominant in Western ideology by the time the post-communist CEE states were establishing themselves.'[5] In a host of the transition countries, corruption scandals related to privatization became a standard feature of news reports during the early post-communist years (Elliot 2002).

It could be argued that the problems of privatization-related corruption are short term. After all, public entities are only available to be sold once (albeit often in various tranches) and are then subject to the rigours and discipline of market forces, thereby supposedly reducing the scope for corruption. There are three problems with such an argument. First, there is no shortage of evidence that the private sector is also prone to corruption (with notable recent examples including Enron, WorldCom, and Tyco). Second, even though privatization may move firms and utilities out of the state sector, the experience of many Western countries is that deregulation has in turn created further opportunities for corruption, as in the case of Enron's manipulation of the electricity prices in California, and has led to calls for re-regulation. Indeed, the rise of the so-called regulatory state is in large part related to market failures.

Third, and most important, is the fact that even if the risk of privatization-related corruption is indeed short term, the impact of such corruption may be very long term. The transition economies provide evidence that the combination of privatization and corruption can have a profoundly damaging impact on the functioning of democracy itself. Here we explore various ways in which anti-corruption campaigns and the promotion of good governance may have undermined, rather than reinforced, the development of democracy in many former communist states.

In regard to privatization, a key issue that has generated disquiet in many of the transition economies is the question of how the process was managed and where investors were able to find the money to buy into privatized state assets. A recent report on anti-corruption reforms in Bulgaria notes that ' ... the privatization process turned into one of the most problematic corruption spheres ... [and] created unlimited opportunities for corruption and abuse' (Coalition 2000 2005: 90–91). As Krastev (2004: 54–56) argues, there were three main problems with the post-communist privatizations. First, in common with many privatizations in the developed world, but even more so, there was difficulty in fixing an appropriate price. In the eyes of many citizens, a combination of Western accountants and the market ensured that state assets were sold too cheaply, especially since the state-owned enterprises represented a source of livelihood for vast numbers of those citizens. Second, and even more important, there was widespread scepticism about how buyers had secured sufficient funds to purchase the privatized assets. According to Holmes (2003: 198):

> The West had limited funds to invest in the post-communist countries. This suggested that privatization would have to take place through the sale of assets to domestic investors. But in the absence of a wealthy capital-owning class, it was unclear how this would happen. ... [M]any members of the former *nomenklatura* ... were particularly well-placed to take advantage of some of the unusual privatization processes, albeit to differing extents in different countries. Many were directly involved in the sell-off of state assets, and benefited both in terms of bribes and kickbacks from those to whom they sold assets at knock-down prices, and by becoming shareholders themselves.

Understandably, suspicion arose about those who secured access to funds and rapidly became the 'new rich' in post-communist Europe – particularly given the *nomenklatura* past of many of them, several of whom rapidly became millionaires (Mason 2004).

A third problem, according to Krastev, is that the very process of privatization was seen as corrupt in the eyes of many citizens. Limited regulatory frameworks – consistent with the shock-therapy tactics promoted by Western economic advisers (for instance, the so-called Lipton-Sachs programme which argued for a 'Big Bang' approach to ending central planning) – ensured that personal gains through privatization went largely uninvestigated, and there were very few corruption-related prosecutions. None the less, the assumption became widespread that corruption was rife throughout the privatization process, and this fed into a wider concern about the stark growth not only in inequality, but also in poverty, which characterized the post-communist states. The number of people living in 'poverty' in the post-Soviet states rose sharply during the 1990s, rising from 4 per cent in 1989 to 45 per cent in 1995 across all the transition economies (*New Internationalist*, 2004).

In the search for explanations to account for the dramatic collapse of living standards throughout many of the post-communist states, and the failure of market reform and liberalization to secure democratic deliverance, many turned to 'corruption' as the key explanatory factor. Indeed, corruption became the explanation of last resort both within and outside the post-communist states for a whole host of problems, ranging from economic failures, growing inequality, and increasing disillusionment with democracy. It has been claimed that post-communist societies are 'simply obsessed with corruption' (Krastev 2004: 43), and it does indeed appear that corruption has assumed the status of being the principal policy narrative in many of the transition economies, used internally to structure political debate and externally to explain the differential success of progress towards stable democracy. In the words of Rose, Mishler and Haerpfer, 'corruption has replaced repression as the main threat to the rule of law' (quoted in Krastev 2004).

Such inflated rhetoric picks up on that used by the World Bank, referred to above. The danger with emphasizing corruption to this extent is that it serves to legitimize its use as a proxy for other forms of explanation. Thus, politics starts to be played out in terms of mutual accusation of corruption: the politics of *kompromat* which involves looking for ways to discredit opponents through finding (or often inventing) compromising material and damaging allegations about them. This in turn further reinforces the sense of corruption being everywhere, and feeds perceptions about the scale of the problem – as revealed in the research by Miller, Grødeland and Koshechkina (2001) on routine corruption in Bulgaria, the Czech Republic, Slovakia, and Ukraine. They showed that citizens in those countries saw corruption as the product of transition to market economies, and that the principal beneficiaries were politicians, state functionaries, and various mafia-like groups. Yet, their findings also revealed that although perceptions of corruption being rife were high in all four countries, personal experience of corrupt exchanges varied significantly and was notably higher in Ukraine, for instance, than in the Czech Republic. The mismatch between perception and experience not only highlights how suspicion of malpractice can easily take hold, but should also alert us to the risks of relying on perception as a guide to reality.

Nonetheless, the perception of corruption being a major problem in the transition economies has undoubtedly become deeply embedded, and has probably been reinforced by the insistence of international bodies, such as the European Union, that it be tackled as a precondition for entry – notably in the case of Bulgaria and Romania in October 2006. By placing such emphasis on corruption as a major problem, the impression is inevitably created that there is both more corruption than in the past, but also that corruption is particularly associated with the post-communist reforms. Whether there is actually more corruption than in the past is less important than the generation of a conviction that corruption has become the major issue facing the transition economies. Corruption becomes part of the narrative of post-communist politics, which in turn generates a sense of disillusionment with the democratic political process. Given the limited apparent impact of anti-corruption initiatives in terms of reducing the perception of corruption (itself reinforced by the lack of significant change in Corruption Perception Index (CPI) rankings over recent years), it is easy for critics to point to the failure: 'If citizens continually read and hear reports of corruption, they begin to lose faith in the democratization and marketization projects' (Holmes 2003: 204).

One result of this emphasis on corruption is that politicians increasingly feel the need to demonstrate their credentials in terms of 'transparency' rather than in specific policy proposals. Political choice itself becomes 'moralized' as corruption-centred politics ensures that the options are presented in terms of corrupt government versus clean opposition (Heywood and Krastev 2006). In such a context, when the trustworthiness of candidates becomes more important than what they are actually saying, political judgements cease to be about political choices as opposed to moral judgements. It is hardly surprising that the transition economies have seen one government after another thrown out by electors as accusations of corruption and malfeasance by those in power becomes the stock-in-trade of the democratic system. In turn, such a focus on corruption leads to the risk of the post-communist states becoming what are effectively protest-vote democracies in which anti-system populist alternatives find fertile terrain in which to prosper. In many ways, the transition economies have seen some of the trends familiar in many established democracies – popular disillusionment with the political class, growing lack of trust, increased personalization of the political process – taken to a more extreme level, without having had the chance to build up a residual belief or confidence in the fundamentals of democratic politics. The risk is therefore that the new democracies will have neither process- nor output-legitimacy upon which to rely for popular support, which may open the way for non-democratic interests to capture the political process.

The most insidious example of such a process is so-called state capture, described in the World Bank's report, *Anti-Corruption in Transition* (2000: 16), in the following terms: 'the action of individuals, groups, or firms in both the public and private sectors to influence the formation of laws, regulations, decrees, and other government policies to their own advantage as a result of illicit and non-transparent provision of private benefits to public officials.' With populations disillusioned by and disenchanted with the functioning of the recently created democracies, the risks of state capture by a variety of actors – including private firms, political leaders, or sectional interest groups – increase significantly. By focusing so relentlessly on corruption, the shortcomings of democratic functioning in the post-communist states have been highlighted in ways that carry significant risks for their very survival.

Anti-corruption in authoritarian states in Asia

This section discusses unintended consequences of anti-corruption measures in non-democratic countries in Asia (particularly Vietnam, but also China). What are the consequences of the dominant anti-corruption approach and what role is played by international donors?

Domestically, it has become increasingly important for Asian regimes to tackle corruption. If it used to be the case during the 1970s and 1980s that high growth rates and increasing per capita incomes were enough to maintain popular legitimacy and support, these days Asian regimes are ever more dependent upon a regime's record on fighting corruption, as demonstrated by recent examples from Thailand, Malaysia, and Indonesia (Bloomberg 2005; Tarling 2005: 14). In China and Vietnam, fighting corruption is seen as vital to enhance the legitimacy of communist rule. The Chinese President, Hu Jintao, has warned of the effects of corruption on governance and argued that improving anti-corruption capacity is an important guarantee for the consolidation of power (Feng 2005).

However, anti-corruption campaigns and good governance rhetoric can be used for purposes other than reducing corruption. In China, at least as important as fighting corruption has been the use of anti-corruption campaigns as an opportunity to get rid of people loyal to previous leaderships. Another prominent feature of Chinese anti-corruption campaigns has been their use to cool the economy, since fighting corruption can be an effective way of controlling money supply by hampering improper lending by state banks and reducing the funds going to other financial institutions (DeWeaver 2005: 3). Moreover, campaigns serve to signal the commitment of the regime to combat corruption and to sow fear about the odds of detection and punishment, which is important if these odds in reality are low and the cadres who escape detection under one campaign may still fear that they might be less lucky next time (Wedeman 2005: 115).

As far as China and Vietnam are concerned, many scholars point out that the rise in corruption and development of new forms of corruption have gone hand in hand with economic reforms and that other reforms have not been enough to check corruption. But on the other hand, the real level of corruption is very difficult to ascertain and therefore by extension so is the impact of the anti-corruption campaigns. There is evidence to suggest that anti-corruption campaigns have had some effect in preventing corruption from increasing still further. In China, campaigns often start with a clemency phase providing an opportunity to admit wrongdoing, followed by a crackdown phase in which offenders are dealt with harshly. Campaigns seem to have been rather effective in keeping corruption under control, but they have also had an impact on the form corruption takes. Mainly it is low-level corruption that has been deterred, rather than high-level corruption, and the size of bribes also seems to have risen (Wedeman 2005: 106).

If anti-corruption is elevated to the status of being the most important issue facing governments, does that contribute to legitimizing an approach in which the end justifies the means, for instance using very harsh means to fight against corruption? This is an important issue to consider when discussing countries like China and Vietnam where the measures to fight corruption sometimes can be questioned in relation to legal security, the risk of arbitrary punishments, and human rights. The death penalty is used even for non-violent crimes such as embezzlement and fraud.[6]

And if the good governance agenda is also a means to introduce democracy or liberal values through the back door, via the fight against corruption, is that really a good strategy? Will the hopes that the reforms lead to more democracy be fulfilled or will the hold on power of existing non-democratic regimes actually increase? On the one hand, anti-corruption might be seen as a window of opportunity to allow people to discuss and criticize politicians and public officials, and to increase the freedom of the press; on the other, there are risks that these measures are not really adopted in depth and instead the anti-corruption and governance agenda are used for other purposes, such as attacking opponents for political reasons. Below, these questions are addressed in the case of Vietnam.

Anti-corruption in Vietnam

The economic reforms, *doi moi* (renovation) that started in 1986 meant that many free-market enterprises were permitted (and later encouraged). The push to collectivize industrial and agricultural production was more or less abandoned. Although *doi moi* was not simultaneously accompanied by increased social or political liberty, the Communist government has nonetheless tacitly permitted many more personal freedoms than in the past (apart from such issues as criticizing the Communist regime).

Internal reasons for anti-corruption?

Corruption is generally regarded as widespread in Vietnam (Transparency International 2005b; VDR 2005: 92). As the country has gone through economic liberalization and rapid change over the last 15 years, with an annual economic growth rate on a par with the highest in the world, the opportunities and incentives for corruption have changed, and despite various reforms corruption also seems to have increased (VDR 2005: 90).

The official stance by the Communist Party of Vietnam (CPV) is that the situation is serious. The unrest caused in the country every now and then due to discontent with corruption and maladministration – not least the uprising in the Thai Binh[7] province in 1997 – have contributed to general worries about corruption and its implications for regime survival. According to Article 8 of the 1992 Constitution of Vietnam (amended in 2001), it is the duty of all state agencies, cadres, officials, and employees '[t]o resolutely struggle against corruption, extravagance and all manifestations of bureaucracy, arrogance, authoritarianism'. Anti-corruption was one of three priority tasks of the government during 2003–07 (Embassy of Sweden 2002: 3). But the measures undertaken so far have not been successful and according to the CPV, '[c]orruption is still very serious and can be seen in most of State management fields under more and more sophisticated forms' (Communist Party of Vietnam 2002).

One way of showing commitment to the cause is by anti-corruption campaigns and the imposition of heavy penalties. So at the same time as economic liberalization indirectly contributes to increased personal freedom, the democratic record remains very problematic. Although previously rather few cases of corruption were brought to trial (Lindsey and Dick 2002: vi) in recent years many corruption cases have been exposed and perpetrators punished. But the application of penalties is regarded both as arbitrary, depending on the position of the individual involved, and too lenient by many Vietnamese, despite the fact that the death penalty is used for corruption crimes (Communist Party of Vietnam 2005). The number of people executed is regarded as a state secret, but in 2004 at least 88 people in total were sentenced to death, of whom six were convicted of fraud, according to official sources. At least 64 people were reported as having been executed (true figures are believed to be higher). Despite reports that the authorities were considering the abolition of the death penalty for economic crimes, two executions for fraud were reported, and some executions continued to take place in public (Amnesty International 2005b).

One of the most publicized cases in recent years, the *Nam Cam* case, concerned an extensive network of gambling, protection, prostitution, and drugs. It was sustained by regular bribes to the police and other authorities.

In the case 154 people were tried, many of them organized criminals but also high-rank party and government officials, such as a former deputy state prosecutor and a former deputy police minister. Five men were executed in 2004.

Other examples of the tough stance taken include the execution in 2006 of a former senior customs officer who was convicted of having taken bribes and assisted in one of the country's largest smuggling scandals in 1997 (Thanh Nien News 2006). In another case, a businesswoman was sentenced to death for embezzling nearly US$1 million from the government-owned company she headed (Associated Press 2002).

Such actions are of course problematic in themselves, but even more so when the rule of law can be called into question and where corruption is part of everyday life since anti-corruption charges may be used against political opponents. According to Tsuboi (2005: 9–10), the structure is set up so that if someone on the inside is likely to oppose or protest against the system of party government, corruption is used to oust that person 'legally'. When almost everyone is involved in some sort of corruption in daily life, corrupt activities are unlikely to be exposed, but if someone displeases the establishment by refusing to take part in corruption or by opposing the system, corruption offers a convenient mechanism to charge such people with violation of the law.

External reasons for anti-corruption

Besides internal factors promoting anti-corruption initiatives, the international donor community has also pushed for reform and improved governance (see Thanh Nien News 2005a, 2005b). Moreover, Vietnam, which has been quite successful in fighting poverty despite increasing corruption, is a country where donors 'compete' with each other to assist and contribute aid to a country regarded as a success story when it comes to promoting development.

Although anti-corruption in Vietnam, as is the case in China, has a punitive base (VDR 2005: 99), growing attention is paid to various governance and accountability measures which have been implemented with the support of various bilateral and multilateral aid agencies. To reduce opportunities for corruption, public administration reforms, such as the granting of licences in business, construction, and land allocation, aim to simplify and reduce administration. Other measures have been salary reform and increased transparency and accountability. The grass roots democracy reforms in 1998 were a response to the Thai Binh uprisings and aimed to provide a legal framework for increased participation in decision-making in communes, state-owned companies, and administrative organizations (Vasavakul 2003). The ordinance on complaints and the ordinance on anti-corruption (1998) aim to give people the opportunity to complain about corruption and misuse of powers and to create a legal base which the courts could use to punish corruption. In 1999 the press law was revised providing a channel for citizens to report on corruption and has resulted in the revelation of several corruption cases in recent years, but it also goes hand in hand with some self-censorship (Embassy of Sweden 2002: 2). There have also been reforms of financial management, public procurement, and new budget and accounting laws.

Recent reforms

The most recent reforms, which have been supported by the United Nations Development Programme (UNDP), were included in the new and quite openly debated anti-corruption law (adopted in 2005, effective from 1 June 2006). An anti-corruption committee has been introduced, but it is not as independent as some of its counterparts, and will be headed by the Prime Minister and members from communist agencies. Other measures include a new requirement for certain officials, and their family members, to declare their assets above 50 million Dong (about US$3,200). The government will be required to report on its anti-corruption work and, similarly at the local level, peoples' committees must report to peoples' councils. Journalists will have the right to ask any organization to provide information or documents relating to corruption and any refusal will require a written explanation. Moreover, retaliation against denouncers of corruption is to be punished and those who fight corruption have been promised rewards (Vietnam News 29 November 2005; Thanh Nien News 2005c, 2005d, 2005e, 2005f).

In 2002 the CPV accepted an offer made by Sweden, first in 1999, of support to undertake a study of corruption. The Swedish government was the only one that the Communist Party wanted to work with, which had much to do with the two governments' long-standing development cooperation. The specific project objectives agreed upon with Sweden were to undertake a diagnostic study of corruption and to identify causes of corruption and the reasons for the ineffectiveness of the measures already undertaken against corruption. Moreover, according to the project objectives, measures to reduce corruption and improve the effectiveness of combating corruption should be proposed to the government, the national assembly, and the party (Embassy of Sweden 2002: 3–5).[8]

The Swedish International Development Cooperation Agency and the Swedish Embassy also acknowledged potential problems, one being its political risks, including the impact on democracy, but concluded that the project did not contradict Swedish policies on democracy and human rights (Embassy of Sweden 2002: 8). One of the more noteworthy risks discussed was whether successful results in 'the project' could be used by the CPV to '[e]nhance its legitimacy and strengthen the one-party state management system', which was weighed against the potential benefits of greater transparency and on easing poverty and promoting socio-economic development (Embassy of Sweden 2002: 8). Another related risk concerned whether the project would provide support for organizations associated with the Communist Party. It was argued that the project required cooperation with the political system as corruption is a political issue, so even if the project would not be supporting political organizations as such, it was seen as necessary to include political stakeholders early on (Embassy of Sweden 2002: 8–9). Despite these high risks, Sweden ultimately supported the project as it was seen (Embassy of Sweden 2002: 10) as giving unparalleled opportunities to:

> [i]nfluence this very sensitive and critical issue, and to support one of not too many positive and promising processes towards core or structural reform including political system reform.

The long-term impact of measures stemming from this project, concerning whether genuine democratic reforms will be the outcome or more repression and a reinforcement of the regime's grip on power, remains to be seen.

Conclusion

This chapter has explored the relationship between corruption, anti-corruption, and democratic politics, focusing on when and under what circumstances fighting corruption can actually constitute a risk to democracy and democratic stability. In exploring these issues it has pointed to the need for a better understanding of the relationship between anti-corruption campaigns and governance, and their impact on democracy. Our main argument is that there are indeed significant risks with anti-corruption campaigns. Moreover, although the tipping point from positive effects to negative is difficult to determine with precision, there is a need for a more balanced perspective than is evident in the approaches that currently dominate anti-corruption initiatives.

The way corruption is understood in the dominant 'good governance' approach and the remedies employed generate a number of potential risks in the context of the emerging democracies of Eastern Europe and also in developing countries in Asia.

First, we have pointed to risks linked to the heavy emphasis placed on seeing corruption as the most important obstacle to social and economic development. In the context of transition countries in Eastern and Central Europe, we point to the risk of politicians and political institutions being regarded as inherently corrupt, which promotes disaffection amongst citizens and a growing fixation with clean politics which in some cases depoliticizes policy choice in favour of a focus on moral propriety. Moreover, as corruption in many cases has become the explanation of last resort, it further contributes to the impression of corruption being everywhere and all officials being corrupt, which makes the democratic process even more fragile.

In the Asian examples, with particular reference to Vietnam but also to China, there is a risk that non-democratic regimes can use anti-corruption as a pretext to crack down repressively on opponents rather than supporting genuine transparency and accountability, and we posit that this is also true for emerging democracies in Asia. And they can act repressively whilst still claiming that they are in line with the focus of the international community and important aid agencies. Anti-corruption programmes may thus risk cementing the existing regimes' grip on power, rather than promoting democracy, despite donor agencies' best intentions to use the fight against corruption as a means of pushing for improved governance, increased accountability, and transparency.

As we have seen in both China and Vietnam, aid agencies see anti-corruption reforms as a window of opportunity to undertake governance reforms and enhance accountability and transparency, thereby promoting liberalization. Indeed, if such reforms turn out to be successful in reducing corruption and improving governance they might contribute to real improvements in citizen welfare. But here too we have to keep in mind the short-term effects and the risk that very harsh and arbitrary measures taken against corruption may be legitimized. And as the example with the Swedish support for the anti-corruption work in Vietnam shows, donors also acknowledge some of the risks involved in a strategy to democratize via the backdoor, although in this case concluding that the pros outweighed the cons.

Second, governance programmes and anti-corruption campaigns can themselves create opportunities for corruption as they may target and discourage some forms of corruption, but create opportunities for others, as both the Eastern European and the Asian examples have shown. Corruption has in many countries come to be seen as an outcome of the reforms undertaken. In the emerging democracies in Eastern and Central Europe, the transition to democracy and market economies is often seen as the reason for increased corruption, whilst in Vietnam and China the liberalization of the economy has been seen as promoting opportunities for corruption. As a result, there is a risk that scepticism towards democracy itself in transition countries will grow, and if anti-corruption initiatives are seen as being part and parcel of democratization in authoritarian or emerging democracies and yet corruption continues to flourish, this may ultimately do more damage to processes of democratization. In short, tackling corruption remains a social, political, and economic priority – but, as we have sought to show, it is one that is fraught with risks.

Notes

1 That is, diagnostic studies of households, public officials, and business.
2 The World Bank Institute is the capacity-development arm of the World Bank.
3 For instance, Record (2005: 7–8) contests the straightforward causal direction going from good governance to economic performance and argues that good governance is not the missing link for take-off into sustained growth among countries experiencing low growth.

4 Governance is measured by six components: 1. voice and external accountability (i.e. the government's preparedness to be externally accountable through citizen feedback and democratic institutions, and a competitive press); 2. political stability and lack of violence, crime, and terrorism; 3. government effectiveness (including quality of policy-making, bureaucracy, and public service delivery); 4. lack of regulatory burden; 5. rule of law (protection of property rights, judiciary independence, and so on); 6. control of corruption (Kaufmann 2003: 5).

5 Holmes goes on to argue that, in practice, neo-liberalism may help to reduce corruption by breaking the hold of former members of the *nomenklatura* on the levers of the state.

6 Amnesty International (2005a) estimated that in China at least 3,400 people were executed and 6,000 sentenced to death during 2004, with the true figures understood to be much higher.

7 That the unrest among grass roots occurred in Thai Binh province (south of Hanoi) was particularly concerning for the CPV as the province is normally regarded as one of those more supportive of the party.

8 The report on the results of the diagnostic survey was presented in November 2005 (Thanh Nien News 2005g).

4 The development of inspection and oversight

Blind alleys and open vistas in the case of American procurement policy

Frank Anechiarico

Analytic premise

An important premise of this chapter is based on the work of Anthony Amsterdam and Jerome Bruner (2000). Since this chapter deals with broad-based reform movements, their consequences, and possible alternatives, we are in the realm of political culture. What are the assumptions about ethics and official integrity that informed the changes that the American Progressive Reformers at the beginning of the twentieth century prescribed and implemented? Were the Progressives expressing widely shared (modal) beliefs about the distribution of power that had become part of American culture? Does the answer to this question help explain the durability of Progressive reform and/or the consequences of the Progressive ethics agenda? Amsterdam and Bruner take up the question of political culture and how we learn and transmit our beliefs about governance. (The collaborative work of Amsterdam, a specialist in civil rights law and criminal procedure, and Bruner, who established the field of cognitive psychology, produces a view of learning about American political and legal culture that might preface any discussion of corruption control.)

Their most salient point for the purposes of this chapter is that there has been, and is currently, little cohesion in the transmission of beliefs about the exercise and control of power. That is, culture, since the beginning of Progressive reform, has been contended ground. The Progressive faith in professions and leadership selection as routes to clean, effective government were built on the beliefs and biases of the relatively small middle-class at the turn of the twentieth century. The received beliefs of the majority of the American population was that patronage, procurement 'brokerage' fees, and other hallmarks of partisan political machines were acceptable, had created jobs, were necessary to initiating and completing the great public works projects of the period, and were little different from the way that the private sector worked in the Gilded Age.

The shifts that shaped the current reform culture in the United States have almost always centred on how to deter, detect, and punish corrupt official activity. The argument below focuses on elements of the cultural shift:

deregulation, professionalization, and modal public sentiment about public administration. However, it is useful at this point to set out a basic chronology of reform. A chronology will focus cultural shifts on parallel historical developments.

The progress of anti-corruption reform in the US[1]

The beginning of public administration as we know it was the civil service reform movement in the 1870s. As will be noted again, the civil service movement began as the moral successor to the abolition of slavery. While it may be hard to see the parallel, after ridding the polity of an epic evil it was clear that the engine of politics, government, and administration would have to be cleansed as well. The system that they sought to replace held sway since the election of President Andrew Jackson in 1828. Jackson successfully displaced the long-serving administrators with party loyalists and personal friends. He argued that what became known as the 'spoils' system (to the victors go the spoils) was a democratic reform. Those holding position because of social status and educational attainment, the argument continued, could not understand the needs of the people as well as those dedicated to the agenda of an elected leader. Loyalists would both understand and act upon the desires of the ordinary voter.

Not improbably the spoils system lead, in short order, to enormous corruption which is well documented by reformers and scholars of the day. The great changes wrought by the Civil War a generation after Jackson cleared the field for the next reform. The next stage of civil service reform was led by politicians and intellectuals like the future President and then young college professor, Woodrow Wilson. The post-Civil War generation looked for modes that would create what they admired in European administration without the upheaval that was required to end slavery. As legal historian William Nelson (1982: 112) puts it:

> The efforts of Jacksonian democrats and antislavery moralists to revo-lutionize American society had had immense costs in governmental instability and in human blood. Having paid those costs, late nineteenth-century reformers wanted a government that brought peace and stability by slowing the pace of change. In the bureaucracy they achieved their aim.

As Nelson indicates, the civil service reform movement, which replaced loy-alism/cronyism with a merit system based on examinations and credentials, was the beginning of bureaucratic government in the US. This is a point worth emphasizing and considering in a comparative context. That is, the desire for 'apolitical' administration and corruption-free government deter-mined the organizational form of public administration. Most often in the US, at federal, state, and local levels, this meant the beginnings of the bureaucracy.

Having begun the cleansing of government, the next reformers, the Progressives, had a broad agenda for political and governmental change. Their contribution, as described more fully below, was an emphasis on professional administration. The argument was that those with the right education and experience would regulate themselves in terms of the values and mores of their professions. This seemed to work for a while. But it required a fairly small government that ran with relatively few, highly trained employees.

With the election of President Franklin Roosevelt in 1932 and the huge public programmes of the depression era New Deal, government grew very rapidly at all levels. The added enormous pressure of America's entry into World War II ten years later (Roosevelt was elected to four, four-year terms) made the US government one of the largest in the world. This required another shift, which might be called internal investigation reform. It was no longer possible to trust in professional training to control the deviant impulses of a great many civil servants who had passed examinations, but who were not trained in any of the recognized professions. Large numbers of clerks, procurement officers, and subsidy and rationing officials were needed quickly. A secondary-school diploma sufficed as an entry-level credential. This brought in the first undercover agents and formal offices of accounting and auditing. The Government Accounting Office, the investigative arm of the Congress, was used to uncover kick-backs and profiteering. At the local level, New York City's Department of Investigation came into its own as an internal law enforcement agency in the City's agencies.

From the end of the War until around the 1970s, public administration was drawn into the scientific movement in academia. Attempts to measure loss and to prevent corruption adopted the efficiency models that were gaining currency in American business. This gave the internal monitors more authority in their quest for absolute integrity.

The addition in the mid-1990s of technological advances increased the reach and intrusiveness of statutory rules that were added after each scandal (which seemed to recur whatever the state of reform). Conflicts of interest and the appearance of such conflicts were outlawed, financial disclosures by a great portion of the civil service were required, federal and local prosecutors established anti-corruption units, procurement regulations multiplied to include a rapid process for debarring contractors for infractions, and whistle-blower protections were strengthened. Following Jeremy Bentham's term for totalistic surveillance, this might be called the era of panoptic reform.

From a reliance on values to the stucture of compliance

The growth of what might be called the anti-corruption project is outlined in the previous section. It should not be taken as lock-step development. Along the way there were disagreements about techniques in practice. A lack of cultural consensus about a primary regime characteristic like corruption control will lead to certain predicable, organizational characteristics and syndromes. The first casualty of contended political culture, according to Adams and Balfour (2004), Brint (1996), as well as Amsterdam and Bruner, is the reliance on value-based ethics in a professional civil service. The background to this reliance was the routinization of specialized work into professions. The expansion and growth of professions invariably entailed an expansion of formal, written codes of ethics to the credentialed members of professional organizations. These were the values that reformers had been looking for and came to rely upon. For example, the American Bar Association (ABA) was established in 1878 for 'the advancement of the science of jurisprudence, the promotion of the administration of justice and a uniformity of legislation throughout the country. ... ' Goal 5 of the ABA is 'to achieve the highest standards of professionalism, competence and ethical conduct' (ABA 2007). Similarly, the American Institute of Certified Public Accountants (AICPA) dates back to 1887 when it was known as the American Association of Public Accountants. The AICPA's code of professional ethics includes a clear statement of the connection between ethics and the advancement of the profession and its members: 'Integrity is an element of character fundamental to professional recognition. It is the quality from which the public trust derives and the benchmark against which a member must ultimately test all decisions' (AICPA 2007).

As the professions became a vehicle for socio-economic mobility and government expanded radically after 1932, the basis in values, rather than compliance, of the professions became less that of a 'trustee' as Brint puts it, and more that of a 'rational technocrat' as Adams and Balfour put it. Slowly, but surely, a compliance (rule)-based ethics regime replaced the Progressive ideal. Value-based ethics remain an important aspiration for many scholars and practitioners. This part of political culture is still very much in contention. Understanding this contention and the historical dynamic of the political culture of corruption control is crucial to evaluating what is necessary and feasible in the next phase of reform.

Predicates of reform

During the golden age of civil engineering a great many wonders of American infrastructure were built under the aegis of partisan political machines. The Tammany Hall political machine in New York City presided over the building of the New York County Courthouse, the subway system (at first, a public/private enterprise), the Brooklyn Bridge, the harbour and East River tunnels, hundreds of school buildings, a university system, and public hospitals (T. Henderson 1976). The standard arrangement was for party politicians (for example, Tammany Sachems) to bring key actors in the public contracting process together with labour from the mass of the party's immigrant constituency. Tammany (or the Daley Machine in Chicago, the Corning Machine in Albany, the Hague Machine in Jersey City, etc.) was the broker and took a broker's percentage (Steinberg 1972). Most often the percentage was high, but accepted. The machines were the municipal procurement agencies of their time and, if grudgingly, most citizens and officials accepted their role in the process. The process made a good many rich, the cities were getting built, and a great many families were provided with relatively stable incomes. Why not vote the rascals back in?

However, there were the not infrequent occasions when the machine overreached. A classical and significant example is the construction of the New York County Courthouse, called to this day the Tweed Courthouse after the Tammany chief who gave new meaning to the machine's brokerage role. With colleagues including the City's sheriff and comptroller, William Maeger Tweed looted the municipal and state treasuries through kickbacks and fraudulent payments. Upon the Courthouse's recent restoration as the headquarters of the City's Department of Education, the *New York Times* (Barry 2000: B-1) reviewed a history that was the beginning of a nationwide change in procurement:

> Officially, the city wound up spending nearly $13 million [$100,000 was allocated] – roughly $178 million in today's dollars – on a building that should have cost several times less, although many historians estimate that tens of millions of dollars more changed hands. Its construction cost nearly twice as much as the purchase of Alaska in 1867. ... The corruption was breathtaking in its breadth and baldness. Nearly every major contractor was submitting fraudulent bills for work that was never done, sometimes in the names of people who did not exist. ... Tweed was profiting in myriad ways, including his financial interest in the Massachusetts quarry providing some of the courthouse marble. When a committee was assigned to determine why construction was taking so long, it spent $7,718 (roughly $105,000 today) on printing its lightning-quick findings that everything was above board; the printing company, of course, was owned by Tweed. ... A carpenter was paid $360,751 ($4.9 million) for one month's labor in a building with little woodwork. A furniture contractor received $179,729 ($2.5 million) for three tables and 40 chairs. And the plasterer, a Tammany functionary named Andrew J. Garvey, got $133,187 ($1.82 million) for two days' work; his business acumen earned him the sobriquet the Prince of Plasterers.

The original publication in *the New York Times* of the cost overruns and plain thievery caused a furore that provided the impetus for Progressive reform of municipal government in general and for the professionalization of procurement in particular. The lowest responsible bidder system, pre- and post-audits of contracts and, by the 1930s, the assignment was made of officials from the City's Department of Investigation – eventually inspectors general – to each municipal agency. With the best of intentions the Progressives divided public procurement and public administration into specialized units responsible for performing public service and other units responsible for public integrity. The division between performance and integrity paralleled the distinction argued for by Woodrow Wilson in the 1880s. Politics, according to Wilson, was a mandate from the people that politicians were meant to interpret and shape into policy. Policy, once it became law, was to be administered in isolation from politics by professional authorized specialists in a bureaucratic setting (Wilson 1887:197).

In spite of its substantial analytic appeal, there are two flaws in the scheme championed by Wilson and the Progressives. First, administration cannot be separated from politics. Even the most mundane task assigned to the executive by legislators or judges requires discretion. The choices made by administrators grew in scope and importance as government grew in the US and elsewhere. By 1947 in the US, it was necessary for Congress to enact the Administrative Procedure Act which recognized the law-making role of civil servants and codified the way in which discretion was to be exercised; in essence, the way that politics was to be conducted in administrative agencies.

Bureaucratic politics and corruption control

It is true, as the Progressives understood, that favouritism and partisanship in administration undermine the legitimacy of democratic governance. Citizens will not appreciate or tolerate the spending of their tax dollars on the friends and loyalists of elected officials, especially since cronyism takes no notice of credentials or other qualifications. The obvious solution, as historians of the civil service movement note, is a neutral institution with codified standards of recruitment and monitoring. In short, bureaucracy. However, as indicated above, bureaucratic inspection and oversight fall prey to the same pathologies that bedevil all such structures: delay, overlap, over-centralization, demoralization of middle management, criminalization of inter-organizational exchange, and goal displacement.

The problem of placing the anti-corruption project in bureaucracy became apparent by the 1980s when the edifice of corruption control was bigger and less effectual than ever. Just after the Mayoral Administration of Rudolph Giuliani had begun to cut the amount of bureaucratic oversight in the procurement process, New York City was faced with one of its greatest crises: the attack of 11 September 2001 on the World Trade Center. Because of the appointment to the Procurement Policy Board of those interested in rational deregulation of public contracting, by 9/11 there were in place mechanisms for emergency selection –outside the required bidding process – of contractors. In the wake of the disaster, four large companies at work on other projects in Manhattan were chosen to move to Ground Zero and begin the difficult and sensitive process of clearing thousands of tons of debris and ensuring that the slurry wall that kept the Hudson River out of the deep foundation 'tub' did not give way. The four contractors, who were selected in the emergency selection of contractors because of their reputations for quality performance under adverse conditions, were among the largest in the US, but they seldom did business with New York City. Conflicting integrity rules and fraud allegations against the four contractors either repelled or disqualified those selected for the Ground Zero job from regular City procurement. The City requirement that the lowest *responsible* bidder be selected indicated that the winning bidder be free of criminal taint or investigation. According to City Comptroller Elizabeth Holtzman, the daughter of one construction principal married the nephew of a mobster, which disqualified the company from City contracts. The four companies at Ground Zero were Tully Construction Company, AMEC Construction Management, Bovis Lend Lease, and Turner Construction Company. Tully Construction, by 9/11, had been disqualified as a bidder for not meeting 'responsibility' criteria, so New York City refused to allow Tully to bid on a contract with the City Department of General Services (Green 1991; Anechiarico 2005):

> Tully ... has [also] been found non-responsible, by [the Department of] Sanitation. As with the earlier finding, the Commissioner's designee found that Tully neither provided information requested nor cooperated with a Comptroller's subpoena, failed to disclose required information on its [background] form, and engaged in improper waste disposal in New Jersey. Sanitation also relied on the fact that Tully's president employed a known organized crime figure in one of his companies.
>
> (City Law 1995: 1, 3)

AMEC also had stains on its record before 9/11:

> In November 2000, Morse Diesel, Inc. [which was shortly to become AMEC] pled guilty in federal court in the Eastern District of Missouri to one count of submitting a false claim to GSA concerning a contract for the federal building in St. Louis, Missouri ... [T]he company submitted a claim that the bond premium had been paid when in fact it had not ... the company paid a fine of $500,000. In a more recent proceeding, AMEC, on February 20, 2002, was paced on the list of Parties Excluded from Federal Programs ... The cases were investigated by the Office of Inspector General, Office of Investigations, and the US General Services Administration.
>
> (US Department of Justice 2002)

In general, companies that cheat and break the rules and are found not-responsible ought not to be trusted with one of the most important construction projects in American history. How would local and world opinion turn if the companies selected to clear what was considered to be consecrated ground were found to be dishonest in their work? The political fallout and recrimination would be epic. Nonetheless, just as the federal government was erasing AMEC from its list, New York City was granting it a huge contract which would be paid with federal dollars.

The political culture of corruption control had shifted in New York and was beginning to shift elsewhere. As a former prosecutor and a senior Justice Department official in President Ronald Reagan's administration, Mayor Giuliani had little patience for bureaucratic tradition. If he could find a way around the delay and other pathologies of large-scale, rule-oriented hier-archies that would still deflect corruption, he would seize it and put it in place (Siegel 2005). Parallel and not unrelated to the anti-bureaucratic ethic in the Giuliani administration was a movement among American public administration scholars that favoured rationalizing and cutting rules and regulations, giving more discretion to programme directors, and privatizing or contracting out many services if the official agency could not meet or better outside price and performance. A great deal of this was brought together from disparate sources by David Obsorne and Ted Gaebler in a book that was published in 1992, just as bureaucratic dysfunction hit its peak at many levels of government. They entitled their influential work, *Reinventing Government: How the Entrepreneurial Spirit is Transforming the Public Sector* (Obsorne and Gaebler 1992).

Osborne and Gaebler say very little about corruption control in their book except to note that it has become the tail wagging the dog. In order to reset priorities in most bureaucratic agencies they recommend an exercise whereby half of the rules guiding operations, including those designed to protect integrity, are considered for deletion. Giuliani appointed agency heads who were in sympathy with Osborne and Gaebler and who did, indeed, cut away a great many rules and regulations. The question was, of course, were they reinventing, not government, but William Maeger Tweed? There was a piece of the puzzle missing that Osborne and Gaebler did not provide: how is integrity protected in a free-wheeling, deregulated, entrepreneurial public sphere?

The professions, integrity, and performance

As noted above, public administration began a long and painful loss of public support in the decades following the Civil War. When President James Garfield was assassinated in 1881 by a deranged loyalist, Congress was pressed toward reform. In 1883 the Pendleton Civil Service Reform Act became law. This was the beginning of the evolution that did not improve the situation, but instead lead to a nadir in public support and to a low-point in the effectiveness of the public service. Osborne and Gaebler's work was widely popular, because it was a plausible, if incomplete, recommendation for confronting this low point in American governance.

But more complete and specific reform proposals were coming. They began with recognition of the shift in the nature of professions away from 'trustee' public orientation. The change in the professions had caused an ethical problem in the American public service at all levels. The compliance regime that replaced reliance on trustee values was, by the 1990s, viewed as undesirable. The compliance regime had the unfortunate side-effect of slowing or stopping the operation of government, by causing intense paranoia among administrators. The problem, which American scholars of public administration toiled over for a generation, was how to structure a system that operated both effectively and honestly. For many observers in America and elsewhere, such a structure was unattainable. Effectiveness and integrity were considered by the skeptics as trade-offs. If you wanted one, you would have to accept a deficit in the other.

The unchartered waters of reforming public administration, not just deregulating it, would have to include regulations and rules that allowed innovation and efficiency that was based on carefully and clearly set out standards of integrity. This reform would be based around new strategies for measuring the outputs and outcomes of effort in American public administration. A key use of measurement in the public sector is to highlight those operations and structures that detract from effectiveness. This use of measurement is linked to the premise that, rather than being a trade-off, the relation of integrity to effectiveness is one of mutual reinforcement. Thus, measurement showing short comings in the approach to a goal would require a thorough audit that included close scrutiny of compliance with ethics regulations.

Finding the missing piece

Responding to the shift in political culture was a group of prosecutors in the New York State Organized Crime Task Force (OCTF). Led by Task Force Director Ronald Goldstock, an Associate Attorney General of New York State, Governor Mario Cuomo of New York assigned the OCTF to study corruption and racketeering in the New York City construction industry (New York State Organized Task Force 1991). In summary, the OCTF found two things that are pertinent to this discussion. First, the City and other governments doing business in the area had managed to encrust the procurement process with so many rules that only relatively small, but 'responsible' contractors would bid on public work. In order to win the work, a company would bid unrealistically low and then make up their margin of profit with multiple requests for 'change orders' which allowed supplemental payments in light of unforeseen circumstances discovered during the process of construction. The definition of unforeseen circumstance became the subject of long, post-contract litigation, which became nearly standard. Thus, the contractors selected might be unblemished under definitions built up over a century, but they were slow and they were among the poorest performers. It got to the point that a school in New York City would take eight to ten years to build. The same structure would be completed in a neighbouring jurisdiction in less than half the time and for considerably less money. The lowest-responsible-bidder system, OCTF found, had created a race to the bottom.

Second, on close examination, many of the blemishes that prevented high performance companies from working for government were the result of 'sting' operations and not reflective of the intentions of a company's management. Still, it was hardly possible to bring them into the fold as they were. But what if they could be brought in under conditions that would join their performance records with high integrity standards? After considerable debate and in the spirit of public/private solutions to political problems like this one, OCTF developed the Independent Private Sector Inspector General (IPSIG).

IPSIGs, often formed as special units of law firms or units of security companies, include forensic accountants, contract lawyers, engineers, and investigators (Getnick and Getnick 2007). Other personnel may be added in contract negotiations between the public agency and the IPSIG it is hiring to supervise the work of a tainted contractor. The core idea is to make it possible for high performance companies to bring their skill back into the public sector, but to leave their sins behind. To stretch the religious metaphor, IPSIGs are the instrument of redemption for both the outlawed construction companies and for bogged down, bureaucratic agencies.

IPSIGs are pre-cleared by central investigative agencies or Inspector General (IG) offices. In New York City, the Department of Investigation pre-clears and assigns IPSIGs.[2] The IPSIG teams – there was one for each of the four companies at Ground Zero – are paid by the company to which they are assigned and they report to the company and to the sponsoring government agency. The obvious and first question must be whether the IPSIG will be 'captured' by the company it is monitoring. This is, of course, possible, but is mitigated by three factors. First, the IPSIG may only oversee a particular company once according to the professional standards of the International Association of IPSIGs. Second, the reports submitted to the government agency allow for post-audits of selected IPSIG assignments, which would readily indicate collusion, kickbacks, etc. Third, IPSIGs are costly to form and develop. A law firm or security firm would jeopardize a substantial investment through collusion, detection, and punishment.

In addition to making sure that basic integrity standards are complied with, IPSIGs also provide written advice (monitored by the official sponsors) on how the company might operate more efficiently, provide high quality service at lower cost, and maintain or increase profits. The consultation function brings performance and integrity together. Director Goldstock reports that the first companies ordered to accept IPSIGs if they wanted public work objected, but eventually gave in. By the end of the work, these same companies, according to Goldstock, found that they had satisfied high integrity standards and finished the work ahead of schedule and within the contracted price. This was also the case for all four companies at Ground Zero in Lower Manhattan after 9/11.

A new politics of integrity

The IPSIG story and how procurement has moved from a highly bureaucratic, low integrity sector to a part of government that now has the tools to satisfy public demand for high performance *and* honesty is only one part of the new politics of integrity. The key is that politics is not and never has been separate from public administration. This has been a heavily contended part of American political culture in Amsterdam and Bruner's terms. If politics is defined as control of the allocation of scarce resources, it will always be the job of administrators to allocate resources skilfully and honestly. The joining of performance and integrity indicated by IPSIGs is happening in other parts of government. As administrators become more adept at measuring performance, as IPSIGs do right on the job site, they will inevitably detect misconduct, misuse of funds, and basic fraud, waste, and abuse. Measurement is no longer confined to adding up the deployment of personnel or the allocation of certain funds; it focuses on the outcomes of public service. The police do not just prevent and detect crime; they provide an outcome: public safety. Measuring that includes citizen surveys, and detailed reports from officers, witnesses, and victims. The New York Police Department's Internal Affairs Bureau has a computerized system that tracks all complaints against officers and holds precinct commanders responsible for following each complaint to resolution and taking clear steps to prevent recurrence. It should be noted that the new politics of integrity is enabled by a new system in New York City. The 911 emergency call system is still in place. There is now a new 311 system that citizens can use to ask questions about service delivery and/or complain about the behaviour of city employees (New York City Department of Information Technology and Telecommunications 2006). The 311 system provides a special sort of transparency – not the kind that allows citizens to see what government is doing, though that is crucial, but the kind that allows government to see what citizens want, dislike, commend, or condemn. It is a democratic innovation that helps weave performance together with integrity.

Notes

1 This section is an abbreviated adaptation of the historical argument in Anechiarico and Jacobs 1996: 3–28.
2 Interviews with the author, November 2001.

Part II

The vices and virtues of governmental anti-corruption

5 Matching workload, management and resources
Setting the context for 'effective' anti-corruption commissions

Alan Doig

Context

The 2005 United Nations Development Programme (UNDP) report (UNDP 2005: 5) on institutional anti-corruption arrangements has noted:

> Several countries have opted for or are currently considering creating an independent commission or agency charged with the overall responsibility of combating corruption. However, the creation of such an institution is not a panacea to the scourge of corruption. There are actually very few examples of successful independent anti-corruption commissions/agencies.

At the same time an Organization for Security and Co-operation in Europe (OSCE) report (OSCE 2004: 175–76) found:

> It is true to say that anti-corruption agencies have met with mixed results. For reasons not yet wholly apparent, they have tended to be much more successful in East Asia – in countries such as Singapore, Malaysia, Taiwan and Hong Kong – than they have been elsewhere. One factor is clear: in each of those countries the agencies have enjoyed high levels of political and public support. They have also had adequate research abilities, and have adopted both rigorous investigative methods and innovative programmes of prevention and public education. One may suspect that some other anti-corruption agencies have been established with perhaps no real expectation of their ever tackling difficult cases at senior levels of government. They have been staffed and resourced accordingly. Some have done good work in attacking defects in integrity systems, but only at junior levels; however, most have had a negligible impact on tackling grand corruption.

The chapter does not discuss anti-corruption commissions (ACCs) as investigative agencies. It addresses the UNDP and OSCE issues by arguing why donors and countries must pay more attention to the organizational infrastructure, development and planning issues that must underpin decisions on the establishment of new ACCs or changes to existing ACCs as follows:

- *Workload*: identifying what is the threat – what types and levels of corruption exist and what threats do they pose to politics, administration, public perceptions, and democratization. These need to be identified in order to develop the strategy and an institutional shape in terms of the likely volume and type of work the agency will be undertaking.
- *Management*: the institutional shape is necessary to deliver the strategy; it will require management capacity and expertise to plan the institutional processes, resourcing, and priorities to achieve this.
- *Resources*: strategy and organizational design shapes management's approach, decision-making and budget processes towards the anticipated successful undertaking of the workload but both will only be achievable if they are based on a realistic assessment of the level and type of resources, from staff expertise to equipment that would be available.

The chapter also includes discussions on two related issues:

- *Transitional countries:* do their socio-economic context and institutional configuration mean that some of the problems to be addressed may require different approaches?
- *'Organizationally-young' institutions:* do donors and governments, in trying to address high-level corruption, expect too much from organizations that do not yet have the organizational maturity, capacity, and competence to deliver?

Why ACCs and why planning?

Article 36 of the United Nations Convention Against Corruption (UNCAC) states that:

> Each State Party shall, in accordance with the fundamental principles of its legal system, ensure the existence of a body or bodies or persons specialized in combating corruption through law enforcement.

In a number of countries, responsibility lies with a police agency or units within such an agency. In others, a specific and specialized agency, distinct from the police, is preferred. In developing and transitional countries, where the police traditionally have not been trusted to deal with corruption, a new agency is often proposed (and usually a preferred option of multilateral and bilateral donors). Table 5.1 indicates the range of agency responsibilities relating to anti-corruption work in a number of European countries;

it is noteworthy that transitional or newly-accessed countries have tended towards a discrete agency. Exactly what processes are used to determine whether or not a specific body is needed (and, if established, what it should do) would involve what are normal business-planning and management assessments. Governments and existing ACCs should consider, as elsewhere in the public sector, the use of such approaches to determine if an ACC is needed or, if it exists, whether it is effective or how it could be improved (Doig *et al.* 2001).

It has been argued that the main features of an effective ACC are well established 'according to the international standards and practices. They comprise of areas such as models and forms of specialization; mandate and focus; legal basis; independence, autonomy and accountability; adequate material resources, specialized and trained staff; adequate powers; cooperation with the civil society and the private sector; inter-agency cooperation'

Table 5.1 Selected ACCs in Europe

AGENCY	POLICE DEPT	PROSECUTOR DEPT	INVESTIGATION	PREVENTION	EDUCATION	LOBBYING PARTY FUNDING	CONFLICT OF INTEREST	SURVEILLANCE	NATIONAL PLAN	PUBLIC REFORM	FINANCE
LITHUANIA STT	-	-	✓	✓	✓	✓	part✓	✓	✓	part✓	-
LATVIA CPCB	-	-	✓	✓	✓	✓	✓	✓	✓	-	-
SPAIN	-	✓	-	-	-	-	-	-	-	-	-
ROMANIA NAD	✓	-	-	-	-	-	-	-	-	-	-
CROATIA	-	✓	-	-	-	-	-	-	-	-	-
BELGIUM	✓	-	-	-	-	-	-	-	-	-	-
NORWAY	✓	-	-	-	-	-	-	-	-	-	-
FRANCE SCPC	-	-	-	✓	✓	✓	-	-	-	✓	✓
SLOVENIA CPC	-	-	-	✓	✓	-	✓	-	✓	✓	-
MACEDONIA NC	-	-	-	✓	✓	-	✓	-	✓	✓	-
ALBANIA ACMG	-	-	-	✓	✓	-	-	-	✓	✓	-

Source: Drawn from a report on anti-corruption agencies for the Organisation for Economic Co-operation and Development Anti-Corruption Network for Eastern Europe and Central Asia (2006).

(Organisation for Economic Co-operation and Development Anti-Corruption Network for Eastern Europe and Central Asia 2006).

Such features are, however, often aspirational. The questions that a business-planning approach would be asking are: are these features appropriate for particular types of corruption, and suitable for specific countries; how are they to be achieved, and in what order; what are the institutional structures, procedures and resources necessary to ensure they are achieved; and how are they to be measured as to their effectiveness or impact? The business-planning approach would fall into two categories; an assessment of external factors (or environment mapping) and, second, an assessment of the added-value of having an ACC.

The first category – assessing the external factors – addresses the key question – what is the context within which the ACC will work or what is the political or law enforcement environment that will shape the design of the organization and influence its ability to deliver its proposed functions:

The threat: What type of corruption needs to be addressed, and how should it be addressed – is the corruption high-volume (such as by traffic police or licence clerks)? Is it high-value (such as procurement contracts)? Is it politically sensitive (involving government ministers). Is it sophisticated (such as money laundering with overseas and organized crime dimensions)? Is it a permutation of all of these?

The response: What are the strengths and weaknesses of existing institutions and how should or could these be resolved – by a new institution, by merger, by inter-agency coordination or cooperation, or by segmented responsibilities?

The added-value: What are the wider political and developmental agendas that will be facilitated or expedited by, or be constrained by, the work of an ACC?

The review undertaken on behalf of the Organisation for Economic Co-operation and Development Anti-Corruption Network for Eastern Europe and Central Asia (2006) noted a number of factors that could be relevant to achieving an effective ACC:

- *Establishment*: the ACC should be embedded in a comprehensive anti-corruption strategy, subject to careful planning and performance measurement, have realistic expectations, receive strong enough political backing (across class/party) to make it effective regardless of (political and personal) consequences;
- *Focus*: the ACC should have a clear focus on prevention and monitoring government implementation of anti-corruption policy (rather than take on a comprehensive mandate), should be mainly forward-looking (with only a limited concern in past cases), carefully select cases against clear standards, and have an emphasis more on probity and reputation of public service than on investigations and prosecutions;
- *Accountability*: the ACC should have a clear legal framework, be subject to judicial review, public complaints and oversight, be accountable to all

branches of government and the public, keep its size to a minimum, avoid too much donor support, and have precise and comprehensive accountability for its expenditure;

- *Independence*: the ACC's location within the governmental structure and its reporting responsibility should be ordered to ensure its independence, there should be clear appointment/removal procedures for top officials to ensure freedom from political pressure, day-to-day political interference should be avoided, there should be direct roles for public stakeholders, and there should be fiscal/budgetary autonomy;
- *Powers*: the ACC should have strong research and prevention capabilities, should be able to access documents and witnesses, have the powers to freeze assets and seize passports, protect informants, and monitor income and assets, have the authority to exercise jurisdiction over the head of state, and be able to propose administrative and legislative reforms on its own initiative;
- *Staff*: the staff should be well-trained and of sufficient number, with highly specialized skills, well compensated, subject to integrity reviews and quick removal, and have a strong ethic of professionalism and integrity;
- *Other resources*: sufficient budget, adequate facilities and assets, high-level information sharing, and coordination with other government bodies;
- *Complementary institutions*: to facilitate dealings with other institutions, there should be adequate laws and procedures, basic features of the rule of law including functioning courts, free and active media, NGOs/public interest groups, and other capable institutions such as a national audit institution and central bank.

The second category – an assessment of the added-value of an ACC – can be undertaken through a number of methodologies and techniques (Johnson and Scholes 1997) to answer, for example, the sort of questions proposed by UNDP (2005) about the advantages or disadvantages of the ACC approach. These include:

Advantages of having an ACC:

- sends a signal that the government takes anti-corruption efforts seriously;
- high degree of specialization and expertise can be achieved;
- high degree of autonomy can be established to insulate the institution from corruption and other undue influences;
- will be separate from the agencies and departments that it will be responsible for investigating;
- enjoys a fresh start as a completely new institution, free from corruption and other problems that may be present in existing institutions;
- has greater public credibility;
- can be afforded better security protection;
- will have greater political, legal and public accountability;

- there will be greater clarity in the assessment of its progress, successes, and failures;
- there will be faster action against corruption. Task-specific resources will be used and officials will not be subject to the competing priorities of general law enforcement, audit, and similar agencies; and
- incorporates an additional safeguard against corruption in that it will be placed in a position to monitor the conventional law-enforcement community and, should the agency itself be corrupt, vice versa.

Disadvantages of having an ACC:

- greater administrative costs;
- potential for isolation, barriers, and rivalries between the ACC and those institutions with which it will need to cooperate, such as law enforcement officers, prosecution officials, auditors, and inspectors;
- possible reduction in the perceived status of other institutions;
- generation of competing political pressures from other institutions or sectors seeking similar priority for other crime-related initiatives; and
- vulnerability to attempts to marginalize its efforts, or to reduce its effectiveness by under-funding or by inadequate reporting arrangements.

In using such approaches, however, to decide whether or not to establish an ACC or to make an existing ACC more effective will also require complementary institutional reforms to strengthen the wider effectiveness of anti-corruption incentives (UNDP 2005):

- Establish independent investigators, prosecutors, and adjudicators that ensure 'equal' enforcement of the laws and regulations.
- Strengthen capacity and integrity of the police as the frontline investigative agency for criminal infractions.
- Strengthen and ensure independence and accountability of the judicial system.
- Provide adequate powers of investigation and prosecution consistent with international human rights norms.
- Integrate transparency mechanisms, which eliminate privileges (or immunities) that have no relation to the needs of the public, and which high public officials enjoy by reason of their office, into the reform of enforcement measures.
- Develop effective complaints mechanisms, whether internally by a public servant or by a member of the public.
- Develop mechanisms to protect whistle-blowers; encourage the development of institutions, laws, and practices that ensure that responsible citizens can report corrupt practices without fear of reprisals; and ensure that the media is empowered to play a pivotal role in holding relevant individuals and institutions accountable.

- Tackle special sectors that are known to be breeding corruption.
- Impose powerful deterrents against would-be corrupt individual or company, such as civil penalties, blacklisting of corrupt firms, extradition arrangements, and other legal provisions that enable the profits of the corrupt individual or company to be seized and forfeited, whether the profits are held inside or outside the country.
- Strengthen the ministry in charge of civil service reform and establish a close relationships between it and other agenices with anti-corruption responsibilities through enforced codes of conduct; increased supervision; results-oriented enforcement; management-based measurable performance indicators; empowering the public through citizens' charters; a credible public complaints system; access to information.

Environment Scanning: planning for the work and the workload

While the two categories of a business-planning approach mentioned above provide material for a template or framework that the planning process should address, the first stage of that process must be: what is the corruption to be addressed? In other words, what is the potential work of the ACC and how should its workload be determined? Until this is identified, developing the strategy and the shape of the institution will be problematic. Addressing this as a business process allows governments to determine strategies – see Figure 5.1 for the model currently being considered by the UK government

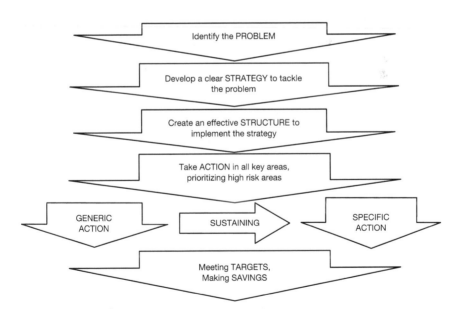

Figure 5.1 The National Health Service outline, currently used by the UK Fraud Review
Source: Fraud Review 2006

for its proposed anti-fraud strategy, drawing on a framework first developed by the UK National Health Service (NHS) anti-fraud service.

This approach also allows governments to assess, if an ACC is to be established (or more focused if already in existence), what type of corruption – the work – the ACC will address and thus what workload it could have (eg, more routine but voluminous cases that do not need too much specialism or more complex cases which, while less in number, may require more time, more specialist staff and more technical equipment). This in turn will allow assessment of whether a separate or new agency is needed, the likely capacity or resourcing required and any factors in terms of the wider operating environment that might inhibit or facilitate the agency's effectiveness – see Table 5.2.

In other words, assessing not only the existing (and future) types, patterns, and levels of corruption, but also whether corruption is 'increasing' or

Table 5.2 Ratings on relevance of a menu of anti-corruption programmes – a selection

Program	Country's Quality of Governance			Comments
	Weak	*Fair*	*Good*	
Raising public awareness of corruption through seminars	Not relevant	Low	Medium	In countries with weak governance, corrupt practices and agents are generally well known.
Raising awareness of public officials through seminars	Not relevant	Low	Medium	Public officials may be aware of corruption but unwilling and/or unable to take action due to incentive problems in countries with weak governance
Anti-corruption agencies/ Ombudsman	Not relevant	Low	Medium	Public officials may be aware of corruption but unwilling and/or unable to take action due to incentive problems in countries with weak governance
Ethics office	Not relevant	Low	Medium	Positive influence may be limited to societies with good governance
Raising Public Sector wages	Negligible	Low	Medium	May have positive impact on petty corruption but little impact on grand corruption. Negative impact if part of problem is excessive public employment

Source: Huther and Shah 2000.

'decreasing', also requires a wider assessment of the development of the governance framework, something currently being reflected in the use of both quantitative and qualitative indicators in a much more sophisticated way than in previous attempts to assess causes, types, levels, and patterns of corruption (Doig *et al.* 2006). Once that is agreed, then whether or not an ACC is required, what the ACC is intended to do, what resources it would need, how it would intend to deliver its goals, and how its effectiveness is to be measured, and what happens once its primary purpose has been achieved can be discussed. This approach has the added-value of being highly country-specific, something that would have been relevant when, for example, the question of whether ACCs were needed in ex-communist countries was raised. Here it was clear that some of the broad assumptions that had applied to lower-income countries, such as those in Sub-Saharan Africa, could need reconsideration.

Issue 1: Are there particular issues for transitional countries?[1]

Many transitional states face some of the same developmental issues of other democratizing countries, but their socio-economic context and institutional configuration has meant that some of the problems to be addressed may require different approaches. For example:

- transition states are institutionally-young and inherit bureaucracies that not only lack many of the regulatory institutions that are necessary for a modern state and economy to function, but also lack many of the conditions necessary for mechanisms of accountability to function;
- there is little or no tradition of established anti-corruption procedures, such as those relating to conflict of interest, and no experience of embedded key institutions, such as the judiciary;
- the overload of tasks in transition – ranging from wholesale privatization to the provision of basic healthcare – distracts attention from ethical and anti-corruption efforts, while the need for wide discretion by the political leadership to carry out transition tasks may conflict with the objective of reducing discretion among those without a developed sense of public service responsibility and accountability;
- political and economic liberalization subjects politicians to a wide range of pressures that are potentially corrupt, with many keen to reap material rewards from office;
- power holders in what are organizationally immature institutions could design the 'rules of the game' to facilitate their exercise of political power and influence. This has particular resonance at a local level where clan structures, family group leaders, and other authority figures from previous regimes can fill the vacuum provided by a weak state and a disempowered society;
- civil societies are weak in transition states and may not function in such a way as to underpin constructive reforms. In many, what has been termed

in Lithuania as 'silence before the official' continues to be a dominant influence on the public-state relationship;

- due to economic concentration, the weakness of civil society and/or the competitive pressures of transition, the private sector may be more aggressive in its relations with the state. In its 1998 report, for example, the European Bank for Reconstruction and Development reported that in Russia, with 'the state's authority and capacity ... ill-defined and inadequately developed, there were ample opportunities for managers and bankers to "capture" politicians and bureaucrats at every level of government. This was a fertile environment for the growth of corruption' (European Bank for Reconstruction and Development 1998: 4).

There are a number of problems specifically related to ethical and corruption issues. Part of the problem lies in the process of state formation. Leaders have to build a new state – at all levels – in the context of the effects of rapid economic transformation that has often taken place before the establishment of an effective democracy. At the same time, they must deconstruct the old state framework, but the legacy of its institutions and cultures often delayed the impact of democratization and reform.

In terms of prioritized reconstruction, there may be strong reasons for not moving too quickly to establish mechanisms of accountability or an over-emphasis on the control environment if a wide degree of discretion combined with good leadership may be more desirable to attract suitably qualified or motivated recruits – of which there should be an appropriate number in many countries – into political and administrative life as pre-conditions for institutional consolidation. A strong and empowered public service may also be necessary to address the impact of marketization and privatization which, in a number of cases, has not only transferred undue influence to private sector institutions but also converted political elites into economic elites. Making assumptions about accountability may seem clear and unproblematic, but an uncritical reliance on compliance and accountability may be less effective than an emphasis on personal responsibility in trying to achieve a balance between compliance and discretion in relation to public office. Here the role of an ACC and its interactions with other state institutions, especially the legislature and the executive, may lead to uneasy relations.

Managing the Organization's workload

Assessment of the context should determine the organizational shape and management structures necessary to translate the strategy into action. The institutional strategy is about 'the formulation, implementation and responsibility for plans and related activities vital for the central direction and functioning of the enterprise as a whole' (Booth 1993: 63) – see Table 5.3.

The strategy determines the organizational design, through 'an understanding of the strategic roles of the divisions, departments or subsidiaries of

Table 5.3 A standard organizational planning framework

Key elements of setting aims and objectives
Define Mission [fundamental purpose] and Core Values [qualities to be upheld throughout all its activities]
Draw Up Hierarchy of Aims [Goals – general in nature] and Objectives [Targets – specific for achievement] for organization and defined operational departments, sections and teams or units
Draw Up Hierarchy of Aims [Goals] and Objectives [Targets] for organization and defined support departments, sections and teams or units
Draw Up agreed level action plans between operational and support areas to deliver objectives
Establish quantitative, financial, qualitative and time-related factors in delivering Objectives to ensure that resource availability supports delivery
Establish means of objective assessment [quantifiable performance indicators]
Establish mechanisms for objective assessment
Establish mechanisms for altering priorities or practicability of Objectives

Source: Doig, Moran and Watt 2001, from Audit Commission 1995.

the organisation, as well as the role of the corporate centre ... there are different styles of managing the *parenting* role of the corporate centre, ranging from the centralised "masterplanner" approach through to a highly devolved approach ... ' – and organizational *configuration* – 'how this is made up of different building blocks and co-ordinating mechanisms ... the issue is the extent to which a particular configuration best fits or supports different kinds of strategies' (Johnson and Scholes 1997: 402).

Design and configuration involves culture management, resource management, and change management approaches to ensure that the ACC has or acquires the resources and expertise to deliver its goals and is able to adapt and develop in the face of changing circumstances. The organization has to be able to 'distinguish between those elements which create the conditions which allow successful change to take place ... , and those which actually comprise the stages (or phases) that individual change projects need to go through in order to be successful' (Burnes 1992: 257) if it is to be flexible and adaptive. See Table 5.4.

Before any effective anti-corruption work can be undertaken, an ACC must embed and integrate five general institutional infrastructural strands – financial and resource management; human resource management, including all training; information and records management; investigation and prosecution management; communication and education management. These should cover the following activities necessary to move the institution forward:

- in-house records, financial and management information systems;
- budgetary, activity and resource allocation and any devolved management and operational arrangements;
- general staff training, team work development and performance, senior management training;

Table 5.4 The policy framework: the components of the process

Gathering The Information: Defining the Aims and Objectives of the Organization

External	Consult Stakeholders; Assess External Perceptions; Liaise With Equivalent Organizations
Internal	Top-Up and Bottom-Down Discussions With Managers and Staff
Aims and Objectives	Output and Outcome-Focused Aims and Objectives of the Organisation
Expenditure	Current Levels on Staff and Non-Pay; Levels Required to Deliver Aims and Objectives
Organization Design	The arrangement of departments, functional units and management structures, together with decision-making and reporting procedures
Business Planning	Developing a Rolling Plan that links Expenditure and Organizational Redesign to Aims and Objectives

Management in Action: Realigning the Organization Towards the Aims and Objectives

Organisational Design	Cascading Aims and Objectives for Discussion, Agreement and Delivery
Decisions, Delegation and Responsibility	Devising organizational decision-making and reporting structures; Operationalizing management ownership of delivery, including staffing and resources
Communications	Devising internal and external communications strategies
Skill Mix/Flexibility	Realignment of staff to workload; flexible working practice; Revised pay structures
Staff Development	Staff Appraisal; Training

Performance Measurement: Moving the Organization Towards Aims and Objectives

Standards and Targets	Quantitative Output and Outcome and Input Targets
Performance Review	Formal Process for Monitoring Performance Against Aims and Objectives
Personal Aims and Objectives	Personal Aims and Objectives for all Staff
Personal Appraisal	Process for Monitoring Individuals' Performance Against Aims and Objectives Identification of Training and Development Needs

Source: Doig, Moran and Watt 2001 from Audit Commission 1995.

- organizational development and communications strategies;
- non-staff resource prioritization and maximization;
- investigation planning and specialist training;
- case management and an integrated prosecutions policy and procedures; and
- performance measurement and appraisal at individual, section/departmental and organizational levels.

This would in turn lead to the development of key internal action plans and procedures to deliver the ACC's overall objectives – see Table 5.5 for an example of an ACC undertaking all three of the traditional functions of investigation, education, and prevention.

The development of the organizational configuration takes place coterminously with the decisions on the *type* of anti-corruption work and thus workload. Unless that is addressed proactively, then the tendency is to assume all anti-corruption activities should be the responsibility of the ACC, from investigation to prevention. In many cases it is almost impossible for a newly established ACC to become effective immediately across a wide range of functions, given limited resources (financial, manpower, skill base, etc.) to give equal weight to a wide range of functions (and the main reason why all ACCs should treat with extreme caution adopting from the outset the tripartite approach of the Hong Kong Independent Commission Against Corruption (ICAC)). Further, even if a full range of functions is proposed for a new ACC (or currently undertaken by an existing ACC), any strategic assessment would need to address another key issue – how to help an ACC develop the confidence, the skills and the experience to act as an effective organization.

Issue 2: Do organizationally young ACCs have development problems?

This issue is crucial for donors and governments to understand. First, how far do the limits on resources and lack of attention to its place in any anti-corruption institutional landscape affect its ability to become established? The creation of a new, and potentially costly, ACC needs to be considered in terms of ensuring the most impact from the organization and use of existing resources, and the following issues should be taken into consideration:

- competition between agencies for scarce resources (not just money, but scarce skills and experience) or donor aid, and the potential for the dilution of the impact of other anti-corruption initiatives;
- substantial additional administrative costs in the setting up and running of the new investigative agency;
- inflexibility in the allocation and use of resources, as well as in responding to changing priorities;
- the need to develop case allocation criteria, and to create and maintain an institutional means of resolving the inevitable 'border disputes';

Table 5.5 The internal organizational structure

Organization and management delivery

Management Teams Responsible for Action Plans in:

Finance and resource management	Human resource management	Information and records management	Investigation and prosecution management	Communication and education management
Senior Finance and Administration staff.	Senior Staff Personnel and Administration Staff	Senior staff Registry and Inspection Office	Directors /Senior Staff of Operations and Legal Affairs	Director /senior staff of Education and Prevention
Member of senior management	Representative from Operations.	Representative from Legal Affairs	Representative from Education and Prevention	Representative from Relevant Agencies such as Audit or Inspection

Key Tasks in Each Action Plan

Finance and resource management	Human resource management	Information and records management	Investigation and prosecution management	Communication and education management
Planning and Development	Staffing Organizational Review	Directorates' Performance Records	Case Intake and Prioritization Policy and Protocols.	Public Education Media Activities
Computerized Financial Information Management System.	Senior Management Development.	Individual/Team performance records	Other Prioritized Tasks.	Public education events
	Basic/Advanced Investigation Training	Investigations Manual Records System	Case Management and Review	Public Relations
Building and Facilities Management Review.	Planned Recruitment and Selection; for secondments and attachments	Investigations computerized records system	Communication, case Transfer and Partnerships with other Agencies	Parliamentary Communication
Vehicle Management/ equipment System.	Performance Management System		Integrated Investigation and Prosecution Procedures	Research Activities
Computerization	Support Staff Development		Communication and co-operation with other ACCs and other relevant agencies	
On-Going Logistical Support for Project Implementation				

Source: developed by David Watt, unpublished.

- disputes over jurisdiction and responsibility between agencies whose activities substantially overlap;
- the development of an elitist culture in the specialist agency, the compartmentalization of expertise, the weakening of police resources and demotivation of police officers (exacerbated by any proposed differential salary structure for ACC investigators);
- arrangements for case distribution;
- arrangements for shared information;
- arrangements for inter-agency cooperation, coordination, and joint working (see Heilbrunn 2004; Doig *et al.* 2006).

Setting up an ACC, or reviewing an ACC already in existence, does not mean that the agency is working effectively *as an organization*, or can deliver across a range of functions, from the beginning. What donors, consultants, and governments overlook, and ACCs often ignore in their wish to respond to their expectations, is that ACCs may be – in addition to the usual concerns that they start their institutional life under-funded, and under-established – organizationally inexperienced or under-developed in terms of process and procedures, culture, expertise and commitment. Young or organizationally immature organizations may be enthusiastic or not, but in either case, lack of planning and prioritization within an appropriate management framework and a robust institutional capacity, as well as the failure to use business-planning approaches to match strengths to functions, may mean the ACC is initially unable to adequately fulfil its core functions, particularly if the focus is on high-level anti-corruption investigations.

In a business context, a focus on immediate high-level success by an organizationally immature institution would be considered high-risk. Institutions might achieve initial success, but ambition – or the ambition of others – would soon see them quickly outstrip their existing capabilities or to take on roles and responsibilities that would not be supported by the organization's existing infrastructure, resources or competences. This – the Icarus Paradox – provides a warning of the need to identify a level of performance that provides sufficient success to complement and support the evolution of organizational maturity.

Thus the initial organizational objective should be for an ACC to do something achievable well within its existing resources and capabilities and, perhaps more importantly, be *seen* to do something *well*. Organizational learning, development, and maturity come from being able to develop sufficiently and linearly to do enough to gain confidence and demonstrate competence. Delivering a defined workload, within an appropriate management structure and with sufficient resources, will lead to a 'good enough' effectiveness. The objective of this approach – which is one that would strike anyone using standard business-planning approaches as common sense – is to seek to achieve an optimal level of performance that persuades donors, peer agencies, governments and the public (and even the staff of the ACC itself) of the instutition's credibility, commitment and future development. In turn, success should be seen through the perspective of country-specific realism rather than a culturally-imported realism – not the effective ACC, but the 'effective enough' ACC in the first instance – as the basis for future progress (see Doig *et al.* 2006, 2007).

Good enough effectiveness: managing resources to deliver workload

In essence, strategy and organizational design are needed to ensure that focus and funding is fully translated into the anticipated delivery of or improvement in the organization's performance. Internally, organizational immaturity and development must be planned for. This will require a generic management process to address issues of: staffing and pay; decision-making and communication; staff development and appraisal; business planning, work allocation, and resource management; case intake and allocation; decision-making and communication; delegation and devolution of operational staffing, decision-making and resources; operational performance prioritization; case review, reporting, and measurement; general work planning and performance measurement. Addressing the organization's decision-making capabilities and financial and management information systems is, then, essential to underpin robust resource allocation procedures. These are needed to ensure that all resources are directed to support core ACC functions, once these have been determined. At the same time, the question of tight-loose financial control (central budget-setting and allocation, with expenditure within that allocation determined by operational parts of the organization) within the context of core activities often requires a very different – flatter and devolved – organizational culture than that current in many existing ACCs.

Similarly, measurement of performance and thus assessment of effectiveness should not be made in crude numbers terms. Thus 'cases prosecuted' may be a success indicator in terms of the workload of the prosecution department. If, however, these do not lead to convictions then the indicator takes on a very different significance. The work of the department promoting education and awareness may be very successful in generating awareness, but there may be adverse consequences for the investigations department if it suddenly adds to their projected workload.

The role of the components of a business-planning process to build toward an effective ACC is thus somewhat self-evident because of:

- the importance of business planning – objectives, targets, and action plans – to establish core functions and to ensure a prioritization process;
- the need to ensure the inter-relations of the priorities – for example, new vehicles and enough fuel and proper maintenance to keep them on the road – and their sustainability in terms of core business;

- the ability of the organization to underpin core activity with the appropriate decision-making, resource allocation, performance measurement, and operational and budgetary responsibilities devolved to front-line departments;
- the need for transparent and quantitative record-keeping and management and financial information systems, to develop a clearer linkage between core indicators, the availability of staff and funding to the relevant departments, and the costing of activities in pursuit of their functions.

Some of the key considerations when determining the organizational structure should be:

- simple line-management arrangements with the minimum number of management layers between the head of the ACC and front line operational staff;
- case intake management criteria and intelligence reviews;
- standard tasking, policy, and review documentation;
- as much devolution and delegation of budgets, staffing resources and case management to operational heads as possible;
- the use of team working rather than creating many compartments specializing in particular areas – e.g. investigative skills should be applicable to most cases handled by the ACC and, where specialist skills are needed in, say, civil engineering or accounting, these could be bought in;
- the use of uniform paper or computerized case-management procedures;
- closer liaison with prosecutors during investigations;
- an organizational structure that gives the appropriate weight to the functions that have been identified as high priority (i.e. the key objectives); and
- an appropriate balance between operational and support staff (generally an organization that has more than 25 per cent of its staff not directly contributing to the achievement of its objectives will be inefficient).

To repeat, the organization's strategic objectives and decision-making capabilities will require functioning financial and management information systems to allow robust resource allocation procedures to be made, to ensure that resources are directed to support core activities in support of the strategic objectives. The purpose of internal performance measurement in this should be to make the links between strategy and objectives and resources, converting the financial details into coherent financial analysis which describes the overall financial position of the ACC and of its work. This financial analysis needs to address:

- how the ACC currently spends its money (and provide a comparison on a year-on-year basis);
- the cost of resources required to undertake planned areas and levels of activity;

- the cost priorities and targets for how they are to be achieved;
- the cost of the capacity development needed to achieve required standards of performance.

Using the financial information the ACC's management can assess where best to place its resources to complete its workload and deliver its objectives. The most appropriate allocation of resources can be assessed and mea-sured – and thus confirm the suitability of the management structure and the decisions on the functions and workload being undertaken. Most agen-cies have indicators which relate to activity and which focus on economy (the unit cost of delivering an activity), efficiency or productivity (the volume of the activity delivered against the unit cost), and effectiveness (the rela-tionship between the activity and the delivery of the agency's stated objec-tives). A number of countries now include a further measure of effectiveness – impact or outcome – which relates the work or the contribu-tion of the agency to wider objectives of the sector in which the agency works. Thus, in relation to corruption investigations, ACCs can be assessed on the cost of investigations, the number of cases investigated, the number of cases successfully concluded (where the indicator is often the number of successful prosecutions), or an increasing awareness of and reporting to the agency by the public. This 'impact' measure may include the reduction of the number of corruption cases or greater trust in government because: the effectiveness of the investigative work of the ACC deters others from becoming involved in corruption, because the public believes that the ACC is effective; the public is convinced the government is taking corruption ser-iously and allocating appropriate support and resources to the ACC; or the other parts of the criminal justice process are also working effectively in conjunction with the ACC. The 'impact' measure thus could be as much a measure of effectiveness as the more orthodox effectiveness measure noted above in that it looks beyond the activity of the agency as an agency (throughput and output) to the effectiveness of the ACC within a wider context.

All four – cost, efficiency, effectiveness, and impact – should be nuanced. Assessment of performance should not be based on crude quantitative indicators, nor focused on only one type of indicator. Thus any approach to developing performance measurement for ACCs has to recognize:

- the interdependence of short-term and long-term objectives (where the latter is concerned with prevention and deterrence rather than investigations);
- the politics of corruption (where immediately trying to address high-level corruption ineffectively through an agency focused solely on investigation could damage the credibility of anti-corruption work when an initial focus on promoting public awareness and education might raise a suffi-cient momentum for reform to put pressure on government to accept the need for an investigative dimension to the agency or another agency);

- the competition between agencies for lead status in a given area and the consequential link between status and funding;
- the accountability dimension, linked to the issue of lead status, in terms of who is responsible for the the overall country strategy to fight corruption and how indicators are determined to reflect the contribution of individual agencies within that strategy;
- the environmental aspect, linked to the accountability dimension and performance ownership, in terms of how to address the effect of issues outside the control or responsibility of the ACC, but which affects their performance;
- the organizational complexity of the agency and how it integrates its work and manages its workload;
- the strategic decision-making and budget processes of the agency relating to the above.

Many indicators are now nuanced in terms of impact. For example, certain investigations may not end in a court case, but the disruptive nature of the investigation may have terminated an ongoing corrupt relationship. Deterring corruption could be measured in terms of funds saved or protecting the public from having to pay for public services. Using investigations to seek recovery of the bribe or the termination of a corruptly-awarded contract (and the refunding of any money paid under the contract) may be more effective in terms of resources than a long court case. What the nuancing is seeking to do is to address the impact or outcome dimension of effectiveness.

Conclusion

Measuring the 'effectiveness' of the organization is only half the process. An organization may be highly effective in terms of internal planning, resource allocation, and delivering on its targets. However, an ACC is established to fight corruption; its work, however 'effective' an organization it is, is of little use if the country is perceived to be becoming more corrupt. Put another way, the *purpose* of an ACC is, as a state institution, is to reduce corruption as part of the wider governance reform process that the current developmental agenda is seeking.

At present, the general approach to development prioritizes a democratic state, promoting short- and long-terms goals towards what might be termed the core components of the liberal democratic model: political legitimacy for the state through universal suffrage and regular elections; the peaceful transfer of power; an effective political opposition, and representative government; accountability through transparency of decision-making and the provision of information; separation of powers; effective scrutiny of financial expenditure and the right to challenge official decisions; effective standards of conduct in public office; official competencies, such as impartially recruited and well-trained public servants; realistic social and welfare policies and low defence expenditure; human and civil rights, including freedom of religion, the right of association, expression, and movement, as well as rights of review, complaint, and redress against decisions or actions of the state; impartial and accessible criminal justice system; an independent free media; and the absence of arbitrary government power (drawn from Doig 1999 and Doig and Theobald 1999).

These components encompass the good governance perspective of the state. Thus, not only does the citizen have the right to participate in the processes that direct and oversee the activities of the state, but the *purpose* of the state itself is to serve its citizens. Governance, therefore, is concerned with not just the organization and activity of government – its economy and efficiency – but also with the ends to which they are put – its effectiveness and impact – in terms of achieving levels of economic, human, and institutional development and of providing its citizens with the basic infrastructures and services for their well-being (such as health, food, education, water and security).

ACCs or equivalent agencies have a central role in that agenda, but often only as one of a number of institutions with regulatory, audit, and investigative functions which also have roles in promoting that agenda. Addressing corruption is often seen to be a major constraint on the delivery of that agenda. If corruption is a key means of assessing change and progress in the development agenda, and dealing with corruption by governments an demonstrator of a commitment both to change and to the developmental agenda, then the ACC may or may not have an effective role in helping achieve this, over and above its own 'effectiveness' as an organization. That role has to be planned for and managed. The failure to match workload, management and resources thus has implications for the context of whether there should be an ACC and, if there is one, whether or not it will be an 'effective' ACC not only in itself, but also for the wider purpose to which all anti-corruption work should be directed.

Notes

1 Some of the issues in this section are explored more fully in Doig and McIvor (2003). The material on transitional countries was primarily developed by Quinten Reed for a briefing paper which accompanied a number of National Integrity System country reports, in relation to which Alan Doig was the project director and Stephanie McIvor was the lead researcher, presented to the Global Forum II conference in The Hague in 2001.

6 Anti-corruption bodies as discourse-controlling instruments

Experiences from south-east Europe

Daniel Smilov

Ideally, institutions should be created with medium- and long-term considerations in mind. They should change the rules of the game of governance in such a way as to maximize the benefits and minimize the costs of collective decision-making. Yet politicians are often driven by short-term considerations and focused excessively on electoral performance and voter mobilization. Therefore it happens that institutions are introduced without sufficient insight into and knowledge of their effects. Hence the widespread talk of 'unintended consequences'. The other side of the same coin is the fact that, in the circumstances of modern politics, institutional innovations often involve a certain leap of faith.

If there is a region in the world that could claim the championship in institutional leaps of faith over the past two decades, it has to be Eastern Europe. Here, since the fall of the Berlin Wall, there have been at least three waves of new institutions. First, there was the universal transplantation of the basic institutions of representative democracy and market economy, starting with free elections and the legalization of private property. This process was a ripple of one of the successive waves of democratization, which by now has been well studied (Diamond *et al.* 1997). Second, and with different degrees of success, there was the introduction of devices constraining the will of political majorities and their representatives. Most of these devices came under the banner of constitutionalism carried proudly by powerful constitutional courts (Prochazka 2002). In their footsteps followed independent judiciaries, independent central banks, currency boards, and other constraints on the will of majorities. As an important element of this trend of limitation of power one could enlist also the increasing transfer of sovereignty towards European Union (EU) institutions in most of the Central European countries.[1]

In this chapter I am interested in the third kind of institutional leap of faith in Eastern Europe, which involved the universal implementation of anti-corruption institutional reforms. An important part of these was the setting up of new bodies designed to create and carry out anti-corruption policies and strategies. First, the so-called anti-corruption commissions gained popularity. They were generally not empowered with investigative powers, but were involved in building partnerships with civil society groups and prepared comprehensive anti-corruption strategies, action plans, etc. The commissions were an essential element of a specific approach to the fight against corruption dubbed by the European Bank for Reconstruction and Development (EBRD) 'omnibus programmes' (Steves and Rousso 2004).

Initially, these bodies had a positive overall effect in raising public awareness concerning the issue of corruption. Gradually, however, publics seemed to grow tired of this type of activity. Probably there is a point of saturation at which public awareness of the spread of corruption turns into cynicism regarding anti-corruption activities as a whole. If this point is reached, which might well be the case in some countries of the region (Tisné and Smilov 2004), an important unintended consequence appears. This is the falling confidence in the political establishment, the rise of populist leaders and parties, and the growing general discontent with the constitutional order and liberal democracy.[2]

The increasing public and external pressure for more tangible results in the fight against corruption has lead to a second phase of the anti-corruption institutional leap of faith in Eastern Europe. Currently, several states in the south-east corner of the region are creating specific investigative and prosecutorial agencies to tackle the problem of corruption. Romania has set up an anti-corruption Prosecutorial Office. (This office was established in 2002 as the National Anti-corruption Prosecution Office and was subsequently reorganized in 2006 as the National Anti-corruption Directorate. The Romanian name is *Direcţia Naţională Anticorupţie*.) Bulgaria (more cautiously) is following suit: in 2008 it set up a specialized agency (The State Agency for National Security), part of whose tasks are the fight against organized crime and grand corruption.[3]

In what follows my task is twofold. On the one hand, I look more closely into the institutional innovations which have been carried out with a specific intention to fight corruption in south-east Europe. The focus is primarily on the experiences of Bulgaria, although illustrations from other Balkan countries, such as Macedonia, Albania, and Romania will be given. Secondly, and more challengingly, I address the question of the motivations behind the anti-corruption institutional leap of faith in south-east Europe. More specifically, I suggest a tentative explanation as to why exactly these specific institutional forms of anti-corruption activities have been chosen.

At the outset, it has to be said that the second question is not easy to answer. When we compare the anti-corruption leap of faith to the first two – the democratic leap of faith and the constitutional leap of faith – there is one substantial and obvious difference. While in the first two cases Eastern European reformers relied heavily on copying the established democracies of the Western world, in the third case there were very few such authoritative precedents. Exactly because of this conspicuous lack of precedent, rare and exotic institutional solutions, such as the anti-corruption commissions of Hong Kong and New South Wales, gained disproportionate prominence in policy debates and discussions.[4]

If Western experience did not offer a model, other justifications and motivations for the anti-corruption institutional leap should be explored. One possible motivation is expected performance. If it is, one should look for performance indicators for anti-corruption institutions. One of the ground-breaking discoveries of the 1990s – the discovery that corruption can be measured – gives hopes in this regard. This hope is rather premature as there have been thus far no reliable performance measurement device tracking the success or failure of anti-corruption institutions in south-east Europe.[5]

Eastern Europeans have been long trained in the Hegelian doctrine of identity of reason and reality, according to which there should be a sound rational justification for everything that is real, anti-corruption institutions included. In this vein, this chapter will argue that local politicians and policy-makers needed these institutions as tools of leverage over the anti-corruption discourse which has become one of the most important instruments of political mobilization. Admittedly, it is a complex argument which could hardly be substantiated in a single chapter. Therefore, the ensuing discussion is sketchy and programmatic. It starts with the idea of the depleting resources of political mobilization, and then proceeds to the presentation of anti-corruption agencies as tools for governmental leverage over the anti-corruption discourse.

Presenting the anti-corruption commissions and agencies as discourse-controlling instruments is not meant to be an argument against their introduction. There is no doubt that in certain circumstances they could produce results which go beyond discourse *per se*. Looking at them as discourse tools, however, gives an answer to the troubling question of why governing parties are at all interested in the introduction of such bodies. The answer suggested here is that these bodies help governments use anti-corruption discourse in the electoral context in their own favour. Anti-corruption, which typically is a topic on which the political opposition thrives, becomes useful for the incumbent who could offer strategies and plans, organize public awareness campaigns, establish links with non-governmental organizations (NGOs), and even initiate corruption proceedings against high profile figures. These possibilities level the playing field between government and opposition in electoral contexts.

Depleting resources for political mobilization

Political parties in most of the liberal democracies in Eastern Europe are in a precarious situation: their resources for political mobilization are running out. I will illustrate this by a short case-study on Bulgarian political life, in the framework of which there will be parallels with other countries. Throughout the 1990s Bulgarian parties relied on three types of resources: ideology, patronage, and state aid (financial and in-kind). Only the third type of resource – state aid – was increasing and became more substantial by the end of the decade.[6] As it is well known, however, reliance on state aid does not always translate into greater potential for political mobilization of voters and sympathizers: on the contrary, it might result in their alienation and the *etatisation* of the parties (Landfried 1994).

The other two resources – ideology and patronage – which have admittedly a greater mobilization potential, were gradually depleting due to a plurality of factors. On the ideological front, by 2000 all major parties in the country had reached a solid consensus on the most important political issues, such as membership in EU and the North Atlantic Treaty Organization (NATO), the desirability of privatization and restitution of property, strict fiscal discipline, and commitment to lower taxes. In practice, this consensus diluted the left-right cleavage in Bulgarian politics. It was no surprise that this was when a new player arrived on the scene – the National Movement Simeon II (NMSII), the party of the former Bulgarian tsar, a charismatic figure epitomizing all of the elements of the emerging cross-party consensus. From then on the other major parties shed most of their remaining ideological baggage, and the ultimate result was a grand coalition between the nominally centre-left Socialist party and the nominally centre-right NMSII, formed after the parliamentary elections in 2005.

The Bulgarian example suggests that the consolidation of democracy in Eastern Europe has paradoxically diminished any clash of substantive political ideas, and encouraged the creation of eclectic, heterogeneous party programmes and platforms (Krastev 2007). In this sea of eclecticism and lack of coherence it is no surprise that the ideologies and programmes of mainstream parties lost their mobilization potential (Krastev 2002).

Patronage was the second most important resource of the Bulgarian parties in the 1990s. Here I use the term 'patronage' broadly to include all practices through which party members and sympathizers gained access to public positions, services, or some other form of privilege. In a giant process of transformation from state ownership to private property in the economy, partisan appointments to senior management positions, governing boards, etc., were inevitable. In the Bulgarian case (and in south-east Europe in general) opportunities for patronage were even more abundant because privatization was delayed and most of the economy remained in state hands until the end of the 1990s (Smilov and Toplak 2007; see also Smilov 2002). Apart from the economy, political parties tried throughout the 1990s to gain control over areas such as the judiciary and the public electronic media, which are supposed to be free from partisan influence.

Patronage practices took a more explicit form in south-east Europe, but they were typical for most of the transition countries. Privatization of state assets by partisan cronies became the reason for major scandals in Hungary, and the Czech Republic: the fall of Klaus as a Prime Minister is an example (Orenstein 1998). But more importantly, as Andras Sajó has argued, the transition was characterized by the existence of specific clientelistic practices around political parties (Sajó 1998).

With the end of the massive privatization processes in the beginning of the new century, the possibilities for mobilization of voters by patronage started to decrease. It is of course impossible to announce the death of political patronage, but there are certain symptoms that suggest that its role is diminishing. The recent local elections in Bulgaria (autumn 2007) illustrate the point. First, they were characterized by a scandalous number of allegations of vote-buying. Secondly, there was a massive emergence of so-called 'business' parties running directly for political positions and bypassing the representation offered by established parties. These developments suggest that the established parties are losing their clientele both in local businesses and among deprived minorities of voters: the former do not want to invest any more in party representation, while the latter want direct financial compensation for their votes.

In such circumstances of depleting traditional resources of mobilization, political actors turn to issues such as nationalism, identity politics, and what is most important for our discussion – anti-corruption. Anti-corruption becomes an election-winning discourse. In the Bulgarian case, all of the parties that won elections since 2001 were seen as anti-corruption fighters. In Romania, corruption also became a central issue of politics: the culmination of this trend took place immediately before and after the accession of the country to the EU in the attempts to prosecute a former Prime Minister on corruption grounds, and to impeach the President.

The structure of anti-corruption discourse

Thus far I have established that anti-corruption discourse has become very important for political parties in Eastern Europe. Now the structure of this discourse – which is by no means a monolithic phenomenon – will be explored. The goal will be to show that different actors have different perceptions of the character of the phenomenon, its causes and effects, and, ultimately, the measures that need to be taken against it. It will be argued that incumbent politicians have an interest to speak in a particular way about corruption. In the following sections it will be shown that the anti-corruption commissions and agencies set up in south-east Europe serve the purpose of instrumentalizing the anti-corruption discourse in favour of the governing parties. The analysis in this section uses the findings of two research projects done by the Centre for Liberal Strategies – a Sofia-based thinktank – in the period 2004–07. In the framework of these projects the understandings of corruption of key target groups, such as politicians, journalists, businesses, NGOs, and the judiciary were studied.[7]

The politicians

No unified definition of corruption exists amongst politicians despite the manifest consensus that corruption is a negative phenomenon that has to be combated. Normally opposition politicians stick to broad public-interest-based, inclusive and inflated conceptions of corruption which go beyond the strict legalistic meaning of the concept.[8] Such conceptions often allege various forms of favouritism in privatization, clandestine state control or tacit state approval of smuggling channels, turning the party into a corrupt hierarchical structure, etc. Few of these allegations could be translated directly into penal code crimes. Yet all suggest abuse of public trust and some damage done to the public good.

Governing politicians, in contrast, usually resort to two strategies in their discourse on corruption. First, they stick to legalistic notions of corruption and require proof beyond reasonable doubt for the substantiation of corruption allegations. Secondly, and much less often, governing politicians try to normalize certain practices which the opposition call corrupt.[9]

Further, corruption discourse is engaged in the separation of power battles between governments and the opposition in the following way. The opposition has an interest in the adoption of anti-corruption measures which limit the discretion of the government in policy-making (transparency requirements, deregulation, limiting licences, etc.). Contrary to that, governments have an incentive to preserve a broader range of discretionary powers.[10]

Finally, governments and the opposition differ in what they see as a proper response to the problem of corruption. The former look for answers in long-term institutional and legislative amendments. The latter are looking mostly for a political change that will bring them to power, which could happen if a scandal leads to a governmental crisis and mass protests. Personnel changes in the government, indictment of key politicians, etc. are also appealing anti-corruption measures for the political opposition.

The judiciary

Not surprisingly, the judiciary normally resorts to legalistic conceptions of corruption and sticks to concepts and definitions in the law books. The paradox is the virtual disappearance of corruption from the discourse of judges. In this discourse the issue of corruption is often renamed and translated into other problems. Thus, in two of the best-known corruption scandals in Bulgaria between 2001–04, the involvement of the courts was marginal: in one of the cases, an allegation of party finance violation was transformed into a libel suit; in the other, an allegation of corrupt privatization was transformed into a problem of pure procedural violation of the privatization law.

In both cases, what stood out was the inconclusive character of the judicial proceedings regarding the major questions at stake in the two scandals. In the party-funding case, for instance, judicial proceedings could not prove or disprove the two competing interpretations of the events: the acceptance of illegal donation versus an attempt by a controversial businessman to set up one of the major parties in the country. The unfortunate lack of conclusive judicial findings creates a fertile atmosphere for the production of myths. For our purposes, however, the important point is that when cases reach the courts, corruption curiously shrinks.

The police and prosecutors

In contrast to the judges, prosecutors and the police are characterized by a very widespread use (including in official documents) of inflated public interest-based conceptions of corruption, such as 'circles of friends', 'favouritism', 'party machines', 'political umbrellas against investigation', 'theft through privatization', etc. Naming ministers as part of Mafia-like structures, calculations of the negative financial impact of corrupt privatization, etc., feature regularly in the parlance and the documents produced by this group. Regrettably, as is clear from the previous section, formal indictments are quite rarely upheld by courts, which creates a significant gap between the discourse and the output of the police and the prosecutors. In terms of conception and perception of corruption this group is closer to the opposition politicians than to the judges.

The media

For the media, corruption is generally an all-embracing metaphor for criminal and bad government. Here, public interest-based conceptions of corruption are encountered in their most inflated versions. The main theme is that greedy and incompetent elites are stealing from the people on a massive scale. Concrete cases are usually blown out of proportion in order to paint pictures of epic theft. As a result, the borderline between investigative journalism, analysis, and storytelling is often blurred and sometimes non-existent. The solutions that the media see to the problem of corruption are, as a rule, repressive in their character: more convictions.

Sometimes one is left with the impression that the real role of the media is not exclusively in the fight against corruption, but also in informing the public of latest developments in the story of grand theft. A cynic might even say that the role of the media is in involving the people in these clandestine processes, making them privy to their intricacies, albeit by means of vicarious participation. From this point of view, it is not surprising that the media tend to show a disproportionate interest in the outbreak and unfolding of scandals, as compared with their resolution. In south-east European context, such attitudes are typical, and not only for the tabloid press and marginal cable networks.

Civil society and NGOs

The main elements of this discourse are the following: corruption is measurable; it is increasing or at least is very high; it is bad for the economy.

This is by far the most sophisticated discourse about corruption, and dictates the fashion in the anti-corruption field in general. Civil society groups stress the importance of institutional change and changes in the incentive structure of important actors in the fight against corruption. Yet, and somewhat paradoxically, although they frame the solutions in terms of substantial structural reforms, often results are expected relatively fast. This urgent feature of civil society discourse dramatically raises public expectations. One of the results of these raised expectations is the dissatisfaction with politicians, the delegitimization of governments, and the creation of a fertile ground for the appearance of new populist political actors.

The business sector

Business generally speaks about corruption, but mainly through silence. It prefers to shift the problem from corruption *per se* to the conditions for the emergence of corruption. These are usually to be found in the domain of legislation and public administration. Extremely popular is the so-called problem of 'red tape' – administrative hurdles for entrepreneurial activities, which are to be overcome by corrupt transactions. Generally, business discourses on corruption are depersonalized. They refer to structural conditions, not to agents and perpetrators. Business is also typically portrayed as the victim of corruption, while the public servants (as an anonymous category) are the potential wrong-doers.

Although the conception of corruption as 'grease' for the economy has been replaced in policy-making circles by the idea that corruption is 'bad for the economy', there is no evidence that the business community has deeply internalized the new credo. In other words, corruption is not by any means excluded by representatives of the business community as a possible means for overcoming unjustified and inefficient government-imposed burdens on business.

Designing discourse coalitions and their political usage

The preceding analysis shows that governmental parties risk losing the public debate if they rely only on the legalistic discourse on the phenomenon of corruption. For example, in 2000–2001 the government of the Bulgarian Prime Minister Ivan Kostov vehemently denied the existence of corruption unless the corruption could be proven in court. This government was swept aside by King Simeon II's movement, which came into office on an anti-corruption ticket. Governments, sticking only to the legalistic conception of corruption, could rely only on support from the judiciary – hardly a vocal player in political life. The government will see virtually everybody talking against them – the media, the NGOs, the businesses, and eventually the prosecutors and the police, if they enjoy a degree of autonomy. Governments, therefore, need to re-examine their discourse coalitions very carefully if they do not want to be left in isolation. In order to break up their discourse isolation, however, governments must take at least some of the following steps:

- First, they must publicly admit and recognize the problem of corruption. In this way they throw a discourse bridge to potential partners in other groups who are not directly interested in political changes, like the opposition, and build partnerships with them around specific anti-corruption measures.
- With regard to civil society, in exchange for the public recognition of corruption, governments could require cooperation with NGOs in a number of spheres, such as measuring corruption, legislative drafting of programmes, action plans, and other normative acts, consultation with experts, etc. The governments will be successful in breaking up their discourse isolation if most of the influential NGOs in the country adopt a 'non-confrontational' stance towards them. This would mean that corruption is depoliticized and that change of government is no longer seen as the key measure to be taken.
- In the case of the media, the situation is more complex. In contrast to NGOs, the media are not that interested in long-term institutional and legislative measures. They frame public discourse mostly through scandal and the personalization of politics. Therefore, personnel changes are indispensable in order to bridge the gap between media and governmental discourse on corruption. For this purpose, governments must involve elements of the prosecutors and the police with the goal of starting investigations about public persons, possibly including members of the governing parties as well (only in exceptional cases, of course). It is important to stress that for the purposes of collaboration with the media, governments need to focus only on the start of investigations since media interest is highest at this point and goes down dramatically at the more complex judicial stages when the intricate procedures are often impenetrable for the public in general.
- Even the opposition could be co-opted in terms of anti-corruption discourse by a skilful government. The key element here is the depoliticization of the issue through the elaboration of a comprehensive anti-corruption plan which requires profound long-term institutional changes in all areas of governance. Ultimately, governing parties will be successful if they obtain the consent of the opposition for these programmes and plans. It is normally not impossible since these contain predominantly common-sense measures aiming at the general improvement of governance. And they reduce the chance of anti-corruption measures being selectively applied to leaders of the opposition. In certain cases, members of the opposition could also become members of watchdog bodies, supervising the implementation of legislative and institutional reforms.
- Finally, the government must tread very carefully in the silent discourse of the business sector on the issue of corruption. The best strategy to

ensure that this silence means support is to lead a policy of downsizing of the state and lowering of taxes. These are the key anti-corruption measures that the business community looks for. Normally, a political crisis and instability are not in the interest of the economic players.

There are several residual problems with these strategies of breaking up discourse isolation by a government. The adoption of legislative and institutional measures – which is the core of what a government can offer to the public and other influential players in terms of anti-corruption – is potentially threatening to governmental discretion in important areas. This alienates traditional clientelistic partners – the role of patronage decreases, but it also leads to a convergence of the acceptable party platforms in the longer run. Cooperation with civil society – understood as a monolithic, non-partisan entity – also leads to a certain depoliticization of politics, which dilutes the dividing lines between the major parties.

Thus, by creating successful discourse coalitions with other influential players, governments resolve their short-term political problems of electoral mobilization. They break up their discourse isolation, and their messages start to find support in what the other actors are saying as well. However, the long-term cost of this strategy seems to be a level of depoliticization and a further undermining of the tools for political mobilization for the established political parties as a group. It is no surprise, from this perspective, that despite the commitment of governments in south-east Europe to the fight against corruption for more than seven years now, there is no visible revival of public trust in the established political parties. In most of the countries, trust in governments and the representative structures of society as a whole is very low. Parties and parliaments are usually most at risk (see Table 6.1). The troubles of the established parties have recently taken two main forms.

Table 6.1 Trust in institutions

	Trust		*Distrust*	
	EU 25	BG	EU 25	BG
Political parties	22%	10%	72%	84%
Parliament	38%	17%	54%	75%
Government	35%	24%	59%	66%
Judicial system	48%	20%	47%	73%
Trade unions	38%	13%	48%	64%

Note: EU25 stands for the enlarged membership of the European Union following the entry of the 10 new member states from Central and Eastern Europe in 2004. The EU now displays 27 members (EU27) following the accession of Bulgaria and Romania in 2007. BG stands for Bulgaria.
Source: Eurobarometer, No. 66. DG Communication / EC (2007) *Standard EURO-BAROMETER 66 / Autumn 2006 – TNS Opinion & Social* (Report). Brussels: EC Publications.

In the Romanian case, the two major political parties (the ex-communist Social Democrats, who control Parliament, and the block of the President Basescu) got involved in a desperate all-out anti-corruption war against each other to win back public trust. Before Romania's accession to the EU, the anti-corruption effort was lead by the charismatic Minister of Justice Monica Macovei, who was closer to the presidential camp. The Social Democrats, who saw themselves as victims of the anti-corruption campaign, retaliated (with the help of other parliamentary groups) by sacking Macovei immediately after the accession of Romania to the EU, and by starting impeachment proceedings against Basescu himself. The impeachment failed because the Romanian people confirmed Basescu in office in a referendum. So far, high-profile investigations against important party leaders on both sides have not lead to convictions. Some of the investigations never reached the judicial phase, while the others have taken considerable time for final resolution. To an external observer, it would be a real miracle if these developments restore public trust in the political process and the representative structures of democracy in Romania.

In Bulgaria, the mainstream parties have adopted another strategy. They have avoided thus far an all-out anti-corruption war against each other, with one significant exception in the first part of 2007 when a Vice-Prime Minister of the Socialist Party was forced to resign, together with the Chief Investigator (who was seen as an appointee of another coalition partner – the Movement for Rights and Freedoms). These two individuals started accusing each other of corrupt behaviour, accusations that remained unproven in court but which had a dramatic effect on the public. This was just an exception to the general rule of avoidance of anti-corruption warfare among the major parties, however. The result of this avoidance is the public perception of all of the major parties as corrupt, which opens the political stage for ever-new anti-corruption populist actors. Accordingly, all new elections bring a new popular anti-corruption hero in Bulgarian politics. In 2001 this was Simeon II and his movement; in 2005 the nationalist Ataka; and in 2007 the charismatic Boyko Borisov – the former bodyguard of the ex-tsar – who made a career in the Ministry of Interior in the period 2001–05.

Somewhat paradoxically, whether avoiding an all-out confrontation on the issue of corruption or not, major parties suffer from a long-term tendency to lose public support in south-east Europe. The long-term trend in winning the public support through anti-corruption discourse strategies is hardly encouraging for the major parties, however. The door for new populist players seems wide open.

Commissions and agencies as discourse-controlling instruments: the experience of south-east Europe

In the previous section the importance of the formation of discourse coalitions for governing actors was explored together with some of its short- and long-term consequences. In this section the structure of the anti-corruption commissions and agencies created in some of the south-east European countries will be examined from the point of view of their involvement in the battle to control the anti-corruption discourse. Although governments must admit the existence of corruption (even if not judicially proven) in order to become players in the discourse battles, they have to do this cautiously. It is impossible for key government politicians to speak regularly about wide-spread corruption, to measure it, and to organize public awareness campaigns as, in the eyes of the public, this will associate the politicians with corruption. Therefore, there is a political need for a semi-autonomous, semi-independent public body to take upon itself the anti-corruption discourse on behalf of the ruling parties. Based on the previous discussion, one could conclude that it would be rational for such a body to have the following structure and powers:

- First, its composition should build bridges with civil society and the opposition. Members of civil society could either participate in the nominations of commissioners, or even sit on the commission. At a minimum, most of the meetings of this body should be open to the public and encourage media coverage and participation of NGOs. As to the opposition, a delicate balance should be sought between its participation and its support for long-term programmatic documents in the fight against corruption.
- The powers of these bodies need to be concentrated mainly in the area of institutional reform, legislative drafting, and coordination among other government agencies. Investigative powers are not needed and, indeed, they could antagonize important groups such as the police and the prosecutors. Still, the commissions may have some limited investigative powers, especially if they are authorized to initiate proceedings which then are transferred to the prosecutors and the police for continuation.
- In relation to the media, the commission should be able to supply them with media-friendly material. The best is the news of started proceedings and possible indictments. In the absence of such data, the second-best option is statistical data on the spread of corruption in society.
- Finally, in relation to business, one could expect that the commission should remain discrete and uphold the two major prongs of the business's silent discourse on corruption: downsizing of the state and lowering of taxes.

My argument is that the adopted anti-corruption commissions in at least four south-east European countries follow closely the ideal type set out above. These countries are Bulgaria, Albania, Macedonia, and Bosnia and Herzegovina.[11] In all of these countries, partly because of domestic political dynamics, and partly because of the pressure exercised by donors (like the Council of Europe, EU, and others), a specific model of anti-corruption institutional reforms was adopted which was aptly named by the EBRD as

'omnibus programmes': a coordinated assemblage of governmental structures and policies specifically geared towards fighting corruption. The main
elements of the omnibus programmes were the following:

- an anti-corruption law;
- a national anti-corruption strategy or programme;
- a ministerial commission, specialized, unit or dedicated agency supervising
  implementation;
- an action plan to implement the programme; and
- a monitoring mechanism.

Here I will focus more closely on one specific case study – Albania. Most of
the conclusions, however, will also be valid for the other three countries, to
the practices of which occasional references will be made.

In Albania, by 2004, a Council of Europe-sponsored project was under-
way, the main purpose of which was to strengthen the newly established anti-
corruption body: the so-called Anti-corruption Monitoring Group. In the
same period, the Macedonian State Commission against Corruption was set
up (with help of foreign donors). Similar commissions were created in Bulgaria,
in Bosnia, and in other countries of the region as well.

In Albania, the national anti-corruption strategy and action plan were the
product of two years of dialogue between the donor community and the Albanian government, which resulted in a strategic document spanning five
reform areas: public administration reform, improved legislation, improvement of public finances management, better transparency in business transactions, and public information and civil society participation. The structure
or agency overseeing the progress of the strategy included an anti-corruption
monitoring group, the Anti-Corruption Monitoring Group (ACMG) –
composed of the legal directors of relevant ministries as well as the Minister
of State – to monitor the implementation of the plan, give advice, issue
recommendations, and suggest improvement to and prioritization of the
plan. There was also a permanent secretariat of the ACMG.

The Council of Europe's approach in Albania was entirely focused on the
implementation of the action plan. The institutional structures that had
been created had no responsibility or powers beyond ensuring the implementation of the plan. More specifically, they lacked powers of investigation,
indictment, etc.

In Macedonia, roughly at the same time, a State Commission for the
Fight against Corruption in Macedonia was set up with slightly more
expanded powers. Apart from the adopting and monitoring of a national
programme for corruption prevention and repression, it also had the power
to summon – in secret if necessary – persons suspected of corruption before
the state commission to clarify their position before possibly starting an initiative before the relevant bodies to discharge, replace, or criminally prosecute
those elected officials or public servants suspected of corruption.

By 2004, the ACMG's achievements in Albania had been limited to passing laws. The Council of Ministers proposed and passed through parliament legislation introducing a code of ethics for public administration and requiring the declaration of assets of public and elected officials. Other laws 'on notary' and 'on advocacy' were passed in the judicial sector and a law 'on the internal audit in the public service' was passed under the public finance management heading. The European Union – in its own monitoring reports on Albania – had been openly critical of the action plan's focus on the implementation of legislation, citing the lack of precision of the indicators used by the ACMG, lack of firm deadlines, lack of institutional cooperation, as well as the poor quality of the requested measures in the draft action plan's recommendations on legal consolidation. Despite these problems, however, cooperation with civil society had been quite encouraging. The United States Agency for International Development (USAID)-sponsored Albanian Coalition against Corruption was given a seat on the board of the anti-corruption monitoring group, and civil society groups contributed as experts in a small number of projects and surveys run by the permanent unit, not least in pushing for the adoption of the declaration of assets law. Involvement and support from the business community was practically non-existent, however. Even at that time there were fears that the adopted anti-corruption strategy had a limited effect as far as the reduction of corruption *per se* was concerned.[12]

If we adopt the view that the anti-corruption commissions are discourse-controlling mechanisms on behalf of the governing parties, the structure, the powers, and the operation of the Albanian and Macedonian bodies will become much more understandable. Their main purpose was to build what I have called 'discourse coalitions' with civil society, the media, and other influential actors. From this perspective, they were quite functional.

First, they managed to gain the support of an umbrella civil society anti-corruption organization, which comprised NGOs from all possible corners of civil society. Thus, the issue of the fight against corruption was practically depoliticized.[13]

The fight against corruption was successfully shifted from the issue of political and personnel changes to institutional and legislative reforms. This was a strategy breeding long-term discontent because the ever-increasing public expectations could not be satisfied with legislative amendments only. But again, from a discourse perspective no one could seriously challenge the government that it was not 'taking measures' against corruption, or not 'recognizing' the seriousness of the problem. All in all, the government had become a player in the corruption discourse, competing with the opposition and others over anti-corruption as a precious resource of political mobilization.

They enjoyed good relations with the media as well. Parts of the activities initiated or sponsored by these bodies and their supportive civil society organizations were actually televised and were quite popular. Hotline telephone lines were set up, TV shows were raising public awareness, etc. In all of these, paradoxically, the respective governments were not always at the receiving end of public criticism, but at times got an opportunity to publicize their own efforts in the implementation of the action plans, etc.

Conclusion

The goal of this chapter was to demonstrate that one of the major reasons for setting up of anti-corruption bodies is control over the unruly discourse around corruption and so should be analysed in the concrete political dynamics of each society. My ambition is not to argue that these bodies serve only or even primarily this discursive function: one could easily imagine cases where anti-corruption commissions and agencies contribute significantly to the reduction of corruption. However, even in such cases the agencies would be successful only to the extent that they build viable coalitions with politicians, judges, prosecutors, media, and the civil society. No matter how powerful and independent these bodies are, they cannot take on the rest of society on their own.

The experience of south-east European countries in the building of viable anti-corruption coalitions around agencies and commissions has been decidedly mixed. Such bodies have taken root in many places in the region and, as shown above, they are seen as functional and useful by a variety of governmental and non-governmental actors. However, their broader effects on democratic politics seem to be rather marginal or even problematic. In any event, sustained anti-corruption efforts by governments have not produced dramatic decreases in the public perception of corruption.[14] Related to this, many of the countries in the region are plagued by very low levels of trust in the representative institutions of democracy: parties and parliaments (Mungiu-Pippidi 2007; Eurobarometer 2005). I have shown that the anti-corruption bodies and strategies adopted by governments have given them a handle on an important resource of electoral mobilization – the anti-corruption discourse. But this short-term success should be evaluated against the longer-term trends of falling electoral turnouts, lack of party membership, and lack of party loyalty and discipline. Finally, we should take into account the dangers of rising populist parties which further undermine the party systems and which campaign not so much against the corruption of a specific government, but against the corruption of the political elite as a whole. These populist parties actually cultivate the perception in the public that liberal, representative democracy is corrupt.

The weakest link in the models of governance in the region is the political parties (Carothers 2006). In this regard, the anti-corruption efforts spearheaded by agencies and commissions have had an unfortunate unintended consequence – they either have contributed to or at least failed to prevent the further weakening of mainstream political parties and the rise of populist players. The future success of anti-corruption efforts, therefore, depends on whether they are embedded in a healthy process of democratic representation. If this is not the case, as it appears to be in south-east Europe, anti-corruption activities and institutional innovations might become a rather risky leap of faith.

Notes

1 Similar processes, albeit to a much smaller extent, could be observed with the membership of East European countries in the NATO, WTO, and the Council of Europe.
2 For the recent rise of populist politics in Eastern Europe see the discussion in Rupnik *et al.* 2000.
3 This agency, which reports directly to the Prime Minister, still has no formal investigative powers. Yet, it has wide powers to collect and analyze information, to design strategies, and to coordinate the activities of other bodies.
4 The author of this article himself has participated in a number of conferences, seminars, and workshops at which experts and politicians from throughout Eastern Europe and Central Asia discussed the experience of the Hong Kong and New South Wales anti-corruption commissions. It is also telling that in the most authoritative handbook on the corruption of the early 1990s (Heidenheimer *et al.* 1989) there is only one article on an anti-corruption agency, again from an exotic country and hardly an established democracy – Singapore (Quah 1989).
5 Such a sweeping claim cannot be exhaustively defended in this chapter, of course. The most authoritative effort to measure the effects of the anti-corruption activities of Bulgaria and Romania were the so-called Regular Reports of the European Commission in the pre-accession process. The series of reports referred to can be found at <http://ec.europa.eu/enlargement/key_documents/index_archive_en.htm> for the period 1998–2003. The so-called 'comprehensive monitoring reports' on Bulgaria and Romania for the period 2004–5 one could see at: <http://ec.europa. eu/enlargement/key_documents/index_archive_en.htm>.
   Since there are no *aquis communautaire* in the area of anti-corruption, the approach of the European Commission was rather contextual and failed to produce truly common standards and concrete performance measurement tools. As a result, for instance, contextual factors such as the appointment and the activities of a committed Justice Minister in Romania – Monica Macovei – seemed to have a disproportionably large impact on the evaluation of the fight against corruption in Romania: the last pre-accession report concluded that Romania (in contrast to Bulgaria) had made sufficient progress in the fight against corruption. With the benefit of hindsight, one could doubt the general soundness of this conclusion: Macovei was sacked immediately after the accession of her country to the EU. For my views on the EU conditionality and accession criteria in the area of justice and home affairs see Smilov 2006.
6 For developments in the area of political finance in Eastern Europe see Smilov and Toplak 2007.
7 Most of the research findings summarized in this section are a preliminary product of the research project Crime & Culture (Sixth Framework Programme of the EC, coordinated by the University of Konstanz). The research included analysis of documents and interviews with representatives of target groups. See Smilov and Dorosiev 2007.
8 For a discussion of public-interest based definitions of corruption see Heidenheimer *et al.* 1989: 10. See also Philp 1997.
9 An extremely interesting case of this kind happened in Bulgaria in 2006 when Ahmed Dogan, the leader of one of the mainstream parties – the Movement for Rights and Freedoms – attempted to sell to the public the so-called model of 'circles of firms', by virtue of which political parties have the right to build circles

of friendly firms, which in turn help for the funding of the patron party. Curiously, this model was advocated by Dogan as a cure against 'oligarchic government'.

10 According to the Bulgarian case studies, it appears that in the framework of privatization, corruption could be understood in different ways depending on the positions of the politicians and their political parties. When in power, politicians tend to praise political privatization where the decisions are made on the basis of political arguments, by elected bodies having extensive powers to decide not only the economic and formal parameters of the privatization offers, but also on a number of other issues, such as possible consequences for the society as a whole. On the other hand, politicians while in opposition claim that political privatization is corrupt and favour the practice of technical/expert privatization based on technical and formal considerations and where appointed bodies of independent experts take the most important decisions following a strict legal procedure. This dichotomy is the main result of the so-called public interest trap. The public insist on fair but also effective privatization. Governments of transition countries have rapidly come to the conclusion that a fair and transparent privatization process does not automatically produce the best outcome in terms of the public interest. This is the reason why politicians while in power tend to shift the focus when defining corruption from the fairness of the process to the quality of the results produced in terms of the broadly defined 'public' or 'national' interest.

11 This part of the chapter is based on Tisné and Smilov 2004. The research for this chapter was done in the period 2003–04.

12 According to the U4 group of donors (a list of which can be seen at <http://www. u4.no/about/partneragencies.cfm>): 'This framework [the anti-corruption action plan] seems very sensible on paper, but if one accepts that the Prime Minister is unwilling or unable to instigate a real fight against corruption, the whole plan with its different levels of monitoring becomes very hollow.' The European Commission's Stabilisation and Association Report on Albania in 2003 noted that:

> Although Albania has developed, in close cooperation with the international community, a number of mechanisms to fight strong systemic corruption, actual progress in this area remains insufficient. Albania has demonstrated its capacity to develop action plans, prepare matrixes, and to set up specific institutions with the objective of fighting corruption. However, declarations of intent and multilateral events are far from being sufficient. Fighting corruption requires full commitment and political will, and full and determined implementation of action plans.

13 The best example of anti-corruption programmes backed by similar umbrella civil society organizations comes from Bulgaria where, again with the help of USAID, the Coalition 2000 was created. This body spearheaded a number of anti-corruption reforms and generally helped successive governments in the creation of their anti-corruption strategies. It has to be stressed that it also adopted a non-confrontational stance vis-à-vis governments of the day, and its aim was to secure their cooperation

14 The Corruption Perception Index (CPI) shows a rather flat trend with marginal improvements for the period 2000–06 for the region as a whole, with the exception of Serbia which however started from very low levels due to the Milosevic rule throughout the 1990s. In 2007, some of the countries reported a rather surprising improvement – for instance, Romania and Macedonia gained 0.6 points each, Serbia and Bosnia and Herzegovina 0.4, Croatia 0.5, and Albania 0.3. Bulgaria gained just 0.1 and appears to be an outlier. It is too early to speculate about the reasons for this improvement in perceptions: the most plausible explanation is that two countries in the region (Bulgaria and Romania) became members of the EU, and Croatia's prospects for EU membership were strengthened.

7 Warriors in chains

Institutional legacies and anti-corruption programmes in Taiwan and South Korea

Christian Göbel

Introduction

For decades, both the Republic of China on Taiwan (henceforth, Taiwan) and South Korea (henceforth, Korea) have combined systemic and endemic political corruption with high economic growth. Economic success, however, did not translate into regime legitimacy. In both polities, the populace expressed deep dissatisfaction with their corrupt regimes even in the restrictive climate of authoritarianism. The fight against corruption became the most important item on the democratization agenda, and did not lose much currency thereafter. While the Taiwanese administration somewhat haughtily likened corruption to dirt that could be simply 'swept away', the Korean government availed itself of the questionable 'war' metaphor to show their determination to fight corruption. However, neither sweeping nor warring was crowned with much success, hence neither polity was rewarded with a significant improvement of its Corruption Perceptions Index score. According to the Gallup polls conducted for the recent Global Corruption Barometers, the overwhelming majority of the respondents persistently see political corruption as a grave problem that they do not expect to lessen anytime soon (Transparency International 2004a, 2005a, 2006a).

While these observations suggest that the decade-long wars against corruption were fought in vain, they were not without impact. Here, the differences between the two polities are more enlightening than their similarities. The Korean administration established an independent anti-corruption agency, which their Taiwanese counterparts had also planned, but failed to achieve. A body of laws aimed to close loopholes for corrupt activities and improve transparency was implemented in Korea, but similar laws were not passed by Taiwan's legislature. On the other hand, more than 12,000 public representatives were prosecuted on charges of corruption in Taiwan between 2000 and 2004, while the numbers prosecuted were negligible in Korea. It follows that the organizational and institutional means to fight corruption are largely in place in Korea, but they remain underused. In Taiwan, on the other hand, these means are found lacking, but the government nevertheless engages in large-scale anti-corruption activities.

What accounts for these differences? This chapter argues that despite their many similarities, the political and social structures underlying corrupt networks are vastly different in Taiwan and Korea. This, in turn, has shaped the strategies that actors have applied in the fight against corruption, and has led to more or less desirable outcomes. The study proceeds by highlighting the systemic constraints that have limited governmental integrity 'warriors' in their professed fight against corruption and examines the birth, development, and impacts of anti-corruption programmes and agencies in post-authoritarian Taiwan and Korea. The analysis shows that corruption in Taiwan was rooted at the lowest political levels during authoritarianism and reached the political centre in a bottom-up process after democratization. Conversely, political corruption in Korea was situated at the apex of political power and percolated to the localities in a top-down process. It is hypothesized that the difficulty in implementing anti-corruption policies in Taiwan after the change in ruling parties was in the durability of its local-level informal networks, whereas in Korea the problem was that central-level leaders had to impose checks on themselves. In Taiwan, the centre could not overcome local-level resistance to anti-corruption policies so it engaged in rather questionable anti-corruption witch-hunts. In Korea, most central-level leaders could not muster the resolve to bid farewell to much-needed funds in the face of intense political competition or did not dare to push anti-corruption campaigns too far lest they become implicated themselves. Although these differences have arguably led to similar outcomes, i.e. the perseverance of corruption in both cases, they are not insignificant. The structured determinants of political corruption will continue to influence the choice of anti-corruption strategies, and they will continue to determine the chance of these strategies to succeed.

The root cause of these constraints does not lie, as dichotomic state-business typologies might suggest, in the differences in industrial organization (coherent family-based conglomerates in Korea versus a dispersed business sector consisting mainly of small and medium enterprises in Taiwan). Rather, it is found in the different types of societies each regime had to face during authoritarianism. While the minority Kuomintang (KMT) regime had to pacify a bifurcated society fraught with deep-running sub-ethnic tensions, the Korean regimes ruled over a much more homogeneous society.

In order to make this point clear, this chapter applies a structuralist approach. As will be shown, the dissimilar initial conditions just summarized led to different interactions between relevant groups in state and society. These differences, I argue, are largely responsible for the distinctive institutional setups in both countries. The chapter starts by sketching the integration strategies each regime has applied vis-à-vis society during authoritarianism and proceeds to show how these strategies have translated into different patterns of corruption. As will be shown thereafter, democratization did not obliterate but increased the scope and intensity of political corruption. Finally, each regime's anti-corruption strategies are outlined and their respective limitations explained. Before the analysis proceeds, however, it is necessary to briefly delimit its underlying theoretical approach.

The structure of corrupt networks

Previous studies seeking to explain the *economic* effects of corruption have focused on both agency and structure, although agency-based approaches are far fewer in number. One example is an approach by Andrew Wedeman, which proposes a typology based on rent-extracting strategies. He distinguishes between *looting* (the systematic theft of public funds and property, with the corrupted sum being immediately consumed or sent abroad), *rent-scraping* (the 'conscious manipulation of macroeconomic parameters in a way that produces rents and the scraping off of these rents by public officials'), and *dividend-collecting* ('transfer of a percentage of the profits earned by privately owned enterprises to government officials in return for policies and services that allow these enterprises to earn profits') (Wedeman 1997: 460). Korea and Taiwan clearly fall into the 'dividend-collecting' category, which, according to Wedemann, is quite compatible with sustained economic growth. Useful as it is, this approach however fails to answer why actors chose a certain type of extraction.

Structuralist approaches seek to provide answers to this question. Based on the principle that unity is strength, David Kang (2002: 177–207) focuses on the cohesiveness of the principal (the state) and the agents (the business sector) to explain why institutionalized processes of corruption take a particular form. He distinguishes between the predatory state (coherent state, dispersed business sector), laissez-faire (fractured state and dispersed business sector), rent-seeking (concentrated business sector, but fractured state), and mutual hostages (coherent state, concentrated business sector). The 'mutual hostages' type seems to be tailor-made for Korea (see below). Taiwan, on the other hand, has a coherent state and a dispersed business sector, but definitely is not a 'predatory state'. In a similar fashion, Paul D. Hutchcroft has developed a typology which is based on the regime type (rational-legal versus patrimonial) and the strength of a state. A developmental state exists where a 'relatively more "rational-legal" state' is 'relatively stronger vis-à-vis business interests', a regulatory state where it is not. The patrimonial state, in turn, comes in the 'patrimonial administrative' and 'patrimonial oligarchic' variants (Hutchcroft 1998: 18–21). Here, Taiwan rather comfortably fits the 'developmental' type. It is much more difficult to place Korea in the matrix because the strengths of state and business are in equilibrium.

In his analysis of the economic effects of various forms of corruption, Mushtaq H. Khan goes beyond the state-business dichotomy and presents a more nuanced variant of the principal-agent-models outlined above (Khan 2005: 467–88). He disaggregates the 'state' into 'politicians' and 'bureaucracy'; and he adds 'non-capitalist clients' to the game. Furthermore, he stresses that corruption need not be motivated by value maximization alone, but that non-economic ends such as race or ethnicity might play a crucial role as well. According to Khan, the number of clients, their homogeneity, and the intactness of the institutions through which they interact must also be figured in. Reminiscent of the structuralist arguments of Barrington Moore

(1966) and later Rueschemeyer *et al.* (1992), Khan's underlying assumption is that 'the distribution of power between the state, capitalists and inter-mediate classes' determine the 'patterns of corruption', which in turn affect economic development. Khan thus cautions that ' … anti-corruption strategies that are concerned with the possible effects of corruption on development have to explicitly identify the underlying political problems' (Khan 2005: 487).

Although this chapter's interest does not lie in the effect of corruption on economic development, a variant of this approach is most suitable for the present analysis. Following Khan, the subsequent sections will identify the relevant social and political groups that have partaken in political corruption and trace how their interrelationship has shaped distinct patterns of corruption and in turn affected governmental anti-corruption strategies.

The beginning: different state-society relations lead to different integration strategies

While Korea was able to reaffirm its independence after the Japanese occu-pation and the subsequent American occupation, the Japanese occupant was replaced by a Mainland Chinese one in Taiwan. Before the Japanese occu-pation in 1895, Taiwan was only loosely appended to the Chinese Empire and was largely independent in conducting its political affairs. After being defeated in the Chinese civil war from 1947 to 1949 however, Generalissimo Chiang Kai-shek, the leader of the Republican Chinese government, instal-led a one-party regime on the island. The Chinese Nationalist Party (Kuo-mintang) legitimated authoritarian rule primarily by promising to liberate the Chinese Mainland from the Communist forces. The Taiwanese popula-tion, which was expected to supply soldiers for the task, did not welcome the prospect of going to war for a cause that was not theirs. Moreover, it was made subject to various forms of discrimination by the Mainlanders. A popular rebellion against Mainlander dominance ended with a massacre on 28 February 1947 in which a great number of Taiwanese intellectuals and other protesters lost their lives. This traumatic incident cemented the sub-ethnic cleavage between the immigrating Mainlanders and the native Taiwanese that has existed ever since (Schubert 1994: 31–32). As will be shown in the next paragraph, elections served as the main mechanism to provide incentives for, and to integrate, the alienated group of native Taiwanese into the regime.

In contrast, the Korean leadership did at first not face such hostility and was very reluctant to hold elections for fear of losing its grip on society. Pres-sure by the United States was the main reason for the introduction of elections. Elections at first did not serve to legitimize authoritarian rule vis-à-vis the population, but vis-à-vis the erstwhile occupant (Kang 2001: 79–80). Accord-ingly, the authoritarian government delegitimated itself and the institution of elections by means of massive electoral fraud and frequent changes of the electoral rules, which heightened the access barrier to the political process just when the opposition believed to have surpassed it (Göbel 2006a: 222–24).

Put differently, elections in Korea became a tool to exclude the majority of the population from meaningful political participation. In Taiwan, however, they became the transmission belt between the authoritarian émigré regime and indigenous socio-political networks with large social influence, the so-called 'local factions' (*difang paixi*). In this way, a large part of the Taiwanese population was directly and indirectly made an accomplice to the authoritarian regime, contributing to its remarkable stability and durability. In contrast, a critical mass of the population kept challenging authoritarianism in Korea, and such popular uprisings frequently led to military putsches.

Corruption in a cage: one-party rule and the emergence of a corruption problem in Taiwan

As was the case in most of Southeast Asia's autocracies, the legitimacy of the KMT one-party state hinged on its ability to deliver monetary rents to various constituencies, to play important actors off against each other without alienating them from the regime, and to prevent splits in its leadership (Case 2003: 245–64).

In order to understand how different social structures have resulted in different patterns of corruption, it is particularly relevant to analyse the mechanisms of rent allocation and the integration of alienated social forces into the regime. Most remarkably, the authoritarian leadership managed to achieve sustainable economic growth without engaging in the large-scale corruption that existed in Korea. Thus, at the central level, politics in authoritarian Taiwan had been rather clean, winning it much praise from the developmental state literature. On the local level, however, the picture looked completely different. Local-level corruption has received considerably less scholarly attention, but is an important explanatory variable for both the nature of Taiwan's present-day political corruption and the difficulties in combating it.

The core problem for the KMT at the local level was to produce regime legitimacy despite widespread hostility by the native populace. The skilful handling of monetary resources coupled with incentives for political competition among the local elites, most notably in county elections, provided the solution. A short introduction to the organization of Taiwan's local polity and especially its basic building-block, the local faction, will clarify this point.

'Local factions' are local-level clientelist networks. Most of Taiwan's counties and municipalities have two or three local factions which compete for local economic and power resources. Factions usually are held together by ties of blood, kinship, and marriage, but also by interpersonal relationships (Chen 1995: 16–18). The KMT made use of local factions by trading money for support via local-level elections. Getting elected at the local level was not very attractive in terms of political power because local government was in the firm grip of the Party State. Political office, however, granted access to local monopoly and oligopoly rights and 'money machines' like the credit departments of the fishermen's associations, the water conservancy associations, and the farmers' associations (Chen and Chu 1992: 89–90). In addition, political protection of semi-legal or illegal projects such as brothels, gambling dens, and karaoke bars guaranteed the local power-holders further resources that could be used at whim and were not subject to financial supervision of any kind. Corruption was rampant, and many of the 'money machines' were technically bankrupt after democratization.

In authoritarian Taiwan, a tailor-made electoral system, its organizational capacity, and its clientelist relationship with local factions enabled the KMT to influence electoral outcomes in a highly effective way. Vote-brokers, who served as the link between a candidate and his voters, played a crucial role. They utilized political campaigns, personal relationships, the mobilization of employees, and, most of all, vote-buying to mobilize votes (Rigger 1994: 94–98, 162–72; for a detailed and first-hand description of vote-buying see also Chan 1999). In order to get elected, one usually had to be nominated by the KMT. The party had the organizational means to coordinate votes and candidates, the financial means to co-finance the costly electoral campaigns, and the coercive means to deter non-authorized candidates from running in a local election. As a consequence, candidates of the various local factions competed for nomination by the KMT, and local alliances against the party were highly unlikely unless they affronted the factions by filing their own candidates. This was backed up by the rigorous enforcement of a policy that forbade factions to conclude alliances beyond the county level (Bosco 1994: 122).

Political corruption in authoritarian Korea

As opposed to Taiwan, where scholars agree that corruption at the state level was only minor, the role of central-level corruption in Korea's development has been the subject of much debate. As Jong-sung You notes, scholars generally characterized politics under Korea's first post-war president Syngman Rhee as predatory, whereas the dictatorships of Park Chung-Hee and his successor Chun Doo-hwan were regarded as prototypes of the 'development state' (You 2005: 4). However, the Asian financial crisis, which plunged Korea into deep recession and unveiled its lack of economic fundamentals, led to a reassessment of the role of corruption in Korean politics.

Political corruption played a vital part in the 'developmental state' of Park Chung-Hee, taking, in Wedeman's terms, the form of 'dividend-collecting' (Wedeman 1997: 461). The leadership coordinated macro-economic policy and co-opted the family-based conglomerates (*chaebols*), which in turn helped the regime to stay in power by providing the necessary funds. However, handing over a fraction of its profits to the political leadership did not automatically guarantee a conglomerate easy access to state funds. Good economic performance was an important precondition. Underperformance or violating the coalition by, say, openly criticizing the government could invite a cutback in government-sponsored loans. In addition, deviant entrepreneurs would often be the victims of selective investigations for tax evasion, as had been the case with the head of the Hyundai conglomerate in 1992 (Moon 1994: 159).

Whereas Taiwan's polity combined an institutionalized, but strictly controlled, clientelist network at the local level with a corruption-free development-oriented central state, Korea's pre-democratic political system was much less resilient. It can be characterized as one in which frequent changes of leadership and highly elitist, though unstable, networks connecting top-level politicians and the heads of *chaebols* stand in an interdependent relationship. Regime change in Korea was of a cyclical nature. First, students and other civic groups took to the streets to protest the regime's declining political performance, their exclusion from politics, and increasing political corruption. Then, the regime would be overthrown by a military junta pledging to end corruption and to lead the country into prosperity. However, the new regime would quickly find itself in need of extensive funds, for which it would turn to the big enterprises. Corruption would get out of control, the masses take to the streets, and another saviour would overthrow the regime (or shoot the President, as happened in 1979).

After the 1960 military coup, which General Park Chung-hee had legitimated by a pledge to rid Korea of corruption (Eckert *et al.* 1990: 361), several hundred entrepreneurs were arrested for graft. Shortly after, however, most of them were set free in exchange for a pledge of allegiance to the dictator and the promise to provide funds (Kim and Im 2001). After this act of subjection, Korea's developing *chaebols* and the Park regime gradually entered a relationship of mutual dependence, a phenomenon that David Kang – as we saw above – termed 'mutual hostages' (Kang 2002: 96ff). On one side, the enterprises were dependent on the government. Enterprise taxes were so high that the *chaebols* were practically forced to evade them. Similarly to the illegal activities of Taiwan's local-level politicians, tax evasion was not only tolerated, but even supported by the central leadership. In this way, selective persecutions served as a powerful tool to discipline the *chaebols* (Chon 2000: 71). In addition, ministries could implement or change regulations relevant to the business sector without legislative approval, which further strengthened the corruptive relations between political and economic actors. Large-scale donations often were the precondition for legal changes or the granting of special privileges.

Under Park and his successors Chun Doo-hwan and Roh Tae-woo, corruption became organized. All established foundations to which the *chaebols* had to transfer a certain part of their profits (Kang 2002: 102). Roh, for example, was able to amass a fortune of 500 billion Won (approximately US $528 million) during his presidency (1988–93). In a spectacular trial in 1996, he was sentenced to a lengthy prison term and his predecessor Chun received the death sentence. Both, however, were acquitted in 1997 by presidential decree. Also, charges of corruption were brought against the leaders of 30 *chaebols*, but only five were convicted (Blechinger 2000).

The donations, the pardons, and the lax enforcement of anti-corruption drives are an indicator of the fact that Korea's top-level politicians were as dependent on the *chaebols* as the *chaebols* were on them. First, the *chaebols* delivered the financial resources that were used not only for personal enrichment, but also to finance cost-intensive electoral campaigns. As opposed to the one-party state Taiwan, partisan competition did exist in Korea, albeit under very unequal circumstances. Korea's opposition parties were disadvantaged not only by an electoral system and campaign rules that largely benefited the ruling party, but also by the huge amounts of money the latter could use to throw banquets for potential followers and to buy votes. Another source of dependence was, and still is, the legitimating function of economic growth for the political leadership, which in no small part depended on the performance of the *chaebols*. In 1988, the combined turnover of Korea's 30 largest conglomerates equalled 94.8 per cent of the country's gross national product (GNP) (Moon 1994: 154). Accordingly, all of these *chaebols* enjoyed considerable political leverage.

Democratization and corruption

Democratization, which in neither of the two cases brought the opposition to power, shifted the balance between politicians and entrepreneurs in favour of the latter. In addition, it fostered corruption instead of contributing to its eradication. In both Taiwan and Korea, elections and in particular electoral mobilization by ways of aggressive campaigning, banquets, presents, and vote-buying played a central role, and the costs of which politicians at all levels could not finance out of their own pockets. Also, the number of elections rose after democratization. In Taiwan, the representatives of the National Assembly[1] began to be chosen by popular vote in 1991; those of the Legislative Yuan in 1992. Since 1996, the President has been elected by popular vote as well, replacing indirect election by the National Assembly. Korea started to hold local-level elections in 1991. Finally, the executive was deprived of the means to coerce its collaborators into submission with the introduction of the rule of law, which further strengthened the economic sector vis-à-vis the government. What David Kang (2002: 193) observed for Korea equally applies to Taiwan:

> Democratization does not change the business sector's generally high demand for rents, but it does affect the supply. With more politicians competing on the supply side, fewer limits were placed on the behaviour of the business sector. ... Democratization led to increased demands for political payoffs as politicians began to genuinely compete for electoral support and to a decrease in the state's ability to resist or contain the demands of the business sector.

Because of the larger number of actors in the KMT's mobilization network, Taiwan displays a situation more complex than that in Korea. Given the limits of this chapter, I will only elaborate on the connection between the party, local factions, enterprises, and organized crime in Taiwan.[2]

With the advent of democracy in Taiwan, the informal rules barring local factions from forming alliances with each other and with enterprises of all sizes were no longer sustainable. The KMT rewarded the support of local factions and native enterprises by granting them access to the tightly controlled land and real estate sector. With the subsequent opening of the financial sector, strong construction and real estate enterprises entered the credit market and made large profits (Chen 1995: 199–203). Many entrepreneurs successfully ran for political office, and parliament became a playground for real estate magnates, representatives of local factions, and financial elites, and a trading-place for political influence and financial resources.

In this environment, the influence of organized crime grew rapidly. Political, social, and financial influence helped organized criminals to win parliamentary seats at all levels. In 2000, Zhu Lilun, a KMT-legislator and professor at National Taiwan University, claimed that 20 per cent of all Legislative Yuan-representatives had connections to organized crime (Li 2000: 74). In 1994, the then-Minister of Justice Liao Chung-hsiung had estimated that around one-third of all members of local legislatures were organized criminals (Hsia 1997). Many gangsters were voted into the Legislative Yuan and therefore not only enjoyed immunity, but were also able to take influential committee positions. Seats on the Financial Standing Committee were especially coveted for their kickback opportunities. Gang leaders became conveners of the Police Administration Group in the local legislatures where they supervised the local police departments (Liao 1997: 179–80). In the Legislative Yuan, legislators implicated in legal suits became members of the Judiciary Standing Committee, for example Lin Rui-tu and Wu Tze-yuan. Lo Fu-chu, the leader of Taiwan's biggest crime syndicate, the Heaven and Earth Society, even served as one of the committee's three conveners. The Business Weekly (*Shangye Zhoukan*) in 1999 reported that legislators with an organized crime background, some of them even accompanied by gunmen disguised as assistants, exerted considerable influence in the Legislative Yuan by means of threats and terror against individual lawmakers (Kang 1999). It is safe to say that the collusion of money politics and organized crime is Taiwan's biggest social and political problem even today (apart, of course, from the tedious relations with Mainland China).

Naturally, the democratization of Taiwan and Korea not only increased the need for political payoffs and therefore gave rise to even more corruption, but it also changed the relationship between those governing and those governed. Corruption became an important electoral campaign topic in both polities. This led to a paradoxical situation: large-scale political funds needed to win elections could not be generated without engaging in corruption, but at the same time the practice took a heavy toll on public support for the ruling party. Still, the conservative elites chose to maintain this system because they feared that disengagement would result in decreasing funds and political support from the industrial sector. Both were necessary to stay in office. The authorities' main answer to this dilemma was selective persecution, which, however, did not achieve much in shoring up legitimacy and lost the ruling parties considerable support of their erstwhile clients (Göbel 2006b: 68–70).

What role did the opposition play in this process? In both cases it was largely excluded from the exchange networks outlined above. Therefore, while the ruling parties engaged in electoral campaigns that were more organizational than programmatic, the opposition had to rely on the formulation of programmatic goals to garner voter support. After taking power, however, Korea's new rulers faced different circumstances than those in Taiwan. Due to the less durable nature of corruptive relations between politicians and *chaebols,* the former could easily engage in clientelist networks themselves. The situation of Taiwan's main opposition party, the Democratic Progressive Party (DPP), was much different. The Party Centre had a vital interest in fundamentally changing the political rules of the game, which had been tailor-made to fit the authoritarian KMT regime. As outlined above, sustaining these mechanisms after democratization had become difficult even for the wealthy and well-organized KMT, and the reliance on money politics and local factions was much less an option for the DPP. Neither did it have the organizational power nor the financial means to maintain such an institutional and organizational setup. The result was that the DPP strove to create a political environment that was more conducive to its survival than the one inherited by the KMT. This, of course, does not mean that the DPP has been free of corruption. On the contrary, some of its city- and county-level legislators have been convicted on charges of corruption and there is ample evidence that local DPP politicians and parliamentary candidates have turned to factions and organized criminals for support (Chin 2003: 154–55). Recently, credible evidence of insider trading and other forms of public-office abuse has surfaced even against President Chen Shui-bian (Yardley 2006). The difference is that these acts were not condoned by the party centre, and they have not taken, and in line with the arguments just presented could not have taken, the shape of KMT-style machine politics.[3]

Combating organized crime and money politics in Taiwan

Making Taiwan's politics fairer and more democratic had been on the DPP's campaign agenda since its foundation in 1986. Although its leadership did not lack the determination to realize these aims, their efforts were seriously hampered both by residue of authoritarianism in the bureaucracy inherited from the KMT era and its minority of seats in the Legislative Yuan. Local factional and business influence in the legislature was especially challenging because institutional restructuring can not be achieved without making adjustments in the legal system.

In July 2000, two months after taking office, the DPP administration started to implement its Programme for Sweeping Away Organized Crime and Corruption in three major ways: fighting organized crime, counter-corruption measures, and investigations into election-related bribery. The programme combined efforts to enact new laws and revise existing ones, and investigate and prosecute corrupt behaviour, and was flanked by personnel reshuffles and the restructuring of government organizations (Ministry of Justice 2000, 2003).

The restructuring of government organizations, no doubt the precondition on which the successful implementation of the whole programme rested, proved to be the hardest one to realize. In his efforts to centralize the Ministry's anti-corruption efforts, the new Minister of Justice, Chen Ding-nan, announced that he would merge the Honest Government Office of the Ministry of Justice Investigation Bureau (MJIB) with the Ministry's Government Ethics Department into an Anti-Corruption Task Force (Chao 2000). The MJIB, which during the authoritarian era was the backbone of the regime's internal security apparatus, still wielded enough political clout to successfully resist this plan testifying to the ongoing entrenchment of authoritarian institutions in Taiwan's young democracy. The standoff between Chen Ding-nan and the MJIB was only ended one year later when its director was replaced by executive order (*Taipei Times*, 15 August 2003). Cooperation was thus improved, but legislation on the envisioned Anti-Corruption Task Force with powers of search, seizure, and arrest was not passed by parliament. Instead, an Organized Crime and Money Politics Investigation Center (OCMPIC) was established from scratch. The OCMPIC, located in the High Court Prosecutor's office, supervises four special investigation sections in Taipei, Taichung, Tainan, and Kaohsiung. It combines prosecutors and investigators and is authorized to issue orders to local district prosecutors, agents from the MJIB, military police officers, and civilian police officers.

This unsuccessful attempt to streamline available resources has two important consequences. First, with the OCMPIC, the MJIB, and the Ministry of Justice Government Ethics Department all involved in anti-corruption work, organizational overlap is now considerable. Second, the creation of an organization that amalgamates executive and judicial powers violates the democratic principle of checks and balances. As will be shown below, this is not only an abstract problem, but has very tangible consequences.

Organization-building was merely one pillar of the anti-corruption programme; institution-building was another. As Taiwan had been an authoritarian state where party directives and informal arrangements were more important than legal stipulations, there was only a weak legal basis on which to build a democratic polity. Although Taiwan had formally become a democracy, the underlying legal framework did not address practices that were incommensurate with democratic principles. Therefore, large scale 'loans' and 'donations' to legislators, influence-peddling, and the abuse of insider-information was clearly considered undemocratic, but was not illegal (Göbel 2001). Building democratic institutions was further complicated by the fact that parliament was still dominated by interests representing the old order. It was hard to come by support for institutional reforms that would counter these interests.

Nevertheless, the Ministry of Justice (MOJ) laid out an ambitious plan for legal reforms with proposals for the revision of existing laws, as well as for the drafting of new laws. The Public Functionaries Election and Recall Law was to be amended to bar convicted criminals, and to prevent organized crime suspects from running in elections; and draft amendments to the criminal law introduced harsh sentences for recidivist criminals. The Civil Servant Services Act was to be amended to make it illegal for civil servants to accept gifts or donations, a revised Public Functionary Assets Disclosure Law would force public officials to put their assets into a trust fund, and an amended Anti-Corruption Penal Statute would automatically assume corruption if a public official earned more than he ought to. Finally, proposals included regulations in the Money Laundering Control Act to establish a citizen bank account data base and the requirement for banks to report large financial transactions to the authorities. None of these drafts were passed, but it has to be noted that the proposed amendments to the Civil Servant Services Act became obsolete with the passing of the Conflict of Interest Prevention Law in July 2000. The law stipulates that public officials cannot abuse their position for personal profit and that they cannot engage in a business relationship with their own agency.

Several other new laws were drafted and it is not hard to see that many of them were directly targeted at the KMT. The Political Party Law would regulate campaign financing and make it illegal for parties to run enterprises and establish subsidiaries in schools and governmental offices. In addition, the draft Political Contributions Law prescribed an 'election period' during which contributions could be made, and set ceilings for individual, corporate, and anonymous donations. The proposed Statute Regarding the Disposition of Assets Improperly Obtained by Political Parties would empower the government to confess assets unlawfully obtained by political parties, which most of the KMT's assets allegedly were. Finally, the ties between business and political parties were to be weakened by a Lobby Law which would require lobbyists to obtain a 'lobbying permit' from the Ministry of the Interior and to publicize the object of lobbying, the resources, and the time span involved.

Apart from the Conflict of Interest Prevention Law mentioned above, only the Political Contributions Law was implemented. Scandals, public pressure, and the KMT's struggle to portray itself as a clean party probably were major factors facilitating the passage of the Political Contributions Law only two days before the 2004 presidential election. All the other drafts outlined above were frequently reintroduced for consideration in the legislature, but voted down by an alliance of opposition legislators who would face severe losses if the new regulations had been passed. Another problem is the lax enforcement of those laws that did pass. Some laws only carry minor fines (such as the Public Functionary Assets Disclosure Law), and some are not strictly enforced (as is the case with the Conflict of Interest Law, the Public Functionary Assets Disclosure Law, and the Money Laundering Law). Reasons for these shortcomings are organizational overlaps, understaffing of the relevant agencies, and small budget allocations (Göbel 2001). Again, blockade politics in the legislature is to a large extent responsible for these shortcomings because both budget and organizational restructuring need legislative approval.

The third pillar in the fight against corruption is the investigations and crackdowns conducted by the Organized Crime and Money Politics Investigation Center and other agencies. Targets were vote-buying, bribery (especially in public construction projects), judicial fraud, and organized crime. Due to the restrictions faced in organization- and institution-building, it was this third pillar that became especially prominent in the fight against corruption. It was widely held responsible for producing the cleanest elections ever held in Taiwan, which, however, came at a price to citizens' liberty rights.

The Legislative Yuan elections in December 2001 were accompanied by massive campaigns aimed at dissuading the Taiwanese populace from accepting money for their votes and by even more massive crackdowns on vote captains and the legislators who had hired them. The MOJ used the number of people indicted as the main indicator of the success of their efforts. For example, the number of public representatives on all levels indicted for corruption and vote-buying rose from 152 in March 2001 to 317 in August 2001, and to 1,876 in October 2004, the last time these figures were published. The total number of people prosecuted was 12,568 at that time (out of 31,893 accused). Of those put on trial, 2,397 were found guilty and 2,220 not guilty (Ministry of Justice 2004).

Despite the fact that the frequent 'sweeps' against vote-buying and organized crime were probably successful in bringing many of Taiwan's most notorious gangsters to justice and served as a deterrent against vote-buying, these figures raise the question of whether these successes have been traded against the protection of human rights. Indeed, individual cases show that prosecutors were overzealous in their fight against corruption, tapping phones without judicial supervision and conducting searches without warrants (*China Post*, 25 October 2001). Also, the administration's draft amendment to the Public Functionaries Election and Recall Law, which would bar organized crime suspects from running in elections, was quite problematic. One reason is that a mere suspect would be convicted politically even before his guilt had been established in a court of law. In addition, this clause would only apply to suspects of an 'organized' criminal background and not to non-organized criminal suspects. This raises definitional problems and discriminates against the former group.

Anti-corruption programmes in Korea after democratization

Immediately upon taking office on 25 February 1993, Korea's first civilian president Kim Young-sam (1993–97) surprised the public by disclosing his financial assets and those of his family members. Naturally, this became a big issue in the mass media, and other government officials were urged to follow suit. This led to the resignation of 'the speaker of the National Assembly, two cabinet ministers, five vice-ministerial officials, and 242 senior administrators' (Oh 1999: 140). 1,363 government employees were subsequently dismissed for 'evident irregularities' (Oh 1999). This was the starting point for the passage of four important laws. First of all, the Ethics Law for Public Officials made asset disclosure compulsory for more than 1,000 public officials. Second, the Real Name Financial Transaction System (passed by Presidential Order) made illegal the widespread practice of registering bank accounts under false names to prevent the masking of illegal political contributions. Third, the Election Malpractice Prevention Act set guidelines for electoral campaigns and significantly lowered the ceilings for campaign spending. For example, a presidential candidate could not spend more than 20 billion Won (about US$25 million) on their campaign. Furthermore, it banned moneyed remuneration for campaign workers, and rendered illegal the mobilization of votes by government officials. Fourth, the Political Fund Law raised the ceiling for individual political contributions to 150 million Won (approximately US$190,000) from previously 100 million Won, and those contributions had to be reported to the Central Election Management Commission (Oh 1999: 140–46).

No doubt, the passing of these laws signified an important milestone in Korean political development as they rendered previous electoral malpractices illegal. It has to be noted, however, that the Korean presidency is limited to one term, so these regulations did not apply to Kim Young-sam himself. Evidence suggests that he had profited from the very system that his administration was banning. Although he did not pocket large amounts of cash like his predecessors did, his party received significant funds for his campaign from then-president Roh Tae-woo. Furthermore, his administration's record and his personal record were tarnished by several corruption scandals that took place just before the Asian Crisis hit Korea. The biggest of these involved the funnelling of $6 billion to the Hanbo Group, whose assets barely surpassed US$100 million, by an alliance of corrupt legislators, bankers, and the president's son (Blechinger 2000). The president's son was found to be involved in other influence-peddling schemes, and allegedly he influenced the staffing of key positions in the presidential office and in intelligence organizations. Finally, it became known that Kim's party spent about 130 billion Won on his presidential campaign, greatly surpassing the legal limit for campaign expenses. Kim himself was proven to have received 60 billion Won from the then Hanbo chairman Chung Tae-soo (Blechinger 2000; You 2005: 37).

Kim Dae-jung, who was voted into the presidency just after the Asian Crisis wrought havoc on the Korean economy, took further steps against corruption. One year after the crisis, in 1998, Kim Dae-jung declared a war on corruption. In 1999, he established the Presidential Commission on Anti-Corruption (PCAC), an advisory body to the president. More importantly, the National Assembly passed the Anti-Corruption Act in June 2000 after arduous negotiations and considerable pressure from civil society. The Act defines corruption as an 'act of any public official's seeking gains for himself/herself or for any third party by abusing his/her position or authority or violating Acts and subordinate statutes in connection with his/her duties', and 'the act of causing damages to the property of any public agency in violation of Acts and subordinate statutes, in the process of executing the budget of the relevant public agency, acquiring, managing, or disposing of the property of the relevant public agency, or entering into and executing a contract to which the relevant public agency is a party' (Article 2, section 3). Obviously, these definitions are geared towards administrative and political corruption and exclude private-sector corruption. However, an amendment to the Act which includes private-sector corruption is under review. The Act further outlines responsibilities of agencies, citizens, and enterprises, establishes a Code of Conduct for public officials, and regulates the establishment of the ministry-level Korea Independent Commission Against Corruption (KICAC) (see below). It contains sections on corruption reporting and the protection of whistle-blowers, and establishes the citizen's right to request inspection into acts they consider to be administrative or political corruption.

Two further Acts were passed: the Act Regulating and Punishing the Concealment of Criminal Proceeds, and the Act on Reporting and Using Specific Financial Transaction Information. Together they are commonly referred to as the Money Laundering Prevention Act because their main aim is to put an end to money laundering. To implement the acts, a Financial Information Unit was established under the Ministry of Finance and Economy (KICAC 2003).

The KICAC is the first comprehensive anti-corruption body in Korean history and has three major responsibilities: first, formulation of anti-corruption policies and supervising their implementation; second, educating the public about corruption and anti-corruption measures and supporting non-profit organizations; third, receiving and handling whistle-blower reports (Article 11 of the Anti-Corruption Act). Its members are appointed by the president. This fact and the fact that KICAC lacks investigative powers have restricted its usefulness. In 2003, KICAC had received a mere 113 cases (KICAC 2004). The fact that the Kim Dae-jung administration was also plagued by allegations of corruption testifies to the fact that petty corruption, which the Anti Corruption Act and the KICAC are mainly aimed at, is not the major problem in Korea's politics. Kim's Prosecutor-General resigned in 2002 after it became known that his brother took bribes, and Kim's sons were arrested half a year later on the same charges (Lu 2003: 130).

Kim's successor Roh Moo-hyun promised to continue the fight against corruption – as had the previous presidential candidates. He set a precedent by relying chiefly on Internet campaigning and small-scale donations by supporters from the general public. In November 2004, a Bill was passed establishing the Corruption Investigation Office under the KICAC, and the main task of which is to investigate high-ranking public officials suspected of corruption (Kim 2006: 247). However, the Roh administration soon faced serious allegations. In 2002, evidence surfaced that some of Roh's top aides accepted millions of dollars in illegal corporate donations, most notably from the Samsung group. Roh promised to step down if it was proven that his campaign had received more than 10 per cent of the illegal funds received by his opponent, which amounted to admitting that he in fact did receive illegal funds (Kim 2006: 249). An opposition Bill calling for an independent counsel investigating corruption in his administration was vetoed by Roh (Freedom House 2005: 584), and he decreed an amnesty for business people investigated for corruption in the 2002 presidential elections in order to 'protect the economy from recession' (Kim 2006: 249).

Although an institutional and organizational framework for systematically combating corruption in Korea is slowly being drawn up, its success has so far been limited. The main problem, according to Taek Kim, has been that 'there was no real coordination network, nor a working linkage handling the anti-corruption drive, which led to a hegemonic struggle among the relevant organizations' (Kim 2003: 373). The KICAC itself does not seem too convinced of its success either: 'The KICAC, for the last two years, made significant strides in establishing the infrastructure for fighting corruption, albeit not enough to meet the high expectations of the people' (KICAC 2005).

Quantitative data, as presented for Taiwan above, is hard to come by for Korea. Nevertheless, a few observations can be made regarding the implementation of Korea's anti-corruption policies. First, the legal and administrative framework for anti-corruption work has consistently improved. However, coordination between the organizations is lacking and enforcement of the laws is wanting. Many observers have noted the inadequacy of Korea's campaign laws. As noted above, the ceiling for presidential and other campaign finances has been significantly lowered during the Kim Young-sam administration, and politicians now complain that these limits are far too low. A report delivered in 2001 found that these regulations were routinely violated. As the new laws were not rigorously enforced, sanctions were not feared, and the practices of vote-buying and paying unofficial campaign workers illegal salaries or subsidies continued (Sejong Institute 2001: 8). In the same report, two Korean researchers summarized the situation as follows: 'spending is out of control, the flow of money is not transparent, virtually everyone breaks the law, politicians are regularly involved in major financial scandals, and voter cynicism is growing' (Sejong Institute 2001: 9).

However, the fact that anti-corruption investigations against presidents, their family members, and their parties are possible and are conducted suggests that the situation has improved since the authoritarian era when corrupt presidents went scot-free.

Conclusion

This chapter has highlighted several important institutional and social structural features of political corruption in Taiwan and South Korea and has demonstrated that these features significantly influenced the genesis and impact of anti-corruption policies. It has shown that political corruption followed a different logic in each country. Political corruption in Korea, both during authoritarianism and democracy, constituted a weakly institutionalized top-down process. In contrast, Taiwan's informal exchange networks were much more complex and more deeply rooted in society. There, corruption during authoritarianism was a local phenomenon, encompassing mostly the township and county levels, but not extending to the central level. In the course of democratization and with local factions, entrepreneurs, and organized criminals entering state-level politics, political corruption reached the centre. With political corruption having thus become endemic at all administrative levels, post-democratization anti-corruption measures at first remained largely superficial and selective in both regimes.

In Taiwan, it was the change in ruling parties one decade after democratization that ushered in a comprehensive anti-corruption programme spanning organizational and institutional measures as well as investigations into and the persecution of corrupt behaviour. Clearly, the new administration's aim was to destroy the long-standing political machine of its predecessor and create an institutional framework more beneficial to the new administration. Due to the fact that localist forces still prevailed in the legislature and parts of the administrative apparatus, however, the central goal of establishing an anti-corruption agency (ACA) could not be realized. Instead, the Chen Shui-bian administration was forced to rely on heavy crackdowns against corruption, which mainly affected, perhaps not incidentally, political opponents. Quite similar to Taiwan, anti-corruption measures in Korea remained selective and focused on political opponents for more than a decade after democratization. Comprehensive legislation for fighting corruption was passed only at the beginning of the twenty-first century, and the KICAC was set up in 2002. Its impact, however, remains weak because political leaders are more reluctant to fight corruption the further their career advances, and the more they become involved in corruption themselves. People convicted on charges of corruption were pardoned. In sum, both the 'sweepers' and the 'warriors' were severely constrained because they were too immersed in the very structures they set out to combat, but in different ways. While in the case of the Taiwanese 'sweepers', one of the hands needed to wield the broom was tied, the Korean warriors had become their own enemy.

It follows that leadership commitment is an important intervening variable affecting the fight against corruption in Korea. If such commitment exists, Korea stands better chances than Taiwan to decrease corruption in a short or medium term; but a relapse into more serious forms of corruption is also possible if such commitment wanes or is absent. The resilience of Taiwan's local level clientelist networks and their large influence in parliament does not suggest an early improvement of the situation.

On a more general level, the analysis implies that there can be no universal recipe for anti-corruption strategies. If the social and political structures that underlie corrupt networks are not appropriately addressed, the effect of such approaches will at best be limited, at worst counterproductive. Even if the differences are heeded, however, policies are not likely to be successful if they rely on combating, fighting, warring, and sweeping. When the decision-makers are directly or indirectly linked to corrupt networks, anti-corruption measures too easily degrade into weapons for political infighting.

Notes

1 The National Assembly's main powers were the election and demotion of the president, and amending the constitution. However, with the constitutional amendments of 2000 and 2005, the National Assembly was successively abolished, concentrating all parliamentary power in the Legislative Yuan.

2 A more detailed analysis of these networks can be found in Göbel 2001.

3 This assumption is even true in the face of allegations that President Chen Shui-bian embezzled state funds between July 2002 and March 2006. In November 2006, his wife Wu Shu-jen was indicted on corruption and forgery charges, and Chen was named as co-defendant. As at August 2008, the matter is still under investigation, and Chen's role in the affair is still unclear. There are no allegations that the sum in question was used to further political aims, nor is it likely that other top-level politicians were accomplices in the corrupt act.

8 Populist anti-corruption and military coups

The clean-up campaign in Fiji 2006–07

Peter Larmour[1]

The literature on corruption and development identifies a 'populist' type of anti-corruption campaign characterized by purges of civil servants, public humiliations and executions, quasi-official tribunals, and Moral Rearmament campaigns that aim to produce 'new citizens' (Riley 1998, Theobald 1990). The populist approach was particularly attractive to leaders of military coups in Africa (Riley 1998: 133; Mbaku 2007). Gillespie and Okruhlik (1991) have analysed the politics of 'corruption cleanups' in the Middle East in the 1970s and 1980s and found six of their 25 cases involving coup leaders undertaking cleanups 'to discredit prior leaders and lend legitimacy themselves' (1991: 84–86).

Gillespie and Okruhlik were writing before the explosion of international interest in corruption and they characterized the literature on cleanups as 'tangential' to the larger body of work on the phenomenon of corruption itself (Gillespie and Okruhlik 1991: 77). The chapters in this book represent new work along this tangent, and it is worth going back to see if the concepts devised in this earlier period are still relevant in our more internationalized, NGO-influenced world. Ideas about populism, for example, appear in critiques of anti-corruption campaigns in Eastern Europe by scholars such as Krastev (2004) and Smilov (in this book). Transparency International (TI) is now often criticized for elitism – the opposite of populism – but its Corruption Perceptions Index (CPI) is a nice example of international 'populism', as defined above, that combines 'public humiliation' (of low-ranked governments) with a 'quasi-official tribunal' of business journalists and ratings agencies who make the assessment.

This chapter focuses on Fiji, where the military coup that took place in December 2006 was the fourth since the country became independent in 1970. Leaders of the earlier coups said they were acting in defence of indigenous rights threatened by democratically elected governments. By 2006, however, demographic changes had given indigenous Fijians a clear majority in the country (57 per cent of a total population of 828,000, Fiji Government 2007a). Prime Minister Qarase's government had won two elections by energetically promoted indigenous Fijian interests. Instead, the leader of the 2006 coup, Commodore Frank Bainimarama – himself an indigenous

Fijian – promised a 'cleanup campaign' against the corruption of the Qarase government.

Bainimarama had his own personal scores to settle, but his forward-looking, anti-racist, and anti-corruption rhetoric attracted sympathy from some people who had been opposed to coups in the past. These included parts of the NGO community and parts of the tourist industry worried about proposed changes to land law that would favour indigenous rights. Non-indigenous citizens – particularly descendants of settlers from India, who now constituted 38 per cent of the population – had felt that their rights were under threat from indigenous majorities. The most unlikely supporter was, perhaps, the director of Fiji's Human Rights Commission who became a vigorous apologist for the coup, and scourge of its opponents (Shameem 2007). The coup also attracted sympathetic coverage from some of the international media (e.g. *Time* 5 February 2007).

Aid donors and development banks have become increasingly vocal about corruption among governments in the South Pacific region (Larmour 2007). While he borrowed their rhetoric of 'good governance', Bainimarama got no support from the Australian and New Zealand governments, or from the EU on whom Fiji relied for concessionary access for its sugar exports. Australia and New Zealand put travel bans on the coup leaders and their relatives, and the EU refused to renew concessions on sugar until the promised date for new elections was brought forward.

This chapter first considers popular perceptions of corruption in Fiji before the coup. The second part analyses the cleanup campaign: the purges, complaints, and investigations which culminated in the promulgation of an Independent Commission Against Corruption (ICAC). The third considers the reactions to the coup of NGOs, particularly Transparency International's Fiji chapter. The final part draws some conclusions about the populist character of the campaign against corruption. I will be using the word 'populism' to mean 'the claim to represent or act in the name of the people, understood as ordinary or common people, the majority, or the masses, as opposed to elites, privileged or special-interest groups, the establishment, or the power bloc' (Collier 2001). That often includes distrust of politicians and the perception that 'they are all corrupt' (Mény 1998).

The extent of corruption in Fiji

'Corruption' is a strong but vague word in English, involving moral condemnation and a sense of decay. The new international concern with corruption is mainly economic. Commodore Bainimarama took a broad moral view, accusing the officials he purged of 'lack of moral strength or incompetence or abuse of power and privileges and funds: Basically they were corrupt' (*Fiji Times* Online 17 June 2007). In the absence of a legal or policy framework, Fiji's anti-corruption campaign initially took a broad, scattergun approach responding to all sorts of rumours and complaints about the public and private sectors.

It is hard to say with certainty how much corruption there is in any country, and particularly in Fiji before the coup. A National Integrity System report, carried out in 2001 by a local consulting firm for Transparency International, identified several types of corruption 'prevalent' in Fiji – kickbacks, greasing of palms, nepotism, rank-pulling, unfair decisions on procurement, and misuse of public funds (Olaks Consulting 2001: 8). But these are types, not amounts. The report was also careful to talk about allegations and perceptions

Transparency International's CPI, which is based on perceptions of journalists and investment risk analysts, rated Fiji in 2005 with a below-average 4/10 for corruption (where 10 was clean and 0 was dirty). Fiji's score is not out of line with other developing countries, which tend to cluster towards the 'dirty' end of TI's scale. Fiji's score ranked 55th out of 158 states, equally with Bulgaria, Colombia, and the Seychelles (Transparency International 2007b).

A populist campaign must presumably take into account popular opinion, and there were popular perceptions of 'corruption' within Fiji. A survey of popular opinion in Fiji carried out for TI's Global Corruption Barometer in August 2006 found 47 per cent of the population believed that 'political life' was affected by corruption 'to a large extent' (compared to 40 per cent for 'business environment' and 22 per cent for 'personal and family life') (Tebbutt Research 2006). People perceived political parties as most affected by corruption and religious organizations least affected. Some sectors were perceived as more corrupt than others (see Table 8.1). However, much smaller percentages of people who had dealings with each sector admitted to ever paying a bribe themselves. Table 8.1 also shows Fiji doing the same, or better, than the worldwide average of bribery experience for each sector. The difference between popular perceptions and experience in Table 8.1 is striking. When presenting the survey, the head of TI (Fiji) commented that 'many of the views seemed to reflect the experience of others because few people said they paid bribes although corruption took many forms other

Table 8.1 Perception of corruption and bribes paid by sector in Fiji

	% who perceived the sector as 'extremely corrupt'	% who paid a bribe (of those who had contact with the sector)	% who paid a bribe (worldwide average inc. Fiji)
Tax revenue	25	3	3
Utilities	25	1	5
Registry and Permits	18	4	9
Police	22	7	17
Medical Services	20	2	6
Legal/Judiciary	19	5	8
Education system	19	1	5

Source: Tebbutt Research 2006 and Transparency International 2006.

than bribery' (*Fiji Times* 24 March 2007). The TI survey found a closer correspondence between suspicion and experience of bribery in the questions that it asked about the legal system. Fifteen per cent of all the people asked agreed that 'the justice system is corrupt'. Seventeen per cent knew of a specific case of bribery (Tebbutt Research 2006). The report of a visiting mission by the Law Association for Asia and the Pacific (LAWASIA) – a regional professional NGO – noted 'allegations of corruption' in the Magistrates' courts, and a danger that it might become institutionalised (LAWASIA 2007: 19).

Academic observers of Fiji, like Brij Lal or Jon Fraenkel, mostly concurred, in a qualified way, with these popular perceptions. Lal referred to the 'massive scam' in the Ministry of Agriculture before the 2001 election, and commented that '"evidence" of corruption (or mere incompetence and sheer carelessness) was everywhere' (2007: 137). Fraenkel (2007: 429) argued that:

> [i]n one sense, corruption under the deposed government was well known; especially in the government tendering process, in the immigration department, in the Native Lands Trust Board, in the affirmative action campaigns and at the interface between foreign investors and government.

Suspicions and allegations are aggravated by gossip and rumour – what Myrdal (1968) calls the 'folklore of corruption'. The lawyer Richard Naidu argued that, in deciding who to investigate and interrogate, '[t]he military seems to be relying on gossip and rumour, just as everyone else in Fiji tends to do' (*Fiji Times* 18 December 2006). Sociologist Steven Ratuva found the rumour-mongering had been worse during the 2000 coup, but the availability of email had provided new opportunities for those for and against the 2006 coup. Members of the educated elite, he said, were the worst offenders (*Fiji Times* 15 January 2007). Fiji also has a lively independent media that is ready to report on untested allegations of corruption, and thus act as a handmaiden to the clean-up campaign.

In Fiji, concern with 'corruption' also has a racial overtone, for example in objections to affirmative action programmes that favour indigenous citizens in scholarships, licensing, and land ownership (Cottrell and Ghai 2007). Fiji's best-documented scandal, over the National Bank of Fiji in the 1990s, had involved concessional loans to indigenous enterprises and to the relatives of bank officials (Grynberg et al. 2002). Qarase and his government had tilted towards indigenous interests, and the coup was initially welcomed by many of those who felt disadvantaged by that tilt: the Indo-Fijians and other minorities.

Populist campaigns often trade on anxieties about race and immigration, claiming that elites have ignored the legitimate prejudices of ordinary people (Mény 1998). But race played a more ambivalent role in this case.

Bainimarama's coup was explicitly anti-racist, and in a speech to the United Nations he called for the abolition of Fiji's system of communal voting and affirmative action (*Fiji Times* Online 30 September 2007). His predecessor's racism was the object of detailed criticism from the Director of the Fiji Human Rights Commission (Shameem 2007). Yet anti-racism had a racial inflection. *Time* Magazine noted that Indo-Fijians were the coup's 'biggest fans' (5 February 2007: 45). It was not hard for its opponents to grumble the coup was 'pro-Indian'.

The clean-up campaign

The clean-up campaign adopted several methods: purges of senior officials and board members; gathering public complaints; and investigations by the police, soldiers, auditors, or *ad hoc* committees. The interim Attorney General Aiyaz Syed-Khaiyum moved quickly to establish the ICAC promised by the Qarase government.

Purges

The military government initiated different types of purges: of the levers of state power; of the governing party, and of Chief Executive Officers (CEOs) and board members of state bodies. Students and staff in educational institutions also questioned their senior staff.

The first purge was essential to any coup, sidelining officials and organizations which might resist the instructions of the military: the chair of the Public Service Commission; the Acting Police Commissioner (the Commissioner was overseas); the Deputy Police Commissioner; the Assistant Commissioner (Crime); the Supervisor of Elections; and the Solicitor General. The head of the civil service stepped down and the only resistance to this first stage was from the CEO of Finance who bravely tried to limit the military's capacity to govern by setting a limit to the amount departments could spend without authorization (he later gave himself up). The army sent the Chief Justice, Daniel Fatiaki, and the Chief Magistrate on leave (though the latter was allowed to return). Fatiaki controlled an important lever of state power, but the army were particularly out to get him for his alleged role in facilitating the 2000 coup.

Members of Parliament were sacked, and the military government also targeted officers of the majority party, which had been established as a vehicle of the interim government after the 2000 coup. SDL political advisers were sacked (*Fiji Times* 19 December 2006). Former officials of the United Fijian Party (SDL) were gathered up with NGO leaders for questioning at the barracks (*Fiji Times* 11 December 2006).

The army also briefly flirted with global con man Peter Foster, who had earlier befriended Fiji Labour Party and SDL figures. Foster claimed to have taped conversations showing that the SDL had rigged the 2006 election by stuffing ballot boxes in Suva, the capital (*Fiji Times* 1 January 2007), and that Qarase had over US$2 million hidden away in offshore bank accounts (which he denied).

A second wave of sackings targeted 13 CEOs and board members of statutory bodies and public enterprises (*Fiji Times* 15 December 2006): the chair, another board member, and the CEO of Airports Fiji Ltd; two members of the board of Post Fiji Limited; two members of the board of Ports Corporation; two members of the board of the Civil Aviation Authority; the executive chairman and chief executive of Air Terminal Services; the chairman of the board of Fiji Electricity Authority; and the chairman of the board of the Investment Corporation. Bainimarama said he was concerned about the number of boards, their overlapping membership, and the opportunities that they provided for political patronage and 'empire-building' (*Fiji Times* 15 December 2006).

In a mild form of the 1960s cultural revolution, staff and students began to ask questions about the leadership of their own institutions. The student union at the Fiji College of Advanced Education asked the Education Ministry to investigate concerns that they had about their social amenities fund. Students had boycotted classes for a day in support of an investigation (*Fiji Times* 21 March 2007). On 30 March 2007 the Fiji Institute of Technology Director was reported cautioning staff against taking files off campus. Staff had apparently 'colluded with their trades unions to illegally collect files and documents belonging to the institute and [transmit] them to the Interim Education Minister's office, as well as the Anti Corruption Unit, to discredit the Institute's council and management' (*Fiji Times* 30 March 2007).

The University of the South Pacific staff association began to ask questions about salaries being paid to senior administrative staff. In March 2007 the Interim Minister for Education was reported to be investigating claims made in emails of 'exorbitant salaries' (*Fiji Times* 27 March 2007).

Generally, the purges created ample opportunity for harassment, disruption, and the settling of old scores. They were populist in the dictionary sense, above: exploiting resentments between elites and ordinary people, and siding firmly with the latter. Recent reforms of long-established institutions like Airports Fiji Limited, the Fiji Sugar Corporation, and the University of the South Pacific had created hostility towards the senior executives targeted by the purges.

Complaints

The second approach taken by the military and interim governments was to invite and gather all kinds of public complaints. An army team opened an office in the government buildings in Suva, where people began to queue up with complaints (*Fiji Times* 3 February 2007).

The new CEO in the PM's office described the mixture of allegations and complaints received by the unit:

They range from various issues like the provision of public services. Some people have been complaining that they had to pay a certain sum of money for certain services and that someone has been deprived the first opportunity because they were not in the good books of some person.

(*Fiji Times* 2 February 2007)

There were complaints about individuals and organizations. According to Major Leweni:

Most cases received by the corruption investigation team at the Government Headquarters Buildings in Suva are old cases that have been pending for years.

(*Fiji Times* 13 February 2007)

By the end of March the unit had received 400 complaints since its establishment (*Fiji Times* 27 March 2007). The *Fiji Times* noted wryly that the unit had been a 'spectacular success – at receiving complaints'. The editorial argued that the unit needed to set priorities and work within rules to ensure accusations held up in court. It also questioned whether it should be straying into the private sector (29 March 2007).

There were many complaints against the military itself. In February an unnamed NGO released documentation on about 200 cases of 'human rights abuses, breaches of the constitution and rule of law since December 5'. People were taken up to barracks, humiliated, made to perform physical exercises, and warned against repetition of a range of often petty offences (on the one hand) and against criticism of the military or interim government (on the other). Soldiers were described as 'short-fused' and 'younger soldiers [were] reported to be assaulting, arresting and detaining persons without any justifiable reason' (*Fiji Times* 25 February 2007). Lawyers also described military interference in civil and commercial litigation. Eventually this arbitrary, sometimes violent, harassment seems to have led to a death of a youth in military custody (*Fiji Times* 26 February 2007). The army, lamely, asked people to complain to it about mistreatment by soldiers. Bainimarama later accepted that 'some guys have crossed the line' (Waterson 2007: 13).

The army also complained about 'civilians verbally abusing soldiers' (*Fiji Times* 18 February 2007). Swearing at soldiers was a popular expression of resistance to the coup. It reminds us that it was ordinary people, rather than the elite, who bore the brunt of the army's crackdown on petty crime. Ironically, in responding to the 400 popular complaints against the government, the army found itself provoking 200 complaints (as collated by NGOs) and having 81 complaints of its own against the public. This spiral of mutual complaint – a petty war of all against all – may be a distinctive feature of populist campaigns.

Investigations

There were three kinds of investigations. The first, initiated by the army, involved soldiers collecting files, and bringing targeted individuals to the barracks, sometimes overnight, for questioning. Investigations of corruption blurred into investigations of dissent or petty crime. Interviews blurred into harassment threats and physical bullying. Lawyer Richard Naidu claimed that the military was picking up people it had already deemed 'unacceptable' and 'no evidence has been produced that they were corrupt' (*Fiji Times* 18 December 2006).

The second followed the initial purge of senior officials, CEOs, and board members. The military initiated or provoked a series of open-ended 'reviews' or 'audits' of public bodies – the Sugar Cane Growers Council, the Ports Authority, the National Provident Fund, Fiji Pine Limited, Fisheries, and the Native Lands Trust Board. Meanwhile, the senior managers of these public bodies were sent on leave.

Not all those accused of 'discrepancies', 'irregularities', and so on went quietly. Two took advertisements in the newspaper to put their case. The free press, which often congratulates itself for its 'investigative journalism' and sees itself as a pillar of the National Integrity System', can also be characterized as one of the 'quasi-official tribunals' in a populist campaign. Ratu Sakiusa Tuisolia, who was among the first group of CEOs dismissed, set out his record of achievement at Airports Fiji Ltd, and argued that the audit:

> was instigated via anonymous letters from various disgruntled people who suffered as a result of our efforts to build and progress AFL ... the AUDIT WAS CLEARLY A WITCH HUNT. ... and DID NOT FIND OR REPORT ANY FRAUD OR IMPROPRIETY.
>
> (*Fiji Times* 16 December 2007)

The CEO of the Fijian Affairs Board (Adi Litia Qionibaravi) defended herself (in English and Fijian) against allegations that she had used Fijian Affairs Board funds to buy vehicles and repair her house (*Fiji Times* 27 December 2007). She was later taken in for questioning by the military.

Later, the sacked CEO of the Public Works Department (PWD) claimed that Interim Minister Chaudhry's allegations of corruption in the Department of Water and Sewerage were 'wild'. Contracts had been made with the private sector because the ministry did not have the machinery to do it themselves. Chaudhry countered that the money was there, but the 'government machines had been deliberately not repaired' to provide opportunities for the private sector – which pointed to a close link between mismanagement and corruption (*Fiji Times* 25 January 2007).

The third form of investigation responded to popular complaints, but these were not necessarily about corruption. A unit in the police – a precursor to the Fiji Independent Commission Against Corruption (FICAC) – launched investigations into a wide range of organizations, and did so mostly in response to complaints. The organizations included a travel agency, a tertiary institution, a private clinic, and the Fiji Sports Council (the last on instructions from the Minister of Finance, who had been alerted by audit reports).

The formation of an Independent Commission Against Corruption (ICAC)

The Law Reform Commission had recommended the formation of an ICAC in 2003. In October 2004, the SDL Cabinet had agreed to set one up, but nothing much had happened since then. In early January 2007, Bainimarama appealed for international help to help the military sift through 'dozens of files' relating to alleged corruption in the Qarase government. A task force was going to be housed in the former Ministry of Information offices in the government offices in Suva

> We need to find a systematic way of getting rid of corruption within each government department. Its unbelievable the stories you hear, the allegations that we get.
>
> (*Fiji Times* 9 January 2007)

The files were 'tangible evidence', and Bainimarama's aim was to set up a 'tribunal' to investigate each allegation and begin the process of reform: 'If we'd left it to the last government to fix they wouldn't have done it' (*Fiji Times* 9 January 2007).

At the end of January 2007, Assistant Superintendent Nasir Ali was nominated to head a new anti-corruption unit (*Fiji Times* 30 January 2007). He would help the military, which was combining its own anti-corruption unit with its 'centre for hearing public complaints' in the Suva government buildings. At this point there seemed to be at least three units for dealing with corruption: two run by the army, and Nasir Ali's new unit in the police.

The interim Attorney General promised a new 'powerful, fully resourced independent investigative body, having new and significantly enhanced legal powers or surveillance in order to be able to successfully investigate, arrest, detain and prosecute offenders of corruption' (*Fiji Times* 1 February 2007). The promised commission would report directly to the President who had been restored to office by Bainimarama a month earlier. Captain Esala Teleni would 'help' and 'monitor' the commission (*Fiji Times* 1 February 2007). He had been a close ally of Bainimarama in his war of words with the Qarase government before the coup, and would later move on to become the new Police Commissioner.

The interim Cabinet agreed to the establishment of an ICAC, and funding of F$1.5 million on 29 March. The legislation was promulgated on 4 April without – in the absence of Parliament – the possibility of a parliamentary debate. A parallel promulgation for the Prevention of Bribery (No 12 of

2007) provided that a public officer who could not explain income or property disproportionate to their earnings would be guilty of an offence. Informers (or whistle-blowers) would also get protection. The focus was on investigation and prosecution; prevention only got a brief mention. The unit was looking for 22 additional staff, and advertised the positions in the *Fiji Times*.

Esala Teleni was made acting Deputy Commissioner of the FICAC, and was responsible for its operations – carried out by Ali – until a Commissioner was appointed. A distinguished Malaysian lawyer was appointed Commissioner, but then withdraw after criticism from his Commonwealth legal colleagues. Mr Mah Weng Kwai was the President of LAWASIA, and he recently led that professional NGO's review of the situation of the judiciary in Fiji (LAWASIA 2007).

NGO dilemmas

NGO groups, including churches, were generally against the coup, and made public statements against it. However some Catholic promoters of social justice were sceptical about the motives of proponents of democracy, and impressed by the Commodore's anti-racism (Lal 2007: 150). NGO officials were called into the barracks for questioning, and several beaten up. As part of an 'apology' to people affected by the coup, Bainimarama explained that 'the military keeps an eye on non-government organisations' as these were 'the only group still going against the military' (*Fiji Times* 29 January 2007).

The local chapter of Transparency International, the anti-corruption NGO, found itself in a quandary. It had followed the general approach of its international patron, Transparency International: lobbying among the elite, commissioning surveys, and drawing the private sector into anti-corruption coalitions. It could hardly be accused of populism. In a press release in 2005 (TI 2005: No 4/05) it had cautiously endorsed the Qarase government decision to set up an anti-corruption commission, though it had wondered about its cost and whether 'instances of corruption that had taken place are real and not just perceptions'. It also argued for a preventive as well as an investigatory approach. TI had joined other NGOs in writing an open letter urging Bainimarama not to proceed with his coup (*Fiji Times* 4 December 2006). TI faced difficult choices about whether or not to engage with a new regime that was ostensibly committed to some of the policies that TI had been promoting for years.

In December 2006, TI Fiji's Chair, Hari Singh, announced that TI had been telling the Qarase government about increasing levels of corruption and,

> [i]f the military is cleaning up corruption, then we are more or less with them on that.
>
> (*Fiji Times* 29 December 2006)

TI then split three ways. Aiyaz Sayed-Khaiyum had been on the board of TI and resigned when he became interim Attorney General in January 2007. Richard Naidu, another influential Suva lawyer who had been brought in for questioning by the military, resigned in February over what he described as 'differing views on the terms on which TI has chosen to engage the Interim Government on corruption issues' (*Fiji Times* 19 February 2007). Hari Singh gave a long interview setting out TI's views on the consequences of corruption, and its prevalence in Fiji:

> Reports and surveys carried out indicate that there is some level of corruption in Fiji. Auditor Generals' reports have been highlighting some corrupt practices that have been ignored in the past ... whether corruption was so serious to warrant an overthrow of an elected government is judgemental and TI Fiji would not like to make that judgement.
>
> (*Fiji Times* 21 March 2007)

TI had told the interim government it did not condone the takeover, but would help with the establishment of an ICAC, including using its networks to identify expertise. TI Fiji had consulted its Berlin office and counterpart organizations in Australia and New Zealand, and decided to engage with the government. It would not condone the military takeover, and would emphasize the importance of the rule of law (*Fiji Times* 21 March 2007).

TI then released the results of the public survey commissioned from a market research company and carried out in August 2006 (and described above). Qarase was reported as describing Singh's statement as unfair, and the survey 'unreliable'. The National Federation Party secretary also criticized the survey, saying they were unaware that it was being carried out, and the result 'was not in any way the true reflection of the political parties' (*Fiji Times* 27 March 2007).

TI's annual report for 2007 noted that it had 'copped some flak' for engaging with the government, but believed some of its advice was heeded (Transparency International 2007). TI did not fall silent. Its call for the introduction of campaign finance legislation before the next election would not have disturbed the military government, already suspicious of party funding. However, its press releases defending the independence of the Auditor General and condemning 'conflicts of interest' among interim ministers – particularly the Minister for Sugar retaining his position as secretary general for the National Farmers' Union – were critical of the regime *(Fiji Times Online* 31 August 2007).

Conclusions

Stephen Riley (1998: 132) noted that populist initiatives in Africa 'have not had much success', pointing out that 'the problem of corruption does not disappear with the removal of those key officials identified as corrupt'.

Gillespie and Okruhlik concluded from their Middle Eastern survey that it was 'unclear' whether or not clean-ups 'actually reduce the incidence of corrupt transactions' (1991: 92). Such campaigns nevertheless had political benefits for coup leaders, particularly through 'short term weeding out of specific opposition leaders and [through] the diversion of attention from more pressing socioeconomic problems'.

In April 2007, Bainimarama listed the establishment of the FICAC among the 'major achievements' of the 'first 100 days' of his regime. The results – in terms of evidence uncovered, or successful prosecutions – have so far been meagre.

The FICAC ran into constitutional trouble when it tried to bring cases to court. In August 2007 the High Court ruled that it had no power to bring cases to court – a power reserved in the Constitution, which the army said was still in place, for the director of Public Prosecutions (Radio New Zealand 17 August 2007). In October, the FICAC announced its investigations were continuing into the Fiji Institute of Technology, the Fiji Sports Council, Airports Fiji Limited, and a number of civil servants, but could not say when charges would be laid (*Fiji Times* Online 31 October 2007).

In December 2006, Leweni had reassured the media that the army would not sack people without evidence, and that the facts would be revealed 'in due time' (*Fiji Times* 19 December 2006). Later challenged to provide evidence, Bainimarama offered a circular argument:

> All you have to do is follow the events of the last six months and see who has been removed from their posts. They have been removed for corrupt practices.
>
> (*Fiji Times* Online 17 June 2007)

Five months later, another military spokesman under pressure to come up with evidence of corruption, argued about definitions and the need for more time:

> People usually think corruption is centred on the exchange of money and that's why people like Qarase are asking for proof. The other facet of corruption which takes time to prove is what we are working on – that is management or leadership corruption. Corruption in government was so rife and they did nothing to address it …
>
> (*Fiji Times* Online 14 November 2007)

As well as pitting ordinary people against the (previous) elite, Fiji's cleanup campaign has elements of the 'populist' type of anti-corruption campaign identified by Riley (1998) – the purges of civil servants (described above), public humiliations (the trial by media), and quasi-official tribunals (the unconstitutional FICAC). There have not yet been the executions, though three people have died after being detained and beaten-up (*ABC News* 8 June 2007).

The Moral Rearmament language has also been present. Bainimarama convened a special church service at which he called on soldiers to fast for a month and counselled them that 'the clean-up must first start from within' (*Fiji Times* 8 January 2007). In June 2007, the interim cabinet met a Kenyan delegation sponsored by Initiatives of Change – the new name for the old Moral Rearmament movement formed by Frank Buchman in the 1930s. They 'shared their experience' and personal stories about ridding their country of corruption (Fiji Government 2007b). As with FICAC, Bainimarama was building on an initiative of the Qarase government, which had permitted Initiatives to Change to hold a conference in Suva in 2006 (Fiji Government 2006).

Moral Rearmament looked for a change of heart. Transparency International talked in a more impersonal language about legal changes needed to prevent corruption, while the military spokesman blamed failures of management and leadership among their democratic predecessors. TI (Fiji), the NGO, was the opposite of populist. While the army's clean-up campaign was populist, in the senses defined above, it was not only populist. Its opponents were subject to public humiliation and arbitrary treatment, but the coup leaders promised their cases would eventually end up in court. The interim government also recognized that the removal of particularly corrupt officials would not be the end of corruption. The FICAC legislation is mainly concerned with investigation, but also requires the anti-corruption commissioner to examine the practices of government departments 'which may be conducive to corrupt practices' (section 12(d) of the Fiji Independent Commission Against Corruption (Promulgations No 11 of 2007)). The interim government also moved to reform public service and audit procedures in order to reduce corruption risks. A senior military officer told the academic, Brij Lal: 'prevention is better than cure', foreshadowing a continuing military role in government (Lal 2007: 151). Bainimarama also stepped back from the clean-up campaign in the second half of 2007, preferring to seek legitimacy in another more inclusive way – the formation of what he called a National Council for Building a Better Fiji, which he hoped NGOs would join (*Fijilive.com* November 16 2007).

Notes

1 Acknowledgement: Parts of this chapter are drawn from a paper in the Pacific Islands Policy Series published by the Pacific Islands Development Program in the East West Center East (http://www.eastwestcenter.org/publications/series/). I am grateful to the editors for permission to reproduce them here.

Part III

The vices and virtues of non-governmental anti-corruption

9 Transnational anti-corruption advocacy

A multi-level analysis of civic action in Russia

Diana Schmidt-Pfister

The anti-corruption literature contains two recurring arguments: the potentially negative consequences of anti-corruption measures,[1] and the tendency to avoid defining 'corruption' in national campaigns and instead to define political opponents as corrupt.[2] More recently, scholars have reiterated these arguments with a view to anti-corruption operations in post-Soviet Eastern Europe and, in addition, increasingly linked them to the international dimension (e.g. Coulloudon 2002, Krastev 2004: xiv, Savintseva and Stykow 2005: 200). It is thus pointed out that the global anti-corruption movement brings together 'diverse actors normally at odds with each other' (Sampson 2005: 110) and that the anti-corruption cause can be exploited to serve the agendas of specific groups (Krastev 2004: xiv).

It is further argued that the anti-corruption movement has been globalized from its inception, beginning at the top and then penetrating locally through a 'projectization of anti-corruption' with the moral campaign issue being 'converted into grant categories and technical assistance contracts' (Sampson 2005: 106–9). The dynamic of this movement, as well as its downside, is thus manifested in what is sceptically seen as an 'anti-corruption industry' that entails a domination of domestic anti-corruption action by donor initiatives and foreign programming (Michael 2004a).[3] In addition, there is growing acknowledgement that the reality of fighting corruption has been a disillusioning experience in Eastern Europe, and even more so in former Soviet countries where corruption situations have only deteriorated (Greenlees 2006; Michael 2004a). While critical observations, most of these arguments remain to be substantiated by systematic empirical analysis.

This chapter contributes to these recent debates with a particular emphasis on the involvement of local civil society actors in the transnational advocacy network (TAN) against corruption.[4] What precisely are the implications for the non-governmental activists, and eventually for the transnational efforts? And how can we possibly study these?

Post-Soviet Russia has been a focus of Western advice and assistance addressing the country's persistently immense corruption and crime problems. In 2000, hopes were raised when Vladimir Putin assumed the Presidency and placed anti-corruption high on his agenda. However, Putin has also established a system of authoritarian governance that negatively affects civil society development in general and the foreign financing of civic advocacy on politically sensitive issues in particular. Corruption in Russia has been discussed among scholars as one of the main issues related to domestic Soviet transformation. The discussion is often implicit, and as a result there is a large body of arguments and findings about corruption scattered among the existing literature on Russia. In addition, after corruption studies had been unable to gather reliable data on corruption during Soviet times, or to use objective surveys on peoples' attitudes to the phenomenon (cf. DiFranceisco and Gitelman 1984, Holmes 1993: 67), the 1990s literature came with new possibilities but also problems. Through extensive writing on Russian corruption and crime problems, it caught up on a lack of information. Fish (2005: 131), however, refers to an 'industry dedicated to recounting the scope of the rod', providing 'a tale of corruption so pervasive' that contributes to cynical indifference, in particular among a Russian audience.[5] Fish, as many other authors recently, has therefore welcomed indices that have simultaneously emerged as presumably objective quantitative measures of corruption and various democratization indicators. Yet the recent belief in index and survey data on developments in Russia seems exaggerated, and all the more since scholars tend to neglect both the underlying methodologies and practical uses of what are in many cases also resources of 'information politics' (cf. Keck and Sikkink 1998: 18–22). Information about corruption, as illustrated below, is often put to use strategically with regard to actor relations, but not necessarily constructively with regard to the presumably common concern of corruption prevention. At the same time, and closely linked, the range and determination of both governmental and non-governmental anti-corruption activities in Russia have earned scant attention among analysts, especially during the Putin era. Earlier research on anti-corruption campaigns in Soviet and early post-Soviet times, by underlining the lack of credibility of governmental efforts (e.g. Coulloudon 2002, Holmes 1993) and the lack of incentives among citizens to blow whistles (Martirossian 2004), seems to have discouraged interest also among scholars to analyse Russian anti-corruption measures. However, these earlier writings failed to consider the interrelationship of national and local efforts with international affairs and foreign anti-corruption assistance that has arrived in Russia since the late 1990s. In these respects, analysis on anti-corruption in contemporary Russia needs to be updated.

This chapter first discusses how research on transnational anti-corruption efforts, in particular that focusing on the involvement of non-governmental actors on the ground, can benefit from using the concept of a TAN that refers to the tripartite actor constellation of international, governmental, and non-governmental actors. A comprehensive view on actors across international, domestic, and local levels, their relations among each other, as well as to the anti-corruption issue, is then presented in the case of contemporary Russia. The chapter thus reintroduces insights gained during a larger research project (Schmidt 2006) that brought together theoretical work on

TANs, anti-corruption studies, and research on anti-corruption advocacy in Russia.[6]

Connecting anti-corruption research and TAN studies

TANs have been conceptualized by scholars of social movements and comparative politics as essentially a tripartite constellation in which domestic groups and international allies put pressure on domestic governments that violate international principles. Some scholars presume, ultimately, that norm-deviant states are successfully socialized into norm-compliance through network pressure (e.g. Keck and Sikkink 1998; Risse *et al.* 1999). Conventional definitions further contain the assumption that 'actors are bound together by shared values, a common discourse, and dense exchange of information and services' (Keck and Sikkink 1998: 2; Risse and Sikkink 1999: 18).[7] Based mainly on evidence from human rights and environmental advocacy, these concepts have never been applied to the realm of anti-corruption or to cases where post-Soviet target states are involved.

The preoccupation with successful outcomes that has characterized TAN approaches would be in line with the views of researchers and policy-makers in the anti-corruption sphere. They tend to focus on assessing the successes in the reduction of the level of corruption in a single country. Most importantly, however, such outcome-oriented views obstruct the view of the socio-political processes involved in transnational advocacy networking. Empirical evidence on developments in the anti-corruption realm calls for analysis that helps to better our understanding of the internal workings of TANs – in addition to, and as a precondition of, their eventual effectiveness (see Table 9.1). Research on Russia further shows that such an understanding could also be enhanced by an analysis of what would conventionally be considered 'unsuccessful' cases (Schmidt 2006). To this end, the changing agendas and actions of TAN actors need to be taken into account by analysing both the advocacy issue and actor relations within their respective contexts – international, domestic, or local. Anti-corruption research may benefit from such a TAN conceptual perspective as long as it is used as a heuristic tool for discovering the more complex ties and indirect interrelations between network actors. It goes further than merely explaining causal effects at the domestic level while presuming agreed goals, shared values, and candid exchange transnationally. In this spirit, TANs are defined here as networks of actors who are working on an issue of common concern while embedded within their various contexts across international, national, and local levels.

The more open-ended approach proposed here sticks to the analytical categories identified by conventional TAN studies, but remains sceptical about the presumed causal and normative assumptions. It encourages students of anti-corruption to re-examine the various actors involved and their interrelations in each case. An analysis of final outcomes resulting from international and domestic bottom-up efforts should not be the primary

Table 9.1 TAN theory vs empirical evidence on anti-corruption advocacy

	TANs	TAN influence (outcome)	Causal mechanisms	Normative bias
TAN theory	State-centred; International norms, shared values	Changing state behaviour	NGOs: pro-active → State: responsive	State: norm-deviant, bad; NGOs: oppositional, good
Anti-corruption evidence	Multitude of actors; Multi-level relations; International/domestic/local values	Changing agendas and actions among international, state, civil society actors	International actors ⟷ State; civil society actors (pro-active and responsive)	Norm-deviance across all societal sectors

objective. As demonstrated in the Russian case, conclusions about the effectiveness of transnational advocacy efforts will change over time. In contrast to conventional TAN assumptions, anti-corruption campaigns do not end (successfully) with the state responding to the pressure from above and below.

Anti-corruption research has also remained rather detached from area studies. Yet, besides studying the emergence of the anti-corruption movement globally, its performance on the ground needs to be understood by integrating profound knowledge of particular country contexts. The Russian case shows that anti-corruption advocacy in the domestic context entails a range of complexities, in particular where various civil society actors are involved and where the action takes place at a local level. Both TAN studies and the international anti-corruption discourse commonly project target countries as a single unit within the international context. However, it is crucial to differentiate between domestic and local as distinct operational contexts. Building on case studies of civic anti-corruption advocacy in three cities in different Russian regions, the research behind this chapter suggests that local contexts provide different conditions for different forms of corruption and changing principles and practices of civic engagement (and thus different transnational anti-corruption initiatives). The insights generated from these case studies substantiate the argument that transnational advocacy potential also varies within the Russian context, depending on the kind and dominance of influences issuing from the international, domestic, and local spheres.

Distinguishing actors, issues, and contexts in the Russian case

The analysis of anti-corruption activities in three Russian cities made clear that, rather than standing as active mediators between international and domestic fronts, activists on the ground are constantly challenged to perform balancing acts between the changing agendas of (potential and actual) international partners, the Kremlin, and regional/local leaders. They are performing reactively more often than proactively. Crucial factors affecting civic anti-corruption engagement include foreign financial assistance and information provision, as well as governmental agendas regarding both anti-corruption and civil society development. These factors entail a range of implications that may both hinder and foster transnational anti-corruption advocacy.

Other research on Russia has described tensions that may result from donor-funded non-governmental initiatives in civic rights and environmental spheres. These include: non-resonant agendas across West–East and international-domestic dimensions; contentious relations of Russian groups with the Russian government; and frequent resentments between these groups (e.g. Henderson 2003, Henry 2002, Sperling 2006, Sundstrom 2006, Yanitskii 1998). However, donor–grantee relations and civil society–state relations have so far been discussed and analysed as separate themes. With regard to local civic anti-corruption projects in Russia, it becomes very obvious that these spheres are interrelated in complex ways and that these overlaps need to be 'considered by any meaningful analysis'.

The international–domestic nexus: Indices are more than measures

It has become quite common to assess any country's corruption situation on the basis of its position or score in the various cross-national indices that have emerged since the mid-1990s, most prominently the CPI (Corruption Perceptions Index) annually issued by Transparency International (TI). This is not the place to review Russia's position in these various rankings. As Fish's (2005) latest contribution illustrates, an assessement of the developments during the Putin era, based on these and other international indicators, could turn into a book-length work. Regarding corruption and anti-corruption in Russia, the analysis of anti-corruption indices eventually leads to three conclusions (Schmidt 2005): first, Russia tends to be found in the lower or lowest ranks in these international assessments. Second, this has not improved throughout the 2000s. Third, the methodologies behind most of these measures do not allow for more accurate conclusions about domestic corruption problems. It is therefore important to accept that the figures provided by the international indices cannot tell much about the anti-corruption achievements or failures in the country, and even less about contextual factors that shape the perceptions of various experts whose opinions those indices measure.

However, when we are assessing anti-corruption initiatives in Russia as a transnational advocacy process, the indices are more interesting from a different angle. Their growing importance as a rhetorical weapon in transnational efforts to advocate for anti-corruption measures at national levels means that the indices are also part of interrelations between various actors internationally and domestically. In combination with available national and local surveys, international indices may indeed be useful for learning about differences and commonalities in the perceptions of corruption problems and anti-corruption priorities. However, these indices are hardly utilized by network actors that are developing anti-corruption advocacy or policy strategies. Instead, in the Russian case, indices and surveys are part of a dynamic that has triggered counter-accusations as well as 'information politics' (Keck and Sikkink 1998). The following paragraphs can only summarize some of these dynamics.

According to all international indices, Russia presents a problematic case. After ranking lowest (21st out of 21 countries) among the leading industrial nations in TI's *Bribe Payers Index* (Transparency International 2002b), Russia also fell in the 2005 CPI.[8] Both international and Russian press took up on this evidence that corruption in Russia has increased. TI views this publicity effect as a first success in its anti-corruption efforts in Russia.[9] In practice, however, anti-corruption promoters, journalists, and scholars tend to ignore that the methodological design of the CPI and other indices limits their explanatory powers.[10] For example, the non-longitudinal nature of most surveys inhibits conclusions about trends,[11] and the reliance on perceptions of experts, often foreign, may ignore other domestic developments.[12] Nevertheless, the CPI tends to be used, even by some scholars, for assessing annual changes and as a basis for drawing conclusions on (the nature, causes, and consequences of) corruption in a particular country, and even on the success of anti-corruption efforts.[13] Additional data sources or in-depth studies of national origin are rarely consulted.[14]

In any case, both international and domestic attention was redirected to Russia's increasing corruption problem in 2005. Here, the influence of the CPI has been amplified by another domestic survey, conducted by the Russian thinktank Information Science for Democracy (INDEM) (2005),[15] the alarming results of which were made public in July 2005 and have since been widely recited in the Russian and Western presses. Russian surveys have revealed a more differentiated picture behind Russia's annual score by referring to various dimensions of corruption in the domestic context, first of all regarding differences between everyday and business corruption, between different sectors, and between administrative regions. They also supplement the perceptions of foreign experts with the views representative of small-to-medium enterprises (SME), as well as of the general population. Still, only the most dramatic findings of the Russian surveys (conducted by INDEM and TI-Russia) were pointed out in accompanying press releases and summaries. For example, it has often been cited that the cost of business corruption has dramatically increased from $30 billion to over $300 billion (INDEM 2005). Similarly, the multi-faceted results of a Russian regional index issued earlier by TI-Russia (2002a) had been reduced to the insight that the Russian map of corruption shows a 'Southern belt' of regions deeply affected by corruption (Chirkova and Bowser 2004: 295; TI-Russia 2002b: 1).[16] Also, in interviews it was obvious that even experts in the field draw their information almost solely from (foreign) news announcements and not from the original surveys, although these surveys are fully available online. Many valuable insights into cross-regional and cross-sectoral particularities of corruption perception in Russia actually offered by these surveys have thus remained out of sight.

Notably increased anti-corruption rhetoric and action proposed by the Russian government since late 2005 might be attributed to the attestation – by both the CPI and the Russian surveys published in 2005 – of a deteriorating corruption situation in the country. Yet other push-factors, such as the 2006 G8 summit held in Russia or domestic developments, have also been relevant here.[17] Still, the government's response is remarkable given that the first INDEM study in 2001, which revealed a volume of business bribery of over US$30 billion (cf. INDEM 2001), merely earned the President's disbelieving note that according to him it should be half this volume (JRL 2005). Also international outreach is actively pursued by INDEM. They presented the first study during the visit of US President Bush to Moscow in 2002 (JRL 2005) and presented the 2005 study at numerous press conferences and expert meetings.[18] It may also be said that the existence of the CPI initially encouraged the development of intra-Russian indices and within-country surveys, in particular the Russian regional index which was among the first projects of TI-Russia and which did not come without some criticism of the CPI.[19] More recently, however, displeased voices from the ranks of a new Russian anti-corruption movement have accused INDEM of feeding incorrect data into the CPI and thus putting Russia's international standing at risk (Protiv Korruptsii 2006b). Given the apparent governmental backing for these critics, one cannot any longer argue that political leaders in Russia are 'affirming these rankings' (Dininio and Orttung 2005: 501).

The international–local nexus in anti-corruption assistance

International anti-corruption programmes that aim at governmental partners and federal-level reforms in Russia are strikingly separate from those that address civil society actors on the ground. Local civic groups have been involved in anti-corruption networks primarily through conventional (foreign) donor agencies and practices. With the exception of TI, which is practically the only specific civil society anti-corruption network, existing grant-providers in various areas have widened their portfolios to include anti-corruption as a new theme. This trend is mirrored at the local level where, with the exception of a few specialized Moscow-based groups, anti-corruption is only a side task added to the mandate of various Russian activists and associations engaged in other fields. This is different from the environmental and human rights movements that are backed by issue-specific groups. In addition to the danger that the anti-corruption movement has been initiated at the international rather than local levels (Michael 2004a; Sampson 2005: 106), there is also a topical piggybacking of projects. Yet while the tapping into existing structures might be beneficial in some respects, it also runs the risk of overstraining valuable resources and competencies of local groups.

As anti-corruption programmes are a side task – and not the main mandate – of most groups, this further blurs the awareness of existing actors and activities in this field:

> [T]here are not that many civil society organisations working on corruption. And this is an unfortunate side. Of course you have journalists that provide a lot of useful information.
>
> (author's interview with representative of the Moscow office of the United Nations Office on Drugs and Crime, 3 May 2006)

This statement by a Moscow-based foreign representative only illustrates one side of the coin. Local groups often do not know which international actors are donors and which are not. It is not necessarily obvious.[20]

Greater exchange of information between international and local non-governmental actors seems necessary to both avoid mutual misperceptions and recognize others' (possible) roles within the network. On both sides, perceptions about each other's existence and changing agendas have remained vague, if not patently incorrect. Moreover, analysis of international documents and evidence from interviews with international/Western anti-corruption proponents and donor organizations reveals an essential lack of clarity as to who actually represents civil society on the ground and how various non-governmental actors ought to be involved. This has entailed an over-reliance on NGOs as local partners and neglected the expertise of others, and has also led to a range of questionable projects. For example, only with hindsight were Western-funded resource centres acknowledged as unsuitable strategic entities in Russian cities where local groups tend to both distrust each other and inspire distrust on the part of the population. In other cases it was discovered that short-term project results could not be maintained after the sudden appointment of a new regional governor.[21] Where envisioned results could not be attained due to the incompatibility between international/Western and local organizational cultures, rather than seeking to solve these dissonances, new grants simply tended to be funnelled to other local partner organizations.

To compound matters, the issue at stake – anti-corruption – remains insufficiently debated. Concerns about corruption bring different actors together, but the networking potential has not been fully tapped through interaction, information exchange, and debate among anti-corruption advocates. While corruption and anti-corruption are not clearly defined in many assistance programmes, discrepancies between international and local expectations frequently surface only while projects are ongoing. Given the inflexible structures of most grant programmes, it is then often too late to engage in deliberations over locally more appropriate strategies. In this regard, more constructive relationships between TI-Russia and the TI parent network or the United States Agency for International Development (USAID) as anti-corruption promoters[22] – for example, in contrast to the USAID-funded anti-corruption projects in Irkutsk[23] – indicate that local expertise is better received when not based on grantee-donor relations. Tensions between donors and grantees may further be amplified where donors see their preferred strategy confirmed by pilot projects in other Russian localities. This strategy of using pilot experiences may indeed serve to develop case-specific approaches in the pilot regions. Yet the cross-regional transfer of anti-corruption strategies through USAID grant programmes, for example, has hardly provided opportunities for open renegotiation of new project plans and adaption to crucial context-specific circumstances in target regions.[24]

The arrival of project-specific anti-corruption assistance affects not only the topical agendas in the field, but also the interaction mechanisms among the actors involved, including local civil society actors, foreign donors, and the Russian state. As for the Russian state, it needs to be taken into account that President Putin has put anti-corruption on his agenda and at the same time established a system of authoritarian governance in Russia that negatively affects foreign-funded civic advocacy on politically sensitive issues in Russia. Despite the move against foreign financing of Russian civic advocacy organizations, some forms of civic anti-corruption engagement have survived or even become increasingly active. TI-Russia continues its efforts as part of a global network; NAK (*Natsional'nyi Antikorruptsionnyi Komitet*) continues advocacy in Moscow and at the federal level; INDEM presents results of cross-regional surveys; USAID-assisted anti-corruption coalitions are active in several Russian regions; and an all-Russian movement *Protiv Korruptsii* (Against Corruption) has emerged since 2005. TI-Russia formally uses foreign grants, and being linked into the international TI movement, it may also access well-organized professional consultation and exchange beyond grant programmes. Both NAK and *Protiv Korruptsii* deliberately distance themselves from foreign financial support, albeit remaining open to international collaboration. NAK works closely with TI-Russia and INDEM; this cluster is critical of the government and is active across several Russian regions. *Protiv Korruptsii* works more closely with government and business, and seeks to integrate anti-corruption experts from all Russian regions. If it comes to signing international agreements, the Duma Anti-Corruption Commission informally interacts with all these groups, as well as with international organizations, whereas the latter tend to be unaware of the various civic groups. While domestic civic groups seek different strategies within the given international and domestic environments, the examples above highlight the importance of seeking a better understanding of the continuing but diverse potentials for civic anti-corruption engagement. This should include an awareness of local tensions building up within the domestic context.

The domestic–local nexus: struggling for status

International donors who are providing assistance to civil society projects have actively fostered the generation of data and independent surveys. Thanks to this, corruption and anti-corruption activities in Russia during the Putin era have become a subject of debate among both international and domestic actors. However, this information provision has also turned into a bone of contention between the state and various non-governmental groups, and information has become a main asset in power struggles among different local groups. Although these increasingly severe feuds take place within the Moscow context, where field offices of all international actors are based, many international organizations hardly recognize these tensions while maintaining bilateral relations with a few selected partner organizations.

Following the government's campaign against foreign financing of advocacy NGOs, the attribute *po grantam* (on grants) is no longer necessarily a positive one in Russia. In contrast to human rights and environmental advocacy, direct governmental repression and harassment are lesser problems for anti-corruption groups. Rather, increasing state control on foreign funding introduces more complex cleavages into relations among Russian and foreign-funded groups in this field. Such cleavages inhibit essential networking domestically, and result in negative implications for international–local relations. For example, if the new all-Russian anti-corruption movement *Protiv Korruptsii* presents itself as a Russian initiative working without foreign funding, on that basis it would have good reason to exclude established organizations such as INDEM and TI-Russia from its activities. In turn, local experts who join the new movement are denied access to longer-standing Russian networks. One should further note that INDEM had to justify itself and the validity of its earlier survey results by proving that its 2005 study was financed by Russian sources (the 2001 study had been criticized for being sponsored by foreign foundations, including foreign government-sponsored ones).

The 2005 CPI and INDEM surveys have incited new anti-corruption bustle with regard to the questions of expertise and information. That INDEM seems to have a monopoly on information about corruption in Russia through its internationally well-received studies is clearly a thorn in *Protiv Korruptsii's* side. The latter perceives INDEM's 2005 study, which attests to rising corruption levels, as 'a fruit either of non-professionalism or political orders' and as a threat to Russia's international standing, not least in the global energy market (*Protiv Korruptsii* 2006b). Articles are posted on the movement's website that openly accuse INDEM, and its president Georgy Satarov, of exaggerating the corruption problem by providing figures in its 2005 study that are deliberately impossible, mere assertions, probably ordered, and without doubt fed into the 'clownish' but momentous international ratings such as the CPI (*Protiv Korruptsii* 2006b). Underlining the problem that there are almost no figures to compare, *Protiv Korruptsii* has become increasingly active in providing additional information on the issue of corruption in Russia, for example by distributing daily email newsletters, conducting online polls, actively engaging with journalists, and inviting experts onto a talk show broadcast on state-owned *Radio Rossiia*.[25] The movement also warned that, as international accusations about the lack of civil liberties had done in the past, the theme of corruption could become 'a new battering ram' against Russia, despite an obviously fundamentally different state of affairs. Today the Russian administration constantly announces measures in the fight against corruption and participates in international anti-corruption agreements. Following the 2006 G8 Summit, it portrayed the international initiative against kleptocracy as an American concept – a new Marshall Plan – while stressing that Russians may opt to fight against their own corrupt officials themselves (*Protiv Korruptsii* 2006a). There is currently a danger that rhetorical feuding in Moscow intensifies while true action against the common target, corruption, gets lost in the noise.

From a TAN perspective, it is noticeable that such status struggles involve both cross-regional (within Russia) and transnational anti-corruption dimensions. Perhaps understandably, foreign donors tend to distance themselves from local cleavages. Yet while anti-corruption assistance programmes continue in Russian regions and at the federal level, it still remains an open question as to which of the Moscow-led anti-corruption initiatives will eventually take the lead in integrating regional activities. Importantly, transnational network and advocacy effectiveness may be disturbed if nodal points across the country are replaced by one (fragmented) centre.

Across contexts: what does 'anti-corruption' now mean in Russia?

With the evolving and expanding activities of the global anti-corruption movement, corruption has become linked to an increasing number of economic, moral, social, and security issues in various ways. However, that corruption is seen as a cause, a symptom, a catalyst, an obstacle, or a consequence of other phenomena has an impact on designing and implementing anti-corruption strategies. On this basis there are many possibilities to frame corruption problems as well as anti-corruption strategies. This may not only create cross-fertilizing overlaps, but may also increase the incidence of contradictory interpretations within the network, which may eventually weaken the network's envisioned effectiveness. Moreover, since most anti-corruption promoters are adopting multi-shareholder strategies, a formal commitment to civil society involvement has become an omnipresent clause. A more detailed analysis of discourses and projects at the international level, at Russian governmental level, and on the ground in different localities, however, points to the problem that neither 'civil society' nor 'corruption' (or 'anti-corruption') are clearly defined in most projects. Such vagueness not only affects the effectiveness of individual projects, but may also foster the problem that there is insufficient awareness among the various network actors of each other's existence, motivations, strategies, and primary addressees.

The Russian case, for example, somewhat contradicts the common perception and critique among observers that governmental anti-corruption moves only hit those at the bottom. From a Russian perspective there seems to be more concern that oligarchs and high-ranking politicians are being removed through spectacular governmental action while the many civil servants who are demanding bribes from average citizens remain disregarded. Fundamental concerns about everyday corruption are fuelled by the stratification of the Russian society into poor masses and rich elites. Accordingly, evidence of corruption considered by local citizens, activists, and journalists includes expensive cars and mansions in exclusive locations and owned by state servants whose official salaries are known to be low. The importance of such local perspectives becomes clearer when considering common housing problems in Russian cities in combination with recent grand construction projects that proceed without consultation of local experts and at the expense of local residents. Yet these concerns are invisible in international or foreign-funded Russian indices or surveys. Similarly, *blat* – the everyday popular exchange of favours, contacts and information – has not yet been targeted by anti-corruption efforts; luckily perhaps, as it would present a form of corruption to foreign experts while remaining a survival strategy for many in the Russian context.[26]

Several anti-corruption measures that have been viewed as effective by some anti-corruption proponents have been seen as counterproductive by others. The most prominent instances inspiring controversial interpretation include the increasingly authoritarian governance style of the Putin administration, the discourse on new terrorist threats, the case against Yukos, and the appointment of regional governors. For example, the authoritarian restructuring of administrative arrangements, although criticized by NGOs, is welcomed by some business actors and those concerned about Russia's investment climate. The journalistic community has been divided on the issue. The anti-terrorism discourse, in turn, has been used by the government to justify some of its unjust manoeuvres against selected opponents as well as against foreign funding of Russian NGOs. At the same time, this discourse has also raised new hopes among some activists that anti-corruption campaigns might experience a new impetus because the issue of corruption entered the anti-terrorism discourse when it became clear that bribes made the 2004 Beslan tragedy possible.[27] Furthermore, Mikhail Khodorkovsky's foundation *Otkrytaia Rossiia* (Open Russia) has been lauded as one of the main Russian donors for civic projects among journalist and activist communities in many Russian cities. In Irkutsk, however, this foundation, belonging to the founder of the Yukos oil company, is perceived less as a supportive donor than as an opponent promoting pipelines at the cost of local communities and ecosystems and 'buying all the politicians and the media along the route'.[28] The fact that the government has meanwhile put *Otkrytaia Rossiia* out of action would thus appear to some Irkutsk groups to be an instance of elite clan infighting. Yet it might be perceived by other supporters of anti-corruption measures as a strike against the beginnings of corporate social responsibility or against support for civil society from Russian sources. Others again might see it as a step towards containing major economic crime in Russia.

These few examples only illustrate how differing expectations and interpretations of effects across levels, across actor categories, and across local settings within Russia may simultaneously strengthen the power of the anti-corruption cause for some proponents and weaken it for others. Furthermore, the multiple interpretations of what 'anti-corruption in Russia' means to one or the other network participant again underline that sound conclusions must be grounded on insights into specific issues, actors, contexts, and issues.

Lessons beyond the Russian case

This chapter has shown that, in the case of Russia, anti-corruption proponents, while interacting through programmes and projects in a constellation that can be regarded as transnational advocacy network, are situated within their various specific contexts. Donors, recipients, and governments thus come together with their different historical backgrounds and situational strategies. Not only does this open crucial windows of opportunity, it may also increase tensions between the various network actors and heighten risks of dissonant interpretations of anti-corruption strategies or achievements. Two factors that have substantially spurred anti-corruption initiatives in Russia have eventually proven not necessarily supportive to civic anti-corruption action: foreign anti-corruption assistance provided to non-governmental groups and international indices measuring corruption in Russia.

To what extent the lessons gained from the Russian situation are exceptional or whether similar patterns can be seen in other less democratic contexts remains to be followed up by further research. This chapter has used the case of Russia as only one example to demonstrate that research on transnational anti-corruption networking, which is yet under-theorized, may benefit from a TAN perspective. Rather than assessing concrete successes and failures, the analysis of an anti-corruption TAN should aim at a better understanding of the interrelations between international, governmental, and non-governmental actors in this field. The most important lesson learned is that the TAN perspective should be more open to tracing processes within the network rather than searching for hypothesized successful outcomes. This is not to argue against the usefulness of analysing anti-corruption success stories in general. However, researchers should be warned against attaching a notion of finality to identified successes in fighting corruption which should instead be seen as no more than steps within an ongoing process.

Empirical evidence further shows that the dynamics unfolded by transnational anti-corruption advocacy differ from those contained in earlier global human rights or environmental movements. Much of this evidence challenges conventional assumptions in the TAN literature (which builds on these earlier movements): that there are clear and stable causal links between norm promoters and targeted states; that normative biases are attached to these actor categories; and, hence, that mutually recognized roles are being developed among those who share common concerns. While specific anti-corruption agreements are reached internationally, and anti-corruption institutions have been created at governmental level, it is interesting that hardly any specific anti-corruption civic organizations have emerged and become active, with the exception of the TI chapters that are spread globally. Anti-corruption is thus most often a side task, which civic organizations and individuals on the ground deal with in addition to their other commitments, duties, and concerns. This makes it even more urgent to open the 'NGO' box within conventional TAN concepts.

Finally, insights into the manifold implications of transnational anti-corruption advocacy for local civil society actors in Russia again highlights the importance of thinking across levels. TI is pursuing a global approach that has always encouraged the exchange of experiences between transition countries in Eastern Europe and Latin America and continues to do so. While such exchange is imperative, civic groups in many countries are dependant on the acquisition of funding through conventional assistance structures. As a result, local anti-corruption projects tend to be short-term ventures that are often conducted under time pressure and with predefined outcomes. Whether these circumstances would allow sufficient opportunity for exchange and reflection before transferring experiences seems questionable. Researchers at least should make use of their opportunity and aim to revisit processes in retrospect, in a comparative and reflective manner, and with due attention to longer-term developments as well as unexpected contextual side effects.

Notes

1 E.g. less efficient government due to reinforced pathologies of bureaucracy (Anechiarico and Jacobs 1996).
2 E.g. anti-corruption measures have often been used as instruments of selective repression and as an alternative to reform under conditions of non-democratic regimes (Huntington 1968: 66).
3 These arguments are supplemented by the literature on Western funding of Russian civil society initiatives in other sectors. Sundstrom (2006: xiv), for example, also refers to a growing 'democracy industry'.
4 It may seem more accurate to speak of *networks* (in plural), given the different actor constellations behind a range of strategies. But even where alliances are clustered, local groups are often linked to the same governmental and international actors. While an accurate tracing of changing links and cleavages is not the central concern here, the overall term (diffuse) *network* is maintained.
5 Fish refers to anecdotal accounts of an 'increasingly familiar story', including the works of Satter (2003), Volkov (2002), McCauley (2001), and Varese (2001).
6 Empirical findings of this study (2003–06) are based on the analysis of documents and campaign material, as well as extensive multi-sited field research, including participant observation at international and local events, informal conversations with relevant experts, and about 116 face-to-face interviews and background discussions with representatives of international anti-corruption and donor organizations based in Russia and abroad (Berlin, Brussels), and with representatives of local associations and individuals working on anti-corruption in three Russian cities (Moscow, St. Petersburg, Irkutsk).
7 Methodologically, Keck and Sikkink's (1998: 6) definition of campaigns as 'sets of strategically linked activities in which members of a diffuse principled network ... develop explicit, visible ties and mutually recognized roles in pursuit of a common goal (and generally against a common target)', contains an equally pre-deterministic set of assumptions regarding TAN performance.
8 The Bribe Payers Index, issued in 2002, assessed the probability that Russian businesses would pay or offer bribes in the country of the respondents as 3.2 (10 = zero propensity/0 = high propensity). In the CPI, Russia's score had worsened from 2.8 in 2004 to 2.4 in 2005 (cf. <http://www.transparency.org/policy_research/surveys_indices/cpi> accessed 23 October 2005). What was reported more

dramatically in the media was that Russia had fallen from 95 (out of 146 coun-tries) in 2004 to 128 (out of 156) in 2005, regardless of the limited explanatory power of that figure. While Russia's descent has been somewhat mitigated in the 2006 CPI (2.5, place 121/163), the 2005 shock effect has been effective.

9 Author's interview, Berlin, 2005.

10 This is not a critique of the existing methodological flaws as such – these have been discussed elsewhere (e.g. Abramo 2005; Galtung 2006); even most index authors have themselves posted their methodology notes online (on the CPI, see Lambsdorff 2005). More important here is the fact that, despite these discussions, the majority of international experts naturally refer to CPI evidence to prove Russia's corruption problem (see the many press reports; also author's interviews and conversations in Russia and elsewhere, 2003–06 – including those where no questions related to this or other international rankings had been asked).

11 TI itself emphasizes that the index is a snapshot rather than a measure of change over time because changing scores may result from varying data sources, ques-tions, or methodologies (Lambsdorff 2005). The significance of Russia's annual position is mitigated by such changes, including changing scores of other index countries and changing samples, so that Russia inevitably finds itself in a different index-neighbourhood from year to year.

12 The criticism that the CPI relies on perceptions of foreigners about a particular country has often been made by lower-ranking developing countries. In response, compliers of the CPI have paid more attention to including the views of experts on the ground 'in order to guarantee a global perspective that is not culturally biased' (Lambsdorff 2005). They underline that correlation of results from polling resident and non-resident experts confirms the robustness of CPI data. However, this hardly matters for the data quality in the Russian case: six of the surveys used in 2005 integrate 'experts in the country' (who might be foreigners), but these surveys are based on two different data sources only. For more details on metho-dological difficulties when assessing Russia's corruption situation using index data, see Schmidt (2005).

13 Indices with more specific measures of *anti-corruption efforts* exist, e.g. the World Bank's Governance Indicators (control of corruption, see <http://info.worldbank. org/governance/kkz2005/> accessed 23 October 2005) or Global Integrity's *Public Integrity Index* (institutions and practices that citizens can use to hold their gov-ernments accountable, see <http://www.globalintegrity.org/default.aspx?act = 13> accessed 23 October 2005). However, these are rarely referred to. For the purpose of assessing the anti-corruption mobilization potential, surveys that also take into account public opinion might be more helpful.

14 As an exception, European Bank for Reconstruction and Development (EBRD) strategies on Russia refer to the corruption issue in more detail and the underuse of Russian studies and expert opinions (e.g. EBRD 2002; 2004; Steves and Rousso 2004).

15 The Moscow non-governmental organization INDEM (Information Science for Democracy) has been devoted to projects on democratic governance since its foundation in 1990. More recently, it has become known as a professional think-tank in the corruption field. Yet its reputation is contested due to its critical position concerning the enormous corruption problems within the given political context and the composition of its team (including former Kremlin officials and a former assistant to president Yeltsin).

16 The indentification of a southern belt is a fallacy since the sampe used for the Russian regional index included more southern than north-western regions from the outset.

17 The 2006 G8 Summit in St. Petersburg triggered a joint international anti-corruption document (G8 Centre 2006) and, in conjunction with the summit, Russia ratified

the United Nations Convention Against Corruption (UNCAC) and the Council of Europe (CoE) Convention on corruption. Domestically, internal power struggles within elite circles have affected official anti-corruption rhetoric and actions, as illustrated by the recent restructuring of the Prosecutor General's office.

18 E.g. transcript of press conference at *Argumenty i Fakty* Press Centre (Johnson's Russia List 2005); author's participation in a presentation at the Levada-Center in Moscow, 2006.

19 Author's interviews, Moscow, 2003–04.

20 E.g. several interviewed groups in St. Petersburg listed TI among potential foreign donors for anti-corruption activities, obviously unaware that TI is not a grant-making organization.

21 E.g. the replacement of governors in St. Petersburg (city level, 2003) and Irkutsk (regional level, 2005) by Kremlin-backed candidates has entailed an increased presence of *siloviki* (chief officials from the security-intelligence services and power ministries). This has not only disturbed ties between regional political and business elites; local civic groups working against corruption have lost crucial personal contacts in administrative circles.

22 TI-Russia has remained in a better position to scrutinize established and largely accepted Western strategies, both within the TI network and vis-à-vis USAID, as TI-Russia has not yet been involved in the grant programmes of these partners (author's interviews with TI-Russia and TI, Moscow and Berlin, 2004–06).

23 In this case, mismatches between the anti-corruption programme proposed by USAID and local preferences have sparked intense debate among local activists. However, these discussions have rarely moved beyond the local level, often ending with the resigned acknowledgement that 'he who pays the piper calls the tune' (author's research on USAID-sponsored anti-corruption coalition in Irkutsk, 2005).

24 Also in Irkutsk, efforts to transfer anti-corruption experiences from other Russian regions (Tomsk, Samara) were perceived as an implantation of alien concepts that did not account for local corruption problems or interrelations between local elites and civic groups (author's research, Irkutsk 2005).

25 *Ochnaia stavka s Olegom Vakulovskim* (Conformation with Oleg Vakulovsky), since February 2006, see archive at <http://www.anticorr.ru/news/news134.html> accessed 22 November 2006.

26 A detailed discussion on *blat* (networks of favour) in post-Soviet Russia can be found in Ledeneva (1998).

27 The Beslan tragedy has been linked to the problem of corruption (bribery) by TI-Russia and the TI secretariat in Berlin, as well as by President Putin after it became known that the terrorists were able to launch this assault on civilians by paying their way through several security checks with only small bribes. TI-Russia and TI believed that this finally changed the indifferent attitudes of many people in Russia towards corruption (author's interviews with TI, 2004). The Beslan hostage tragedy that ended with a firefight between Russian security forces and Chechen hostage-takers left over 325 people dead, almost half of them children (see, e.g. Human Rights Watch 2004).

28 Author's interview with environmental and anti-corruption activist, Irkutsk, 2005.

10 How do international organizations scrutinize transforming states?

The case of Transparency International and the Baltic states

Matilda Dahl

At the international level there is no single regulator. Even so, states continue to follow rules made up by various 'others'; (Meyer 1996). These are often different types of international organizations. One might even claim that states are following scripts (Jacobsson 2005). Models and ideas from outside are seldom diffused as they are. Instead, they are reinterpreted into the local context through a process of translation (Latour 1986; Czarniawska 1996). If the rules are translated, rather than merely diffused, the translation process itself is open to influence by the receiver and other parties. The process of translation itself can also be transformed by the regulator, and by the object of scrutiny. Hence the scrutiny of the adaptation process of the Central and Eastern Europe (CEE) states affects how they transform (translate) the models from outside – for instance, what models they choose to follow and which issues are prioritized.

In a given scenario, we tend to act in a manner that is suitable and proper for that situation; in other words, according to the rules of appropriateness (March and Olsen 1989). What is conceived as appropriate is, in turn, institutionalized; that is, determined by norms that we take in from our environment. Some organizations take this further by playing an active role in shaping the norms according to which it is appropriate to behave. There seem to be organizations that are more knowledgeable than others, and whose expert advice or standards others are willing to follow (Tamm-Hallström 2004; Brunsson and Jacobsson 2000). By living up to rules set by reputable organizations, states allow themselves to be evaluated by these organizations. By doing so, they open themselves up to influence from external actors or so-called 'others'. In other words, the scrutiny of 'others' may also influence the way in which states transform.

States adapt to ideas from their environment through different mechanisms. One of these mechanisms is described as making the transformation visible, by auditing how states transform (Jacobsson and Sahlin-Andersson 2002). Making actions visible implies a possibility of holding actors accountable, which is one of the core concepts of modern democracy.[1] Yet, in the case of the transformation of CEE, the issues that have been put under scrutiny are more complex to measure than the accounts of a business enterprise.

During the process of consolidating democracies and transitioning to market economies, the lack of public transparency and the existence of corruption have been great concerns in the countries of CEE. Corruption, in particular, has been viewed as a major obstacle to democratic transition, market economy, and overall development (Brademas and Heimann 1998). As said by the former Estonian Prime Minister Mart Laar: 'you cannot make transition if you have corruption' (Hiatt 1999). Combating corruption has been important for these states to become accepted as 'modern', not least in terms of their desire to become members of the European Union (EU).

Indeed, the EU candidates were bound to take 'measures against corruption' in order to live up to the political criteria of EU membership.[2] Corruption was continuously brought up in the Regular Reports of the European Commission. Framed under 'democracy and rule of law', a standard headline included every year was 'anti-corruption measures'. Although the European Commission noted that the CEE countries made great progress on the matter since they applied to the EU in early 2000, corruption, particularly in Latvia and Lithuania, was still seen as a central problem and potential hindrance to EU membership (Regular Reports 2001 and 2002).

In comparison to the administrative criteria, which relied on the reports from national civil servants to the European Commission, the evaluation of progress within the political criteria relied to a larger extent upon information provided by non-governmental organizations (NGOs).[3] One such NGO was Transparency International (TI). During the years of adaptation to the EU, and the intense pre-accession process these states were included in a so-called 'international anti-corruption regime'. Evidence of this has been the local presence of the international NGO Transparency International in Estonia, Latvia, and Lithuania since early 2000. Within the theoretical framework set out above, TI can be viewed as a kind of 'other' that scrutinizes and produces accounts from states.

This chapter analyses the work of TI in order to characterize this kind of scrutiny of states. The history and character of TI are described in other chapters of this book. Here I will focus on its connections with other international organizations, and its activities at the local level in the Baltic states. The following section describes the different kinds of accounts and measurements produced by TI. The last part analyses the characteristics of the process of scrutiny.

TI's connections with other organizations

Reflecting on the state of democracy in the last century, Ann Florini concludes that unless 'global integration comes to a screeching halt ... transnational civil society is in no danger of running out of targets' (Florini 2005:136). The meetings and activities of governments, intergovernmental organizations, and corporations outline goals and principles towards which NGOs like TI can aim their activities. Referring to the work of international governmental organizations (IGOs), such as the EU and the Organisation for Economic Co-operation and Development (OECD), seems to be a way in which TI frames and promotes its own scrutinizing activities.

Transparency International marshalled support for the OECD anti-corruption convention at an early stage (Brademas and Heimann 1998). TI has also been closely connected to international financial institutions, in particular the World Bank. At the 1996 annual World Bank meeting, the president James Wolfensohn made combating bribery a top priority. TI contributed to the World Bank's anti-corruption strategy. Today, TI stresses their connection to other organizations, as expressed to me by a project manager:

> There are a lot of organizations supporting TI. There is the EU, the Phare projects, there is an Open Society Fund and to a certain extent the Open Society Institute. And then a lot of other foreign institutions, the World Bank, the EBRD [European Bank for Reconstruction and Development] etc.

'Supporting' should here be understood in a broad sense, not only in financial terms, but also in terms of networks.[4] Referring to IGOs is a way to stress that TI is successful and accepted by the international community. In a sense, TI borrows legitimacy from other organizations, by identifying its own activities as in 'line with' or 'supported by' highly legitimate organizations such as the OECD or the World Bank (and vice versa). To monitor rules issued by intergovernmental conventions is thus a way to create legitimacy for oneself.

TI in the Baltic states

The Baltic states provide another case of how TI connects itself to governmental organizations, in particularly the EU. The EU regards addressing corruption as vital to developing the capacity necessary for membership, and consequently there is a demand for anti-corruption activities. The Commission cannot accomplish this task on its own. For example, TI's regional report about the CEE and the Baltic states (Transparency International 2003d: 177–79) mentions that: 'while the EU has enormous political and economic power in the region, it has not formulated a comprehensive anti-corruption policy.' Identifying a gap in the knowledge of the European Commission, TI frames its own work as a way to fill that gap. The view that TI is needed and has a role to play is reflected in comments by TI national chapter (NC) project managers; for example:

> They [the European Commission] are always asking about our opinion. The people the most of them are reading our reports, if they need some advice or something they just pick up the phone or write us an e-mail and we are writing back but it's not that formal.

The quote above reflects the eagerness of TI to be perceived by the EU as an important actor. TI national chapters' websites show themselves as leaning on support from organizations. For instance, the Latvian NC links to the web pages of the United Nations Development Programme (UNDP), the Council of Europe, the World Bank, and to the Open Society Institute under the headline 'International organizations' on their home page. Placing itself in the middle of a network of highly legitimate organizations, the organization creates an identity through asserting sameness with others (Czarniawska 2002).

Spreading the message

The media play an important role. If 'everybody' is talking about corruption, more people will listen to what TI has to say. At the same time, there is a need to reveal corruption since corruption is so hard to detect: there is a need for enhanced transparency! The discourse of the interviewees often refers to the *raison d'être* of the organization, and how and why TI has an important role to play.

A large part of the work of TI's International Secretariat is devoted to external relations. A crucial issue for the organization seems to be managing the media and agreeing upon statements concerning the position of TI on various policy issues that have a 'transparency' or 'corruption dimension'. If there is a corruption scandal somewhere in the world, TI is often asked by journalists and the media to make a statement – they are given a preferential right of interpretation. As an example, the public relations department was developing TI's position with regard to the issue of foreign aid and debt release (my observation at the time of the Global Aid Gala on 3 July 2005). The question was formulated by the public relations department as how to make a statement 'in order for us to be allied with the right organizations'. The international work of TI thus has much to do with the positioning of the organization. It is often crucial to be influential without being hijacked by bigger actors in the field, especially if the issue is controversial. This means that others might use the opinion or statement of TI for other purposes, thereby 'hijacking' it.

Another aspect of the Secretariat's work is to facilitate the transmission of knowledge gained from local experiences from one country to another. At several times during a personnel meeting I witnessed, the importance of learning from others was stressed. This might be seen as another way to connect the international body with its NCs.

We are networking with other chapters and other institutions and maybe just let them comment upon our ideas, if they think that our ideas are fruitful are they for something, or are they useless … this is also a sort of learning from each other.

(interviewee, Latvian NC)

The national chapters in the Baltic states

The name national chapters (NCs) could suggest that these local branches are closely connected, building upon each other, constituting a sort of 'World Book'. This is not at all the case, however. Rather, they are independent national NGOs and are presented as being loosely coupled to each other and the head office in Berlin. Officers at the International Secretariat explain that the whole idea is for chapters not to be seen as 'extended arms' of TI. As explained by one of the senior officials at the secretariat:

> It is a philosophical issue. Many of the TI founders came from the development industry and they were all too familiar with what you call 'dependency'. If you open up a local branch, then you start funding them. They will sort of depend on you, the funding source. And ... that will become a problem over time.

The relationship between Berlin and the national chapters is discussed in more detail in Luís de Sousa's chapter in this book. Here I focus on the Chapters in the Baltic states.

The Estonian NC

The head of the TI chapter in Estonia explained that the Estonian chapter is not an NGO 'on its own' explains the head of chapter. It is a society that is a part of a well-established national institute (the Jan Tönisson Institute). The Jan Tönisson Institute was created in 1991 and became affiliated with TI in 2000. The creation of the Estonian chapter is described as a 'special' organizational solution. With the help of the TI secretariat, the Jan Tönisson Institute (JT Institute) created a society called Corruption-free Estonia. As described on its website, the society is an 'anti-corruption coalition under the slogan of the Estonian National Chapter of the Transparency International'. The use of the term 'slogan' is telling and recalls the reputation value of the TI brand.

The reason that was given for this particular organizational construct was that there was not room for another organization in the Estonian anti-corruption field since the JT Institute already had corruption on its agenda. Being part of an international network has meant increased opportunities for the Estonian chapter to attract media attention, as described by the head of the Estonian NC:

> After joining TI we have got some more opportunities to go to mass media in Estonia. They are like our 'foreign advisor' ... A couple of times top-level people from Berlin visited us. When they were here they got attention through mass media, which means that we got a little more attention as well.

The administration of the chapter is relatively small. Only one full-time employee is working with TI questions. The main activities consist of organizing discussion groups and seminars. People from other NGOs, the local government, other official state institutions, the private sector, universities, and media were invited to join the society. Since there is only one full-time employee at the centre working with TI, there are not enough resources to do any independent monitoring; instead 'information is used from the network persons', as explained by the young and enthusiastic Director, Triin Reinsalu. The society is her main network to which she turns when she needs advice or a recommendation of an expert to write a report, for instance. She also has some contacts in the local government 'with whom I can discuss any problem or any question I need'.

In the Estonian NC, as in the other NCs, they are not using the Corruption Perceptions Index (CPI) to any great extent. Estonia has had the same index (5.6–5.7) for quite some time, but its place in the ranking might change. The employee of the Estonian NC sees the CPI as one opinion among others, not the only one and not necessarily the most correct one. It might even be a problem for the Estonian NC that they have such as a relatively good CPI rating, especially in relation to contacts with international organizations from which they are seeking support. The high rating is actually used as an explanation why relatively few international organizations are interested in supporting TI Estonia:

> For us the main problem is to explain why we have such a good rating in the CPI, why it is so good here in Estonia compared to other accession countries, that is all. And no one has had any interest to do anything here.
> (Head of Jan Tönisson Institute)

> There are not many organizations which would grant us as an Estonian NGO [dealing with corruption]. Because the problem of corruption is not so important in Estonia as in let's say Latvia according to CPI. So it's harder for us to get grants.
> (Head of TI Estonia)

The relatively low corruption perception for Estonia is thus brought forward as part of the reason the NC has difficulty in attracting funding. But the relatively high ranking does not mean that there are no problems with corruption. The main challenge is rather to bring attention to those problems, which would theoretically encourage more funding for TI. More media attention is seen as one way to attract funds and raise public awareness. The employee of the small office regrets that they do not have the capacity 'to do any monitoring', and also explains that they would like to be able to hire external experts. If corruption is perceived as a relatively small problem (compared to other countries), then fewer people will demand the 'solution' that TI has to offer.

The Latvian NC

In Latvia, in contrast to Estonia, the TI National Chapter is a relatively well-established NGO. It is commonly referred to by its local name, *Delna*, which means 'an open palm of a hand'. It was founded in 1998 by a journalist and at that time it was the pioneering NGO in the field of anti-corruption in Latvia. In 2004, *Delna* employed four full-time paid staff, and six part-time, and had 50 members. The Board consists of five people. A particularity of the Latvian NC in 2004 was the organization of the leadership: the same person was both the chairperson of the Board and the executive director of the chapter, a solution that was somewhat unusual (and as of 2008 has been changed).

The Latvian chapter is seen by the International Secretariat as relatively successful. Advocacy and lobbying constitute a major part of the activities in this chapter. This relatively high profile is reflected by repeated attention in the local media. *Delna* has monitored the privatization of former state-owned firms and has advocated for a change of laws. The ambitions appear to be far-reaching. According to the head of the Latvian office:

> We are trying here to answer *the* questions, *the* needs for society, this is why we are so influential and respected today. We have played the politics.[5]

The NC had a 'fortunate start' according to the head of the Latvian office since the initiators were committed to it from the very beginning, according to the highly engaged chairman. She was eager to point out that the success was not dependent on the funds available. It was rather based on people, who were committed to do something about corruption in Latvia. 'embracing the idea' wholeheartedly from the very beginning. Accordingly, the creation of *Delna* was not dependent on a 'push' from Berlin. As the head of the Latvian NC said during our talk:

> I was very clear about the issue that we are here because we think corruption is a problem, and we believe that civil society can do something about it. We do it regardless of what Berlin would say. If they do not like us, fine.

There thus seems to be a need to show that the local NGO stands on its own feet. At the same time, the interviewee expressed respect and admiration for the TI movement. To highlight independence seems to be part of the Estonian National Chapter's organizational identity. Comparison to its neighbouring NCs was brought up in relation to different topics during the discussion. According to its chairman, the Latvian NC has managed to establish a platform from where other NGOs can act:

> We have fought for the platform so now I think that any NGO could take it and fight for their interest in society.

The confidence expressed by the Latvian NC seems to be based on experiences in the recent past where TI has been invited to participate in the supervision of privatization processes, for instance that of a Latvian shipping company which ended up in a corruption scandal, and which in turn put TI 'on the front page news' for quite some time. The high profile of the Latvian NC seems well in line with the high perception of corruption in Latvia (and low ranking on the CPI). According to a survey done by TI Latvia, however, a considerable amount of what is perceived as corruption by the public in Latvia is not corruption according to the TI definition. As explained by the head of the NC, when comparing Estonian and Latvian attitudes towards corruption:

> Latvians are very politicized and for us it was very easy to start to work because people all thought corruption was a problem ... Last year they had a survey; 80% of Estonians could not even mention one corruption scandal. And it doesn't mean that it hasn't happened. Experts in Estonia can tell you about it. In Latvia they could mention five out of which three are not corruption but they would say they were.

This kind of argument pinpoints the fact that perceptions matter and have consequences. If corruption is perceived as a problem, then anti-corruption activities are perceived as more legitimate and useful than if there is no such perception. This seems to be illustrated when comparing the Latvian NC (where perceptions of corruption were high) with the Estonian (where they were low).[6]

The Lithuanian NC

TI Lithuania does not seem to be as forceful or as much of an advocate as the Latvian NC, but it does not lack resources to the same extent as the Estonian NC. It has, instead, a history of closer cooperation with state institutions. In 2000, when it was launched, the Lithuanian NC was closely connected to academic circles.

It was founded by a professor in sociology and was run by two sociologists. But since 2003, when the majority of my field studies were done, the leadership has changed. It is quite uncommon for a TI chapter to receive funds from government agencies. The Lithuanian case is an exception. The TI chapter has been cooperating with the national anti-corruption bureau, called the Special Investigation Service (SIS), and has even been financed through their projects. This might be seen as an illustration of the differences amongst the chapters and even the national contexts.

One example of a project financed through the anti-corruption bureau, is the Corruption Map. It is an in-depth study of corruption in Lithuania, and relies upon sociological methodology. The map was created in cooperation with Vilnius University Institute for Social Research, and in 2003 it consituted a third of the activities of TI Lithuania. Initially, the Corruption Map was a project financed by the American and the Finnish embassies in Lithuania. This first map was, according to a project leader at the Lithuania NC, 'presented to the government and the parliament members, to the president palace, to all main institutions'. The Corruption Map is referred to as the turning point in the history of TI Lithuania, and was described as the 'face of the organization' by the same person. Since it is relatively unusual for a TI chapter to receive such a large amount of financial support from the government, the funding or the Corruption Map was considered to be an achievement.

> This project was very successful. Because there was a big reaction from state organizations, public officials, government, parliament upon this project.
>
> (Project manager, TI Lithuania)

Recognition by state organizations thus seems to play a role in the Lithuanian NC context.

The methodology of the Corruption Map consists of two surveys measuring both the perception and the experience of corruption. The first survey is directed towards the general public and the second towards business people. One of the main results is that there is a difference between perception and the actual experience. In general, respondents have a higher perception of corruption than actual experience of it. And as put by the project manager at TI Lithuania, it therefore becomes important to investigate from where the public get this perception.

Accounts and procedures

As we have seen, the problems and achievements of a NC are partly perceived as reflecting the situation in its particular country. But there are some common features and principles according to which the scrutiny of states takes shape, independently of any particular country.

As examples of accounts produced by TI, I have chosen the *Global Corruption Report* the *Corruption Perception Index* and the *Source Book*. These accounts are issued on a regular basis and are relatively well-known in the field of anti-corruption.

The Global Corruption Report

The *Global Corruption Report* (GCR) is a well-known report issued regularly by TI. It assesses the state of corruption worldwide, drawing upon experiences of national chapters. It has been issued since 2001 on almost a yearly basis (every year except for 2002). The GCR can be downloaded at no cost from the TI website and is distributed quite generously by TI at conferences and workshops. Each report has a 'special focus', which is a thematic topic.[7] The themes can be seen as a way to link corruption to other issues facing society. In this way, the damage caused by corruption is illustrated by concrete examples and by looking at a sector that is familiar and accessible to the public. The health and construction sectors are such examples. The GCR thus translates an abstract concept – 'the corruption problem' – into something more down to earth by using practical examples. The organization of the GCR has changed somewhat over time. As one of the editors explained, they have been through trial and error from year to year.

The second part is devoted to Country Reports. For example, the 2005 GCR covers 40 countries. In the first reports, these were called 'region reports', but the region was represented by one or two countries. This was considered to give a sometimes unfair representation of the various regions. A reason to have country rather than regional reports was, according to the editors, for the chapters to 'feel ownership' of the GCR.

The reports are written in a similar format; each country report begins with the its CPI ranking, followed by a list of signed or ratified conventions,[8] and a short paragraph on 'legal and institutional changes' which is a critical review of recent anti-corruption legislation implementation. Then follows an account of specific topics, often recent corruption-related events in the country and a description of what occurred in the aftermath of those events.

The last part of the GCR is devoted to Research on Corruption. The articles result from a general call for papers and from more personal contacts, so the majority of the contributions come from people who have previously worked with TI. Finding the right authors is a constant challenge for the editors. On the one hand, TI wants to commission texts about a certain topic; on the other hand, the person who writes the article needs to be considered an expert on that topic. This tension is expressed in the following quote:

> It was difficult to identify experts, it was difficult to deal with them once we identified them because we were making them write what we wanted from them rather than what they knew.
>
> (Project leader, GCR)

The last section of the GCR also includes the Corruption Perceptions Index, for which TI is well known.

The Corruption Perceptions Index

TI scrutiny makes the state's development visible through the Corruption Perception Index (CPI). The CPI ranks states according to how corrupt they are perceived to be by business people and country analysts (Lambsdorff 2003). The CPI is based on different comparative surveys. The score ranges between 0 (highly corrupt) and 10 (highly clean). All states are ranked accordingly. High scores (i.e. 'cleaner' countries) get a low rank. The least corrupt state is ranked as number one, the second least corrupt as number two, etc. Ranking is a particular form of comparison. Its foremost function is to convey information on the number of 'better' countries than the country in question. Ranking represents exclusive comparison: if one country receives a higher rank it means that another receives a lower rank even if it has the same score.

The CPI is a so-called composite index, where each score is based on at least three independent survey sources. For the 2004 CPI, 18 data sources from 12 institutions were used.[9] The methodology was developed by an economist at the University of Passau, Germany, Professor Lambsdorff. He is also the director of statistical work on the CPI.

All TI representatives I have talked to reflect critically on the CPI. It is described as 'one perception out of many'. In this way they show that they do not take the CPI at face value – quite the contrary. Many seem to view it primarily as a good way to garner media attention. The CPI is also one of the most well-known TI ideas. Many interviewees refer to the CPI when explaining the success of TI as an NGO. The reason the CPI became such a widely accepted measure, according to TI representatives, is its ability to translate a complex problem into something easily understood and 'media-friendly'. This ranking is often presented in major newspapers, especially on the day when it is published worldwide. The CPI's main contribution is often described as giving the best available overall picture of corruption.

The TI Source Book: Almost like a bible?

My third example of an account is the *National Integrity Source Book*, commonly referred to as the *Source Book*. It was issued in 1999. The national chapters translated versions in their respective countries. The *Source Book* describes and proposes practical reforms that can be applied to each sector of society in order to fight corruption. It reviews various lessons learned so far in the global fight against corruption, and provides a compilation of emerging best practice. The *Source Book* might be seen as a set of standards to which NCs can refer in their work.

The *Source Book* therefore appears to serve a double purpose. On the one hand, it provides ideas on what sort of activities a national chapter might engage in. It can thus be used as a support in the daily work at the national chapters: project leaders can find theoretical grounding for their projects by reading the *Source Book*. This seems to be in line with employees' own views; an employee explained that people working for TI tend to share the basic principles spelled out in the *Source Book*, 'in our head, in our blood'. Another spoke about it as a 'bible' that one has to know by heart.

> Everything [in the *Source Book*] is about not to cheat, not to betray, to be as good as possible, don't take money which doesn't belong to you ... actually it's like a bible.

Yet another of the interviewees described the *Source Book* as an inspiration for new projects and for activities that could be undertaken by the national chapters:

> We use it as an inspiration of what can be done. Of what institutions can be changed … Of course some countries need special solutions, but it gives you a very strong idea how that should be dealt with.

Characterizing scrutiny

By quantifying performances one can create a sense of objectivity. The numbers quantifying the developments in CEE states might play a constructive role in the sense that they influence how states and states developments are perceived in relation to each other and over time. As in other spheres of human activity, the reports on the 'reality out there' (in this case, the transformation of the CEE states) can be seen as constructing the reality it depicts. The transformation itself is entangled with the accounts of transformation. Some comparisons, but not all, imply a translation into numbers. For instance, TI's CPI is both a cross-country comparison and a translation of a complex problem (corruption) into a numeric index. (The TI Global Corruption Barometer – not discussed above – compares countries but does not quantify their performances.)

Audit processes transform performances into numbers. This act of quantification has a constructing role; audits construct certain realities. Making things quantifiable can be seen as constructing them anew: 'with numbers one can often make new things, or at least transform old ones' (Porter 1996: 46). This case study exemplifies a quantification of the performance of states in the field of anti-corruption. The CPI ranking is the result of a weighting of several opinion polls into a score. The score is then directly transformed into a rating. By becoming comparable to each other, states can be constructed as more or less similar to each other. The *Source Book* sketches out how to reach a much-desired situation which perhaps might be seen as an ideal: a society free from corruption. However, states are also constructed as moving towards other ideals. The transformation process in the CEE states is seen as a move towards a Western liberal democratic ideal society. This can be seen as a rationalization process.

The scrutiny of TI can be characterized through three processes: mediatization, marketization, and glorification. In the following sections, I will explain these three concepts and describe how they can be used to characterize the scrutiny of states in the organizational context of Transparency International.

Mediatization

Mediatization refers to the phenomenon whereby organizations follow a 'media logic'. Hence, they are consciously formulating messages that appeal to the media (Altheide and Snow 1979). The media often rewards simplicity and 'catchiness'. Mediatization supposedly leads to a simplification of the form that the messages take on. How an organization presents itself will affect its self-image, which in turn influences what it is expected to do according to the logic of appropriateness which we discussed above (March and Olsen 1989). Consequently, the media logic should not be seen as an incidental feature of the organizations work, but will rather be an influence on how the organization constructs itself and its activities. This process appears clearly in the TI case.

Media attention is a central feature of the context in which scrutiny by TI takes place. The activities of the national chapters and of the Secretariat are made visible through TI reports and its website, and are also reported on by the international media. People working for TI often refer to the media when they describe the organization and what they do. To spread messages via media is important and seems to guide the way messages are formulated. As a programme coordinator in the Secretariat said: 'we need to keep on saying interesting things so that people listen to us.' In order to be able to act, TI needs others to listen to what it has to say. Because the attention span of the media is short, media friendly 'products' or translations into numbers (such as the CPI ranking of states) are seen as central to gaining attention. As said by an employee in the Lithuanian chapter:

> We want to measure perception and experience and we see a big differ-
> ence. We also want to measure different sources of information, from
> which source do people get information about corruption, and of course
> the main source is mass media.

Measuring perceptions of corruption has an endogenous effect: if people read in the newspaper that Lithuania is perceived as a highly corrupt country, this will influence their own perception of corruption in Lithuania, which then is measured in another type of, or later, survey. The results of such measurements are thus being reproduced and reinforced. Indeed, media and public agendas are often highly correlated, with the former tending to shape the latter (McComb and Shaw 1972).

Further, a competition for attention seems to be a central concept used by several of the national chapters to describe themselves. The success of a chapter is seen as dependent upon whether or not there are other local organizations in the anti-corruption field. This view of competition seems to be in accordance with a market logic. Thus, the scrutiny of TI will be additionally characterized with the help of the concept of marketization.

Marketization

When describing how TI has developed over time, people working for TI often refer to anti-corruption as a kind of market. First, the history of TI is described as the creation of a new market for anti-corruption, where TI had a product to supply. Before corruption was perceived as a problem for economic development, there was no 'demand' for it to be solved. So the founders of TI participated in creating this market by defining corruption as an impediment for progress and by organizing an anti-corruption movement in response.

Anti-corruption is also described as an expanding market, where demand has increased to such extent that TI cannot fulfil it anymore. Hence, we see the entrance of various consultants. At the local level, the picture is somewhat different, but the local chapters still seem to view themselves as acting in competition. The relatively successful start of the Latvian chapter is partly explained by the fact that at the outset there was no other anti-corruption NGO in Latvia. The TI chapter therefore had a privileged position from the beginning. In Estonia, corruption is not perceived as a significant problem, especially in comparison to other countries. Hence, there is less demand and fewer opportunities for the TI chapter to attract resources and attention.

The above examples are to be seen as an illustration of the marketization of the field in which TI acts. This perception of the organization as being surrounded by an environment that is characterized by competition is in line with the view of the market logic. The third aspect of the scrutiny of states in context of Transparency International could be characterized by the concept of 'glorification', which will be developed in the next section.

Glorification

TI monitors corruption, but also establishes how a country should be organized in order to minimize corruption. This ideal is described in various accounts produced by Transparency, for instance the *Source Book* and the *Corruption Fighters' toolkit*. As it may seem, these accounts have a strong positive meaning within the organization. The employees should have the ideas (or ideals) 'in their blood'. The ideas are described in somewhat religious terms. They are about how to behave in order to be a 'good person' (or organization or state). The anti-corruption solutions and their propagators seem to be glorified through the scrutiny that TI directs towards states. Another sign of this mechanism is the glorification of the employees' efforts, through stressing the value of each individual's contribution.

We can thus observe a glorification both in terms of the aim (a 'clean' state), the means (the so-called 'tools'), and the organization as a whole (the doctor that 'cures' society). On the one hand, these values have an impact upon actual practice. On the other, they are constructed by the people working within the movement. It is the second aspect that has been discussed in this paper. The glorification of anti-corruption and the consensus created around its practice – represented through artefacts such as rankings, reports, and tools – are central features of the scrutiny provided by TI. But how will this scrutiny take shape in the future. And does more anti-corruption mean less corruption?

The end of scrutiny?

To conclude this chapter, I will say a few words about how the final stage – during which no more scrutiny would theoretically be needed – can be characterized for TI. The goal, or the standard of scrutinizing activities, concerns higher values. However, the ideal of completely eliminating all kinds of corruption is not only difficult to achieve, it is also difficult to measure. So there is no clear picture of an end stage and, accordingly, even less of a defined time in which things ought to change and pace by which they should change. In the absence of a clear goal or an end stage, the time frame is less pronounced as well. The two might be seen as being connected. The goal towards which TI strives can be formulated more as a vision, expressed, for instance, in the *Source Book*. The measurements made by TI emphasize the relative achievements of states compared to those of other states. The ranking highlights differences between countries, not between different points in time, or different points on an independent scale. A country might thus receive a higher score, but nevertheless might receive a lower ranking than before, if other countries have received higher scores than before. The ranking therefore expresses that a country only ever does better than others, rather than bettering itself in an absolute way.

Transparency International has an institutional incentive to keep demand for anti-corruption measures high. An end stage of the need for scrutiny – and hence of TI activity – is not discussed. It often seems that the number of places where corruption is perceived as a problem is increasing, not decreasing. When this study began in 2002, a TI office opened in Norway, and since then a Swedish NC has been started. Apparently, we will have to wait for the day when increasing anti-corruption measures will be reflected by less recorded corruption. Both seem to be on the rise.

Notes

1 The link is closely connected to the rule of law principles of modern democracies. Indeed, accountability and transparency are defined by the OECD as key components of governance in democratic countries and constituting an important part of the 'European principles for public administration' that were described in the guidelines of how candidate countries ought to effectively implement the *acquis communautaire* (Sigma paper No 7).
2 'EU candidates' refers to the ten countries that applied for membership of the EU in the middle of the 1990s and became full members in May 2004.
3 Especially compared to the monitoring of the other two sets of EU membership criteria (economic and administrative), according to an interview with an official at the Commission (Enlargement Directorate).
4 In her dissertation on the authority-building of standard-setting organizations such as the International Standard Organization (ISO), Kristina Tamm Hallström concludes that it is through networks with other organizations that the standard-setters gain their authority.
5 Half a year after this interview was conducted, this 'play' was boosted in the form of a major political debate and questioning of the role of NGOs in general and of

Transparency International in particular by the Latvian president in the context of the nomination of the Latvian commissioner, Ingrida Undre.

6 This relationship might also work the other way around as is shown in the chapter by Andersson and Heywood.

7 In 2001 there was no special focus; in *GCR* 2003 the special focus was 'access to information'; in 2004 it was 'political corruption'; in 2005 the topic was 'corruption in construction'; and in 2006 it was 'corruption and health'.

8 Examples of conventions frequently figuring in such lists are: the Council of Europe Civil Law Convention on Corruption, the OECD Anti-Bribery Convention, and the UN Convention against Corruption.

9 (1) the World Economic Forum; (2) the Institute of Management Development; (3) the Economist Intelligence Unit; (4) Information International from Beirut; (5) the World Market Research Centre; (6) Gallup International on behalf of Transparency International; (7) Freedom House's Nations in Transit; (8) the Merchant International Group Limited (London); (9) the Political and Economic Risk Consultancy (in Hong Kong); (10) Columbia University; (11) a multi-lateral development bank; and (12) the Business Environment and Enterprise Performance Survey of the EBRD and the World Bank.

11 Corruption and anti-corruption in Southeast Europe

Landscapes and sites

Steven Sampson[1]

Introduction: Everyday corruption

In a paper on anti-corruption in Southeast Europe, it is appropriate to set the stage with a recent report from Romania:

> Romanian public TV station TVR broadcast ... a video recording which shows Agriculture minister Decebal Traian Remes receiving an envelope from the former Agriculture minister, Ioan Avram Muresan. Prosecutors claim that the envelope contained a 15,000 euros bribe, paid by businessman Gheorghe Ciorba. TVR [Television Romania] also broadcast two audio recordings of tapped phone conversations that Muresan had with Ciorba and Remes.[2]

The video and the recordings were part of an investigation of high-level corruption conducted by the Romanian anti-corruption agency, the National Anti-corruption Department (DNA), with the collaboration of Mr Ciorba. The video of a minister receiving an envelope full of cash from an intermediary – himself a former minister – set off shock waves in Romanian political life. The implicated minister, Mr Remes, was forced to resign. The former agricultural minister and erstwhile intermediary, Mr Muresan, was detained by the police. The EU threatened to withhold 110 million euros in agricultural subsidies. A chorus of politicians, pundits, and civil society activists are calling for a concerted anti-corruption effort to cleanse the government of corrupt politicians. Muresan has responded, calling this a smear campaign reminiscent of the 1950s. Foreign diplomats and the EU are now scrutinizing Romania's commitment to wipe out corruption, which was a key requirement for Romania's accession to the EU in January 2007. The Romanian government, envisioning further embarrassing inquiries, is now considering merging the DNA with another Romanian agency. To complete this story, there are reports that a private viewing of the incriminating video was held for selected journalists at the offices of the Romanian affiliate of the American NGO Freedom House. Freedom House-Romania had already come into the public eye some weeks earlier when it was accused of suspiciously obtaining a 2005 contract to assess Romania's anti-corruption strategy.

We have here a typical corruption scandal. The cast of characters in this drama is familiar: the arrogant minister, the unscrupulous businessman, the crafty middleman, the gloating media, the angry commentators, the watchful foreign donors, and, of course, the disillusioned public. This ongoing drama is unfolding not in some Third World backwater or 'failed state', but in an EU Member State, albeit the most corrupt among the current EU members.

How are we to understand corruption and anti-corruption in a place like Romania? In what way is this a local story, and in what way is it the result of international pressure to compel Romania to conform to 'global standards'. What conceptual frameworks can help capture both the dynamics of corrupt behaviour and the drama of public exasperation in a country where anti-corruption campaigns are a policy priority, but where one scandal replaces another in endless succession? The purpose of this chapter is to place the relationship between corruption and anti-corruption into the same analytical framework. I propose to do this by viewing this relationship in terms of two topographic metaphors: that of 'landscape' and that of 'site'. The anti-corruption 'landscape' denotes the transnational flow of resources, people, and ideas – an uneven flow to be sure – which make up the global anti-corruption project. The metaphor of a 'site' helps us understand how these forces play out in a specific local setting, as in the Romanian case. Using the metaphors of 'landscape' and 'site', we can better understand the interaction of local corruption, local anti-corruption fighting, and global anti-corruptionism. This global–local nexus is particularly important for understanding anti-corruption in transition countries, where local political forces are subject to external donor pressures. Using 'landscape' and 'site', we can achieve a better understanding of how corruption occurs in a world full of anti-corruption talk and anti-corruption measures.

Researching anti-corruption

An anti-corruption site is a bounded setting where interests are articulated, resources exchanged, power exerted, and alliances formed. The site has its players, their goals (what is at stake), resources, strategies, and tactics. In examining the summit of the anti-corruption landscape, we can identify how policies are formed. In the valleys and enclaves of this landscape, however, we can observe how these same policies are implemented, distorted, or subverted by local actors.

Focus on specific sites, however, prevents us from observing the extensive similarities between them. Certain strategies and resources (and of course, discourses) seem to circulate beyond the control of local-level actors. Some other analytical framework is needed. I call this framework a 'global anti-corruption landscape'. I have investigated this landscape by carrying out brief periods of fieldwork in several countries of Southeast Europe

(Romania, Bosnia, Kosovo, and Albania), mostly between 2003 and 2006. In order to obtain a better picture of the global anti-corruption landscape, I have also carried out documentary research, interviews, and participant observation with global actors such as the anti-corruption non-governmental organization Transparency International (TI), interviews with anti-corruption consultants and aid officials, and I have attended various international anti-corruption events.[3] In this sense, I have acquired some knowledge of how Southeastern Europe became part of the anti-corruption industry.

The anti-corruption industry

The global anti-corruption industry now channels hundreds of millions of dollars in anti-corruption assistance projects to over 100 countries.[4] Using various corruption indices and governance statistics, we can track the dynamics of corruption in most countries of the world. Western donors and NGOs can now invoke the UN Convention against Corruption to pressure certain countries to sign or ratify the Convention, and then monitor them for their compliance using various 'good governance' indices. The anti-corruption industry intersects with movements for global ethics, corporate governance, public administration accountability and transparent management, as well as more established projects of democracy promotion, economic development, and state-building (Florini 2000, 2007; Carothers 2000; Carothers and Ottaway 2005; Ottaway and Carothers 2000; Fukuyama 2004).

In the developing world, anti-corruption assistance is now a standard part of any kind of foreign aid package. Recipients of aid must commit themselves to statements of purpose, policies of integrity, and guidelines for efficient public administration. Anti-corruption aid includes activities such as raising public awareness, revising laws, formulating good governance strategies, setting up watchdog agencies, streamlining administrative procedures, conducting training courses, carrying out surveys, monitoring progress, and evaluating impact. The combination of discourse and practice comprises what we might call 'anti-corruptionism'.

While corruption was always seen as an impediment to development efforts, it is only in the last decade that anti-corruptionism has become a truly integral part of the global discourse of development, state-building, and democracy. Hence, new anti-corruption policies are announced, and new accusations of corruption are broadcast as well. Corruption has now become a part of local politics. Definitions of what constitutes corruption, and assessments of the effectiveness of 'fighting corruption' are sufficiently vague that they can be integrated into many political agendas or private projects. Anti-corruption discourse thus fills political vacuums or serves local interests. This kind of inflation of concepts has occurred before: think of the 'career' of concepts such as 'human rights', 'civil society', 'democracy promotion', 'good governance', 'organized crime', 'transparency', 'accountability', and, of late, 'trafficking'. In each of these policy areas there are academic debates about precise definitions, typologies, and borderline cases, and discussion about causes and effects. Nevertheless, human and financial resources are mobilized as if all the substantive issues are already settled. Vague concepts discussed in thinktanks become budget lines, and budget lines are 'exported' as projects to a dismal provincial town in Albania or a government department in Romania. The journey from academic seminars to awareness-raising campaigns and training sessions is long and convoluted. How do these vague concepts become budget lines? How do these budgeted programmes become projects? How do these projects affect the local political field? And how are they manipulated by local interests?

In this context of 'anti-corruption export', we need a framework for understanding how corruption and anti-corruption can coexist. Such a framework would outline the resources available to the anti-corruption actors, the strategies these actors employ, and the consequences for society at large of the anti-corruption projects. This framework would help us to understand how anti-corruption operates to inhibit or prevent corruption in some areas, and it would also describe how anti-corruption resources are manipulated in local political space as a partisan political tool (the politics of anti-corruption). It is such a framework that I call a landscape.

Landscapes have summits, enclaves, and nodes where intermediaries can steer resources. One of the nodes on the anti-corruption landscape is Transparency International, an advocacy NGO headquartered in Berlin. With a secretariat of about 45, a budget of £6,000,000, and with 90 national chapters, TI is the major non-governmental player in the anti-corruption industry. Here I will describe how TI operates as a global NGO in the anti-corruption landscape, and continue with a description of the anti-corruption site in Romania, I will try to demonstrate that the metaphors of anti-corruption landscape and local site can be useful tools for researching the interaction between corruption and anti-corruption. By analysing the flows of resources and the actors involved, we can begin to solve the basic riddle of anti-corruption programmes: their lack of impact. Despite hundreds of millions of dollars, and hundreds of programmes, projects, and campaigns, conducted by an army of anti-corruption specialists, experts, and trainers, we have very little evidence of any decline in corrupt behaviour, or even a decline in public perceptions of corruption. It is as if anti-corruptionism persists independently of its goal. Perhaps we can understand this lack of impact by viewing anti-corruptionism as a configuration of landscapes, resource flows, and local sites. Let me start, therefore with TI and what is called 'the TI movement'.

What is a global movement?

As a global project, anti-corruption has aspects of social movement and of structured institution. The 'global anti-corruption movement', as its proponents call it, includes political reformers, international donors, enlightened foundations, civil society organizations advocating transparency, journalists uncovering abuse, and private-sector businessmen calling for more integrity. The fight against corruption takes place in political life, within public administration reform, in the efforts to monitor international trade, and in programmes to make development aid effective and accountable. The remedies cited by anti-corruption reformers, donors, and activists is to build strong state institutions, enhance the rule of law, stimulate public integrity, and raise citizen awareness. Doing this will not only make development more effective, it will keep politicians and unscrupulous businessmen in line.

Anti-corruption ideology, i.e. anti-corruptionism, is not only promulgated by activists. The activists are in fact only a minority. There are also 'professionals'. The professionals are members of, or work for, transnational organizations, aid agencies, policy and training institutes, and private firms.[5] Professional anti-corruption fighters know how to lobby for new conventions; they know how to conduct training programmes for officials, how to carry out awareness-raising activities, how to assess corruption problems, and how to obtain grants and aid contracts from Western governments and foundations. At local levels, we find the hundreds of programmes and projects run by local NGOs or by hastily assembled project management units (PMUs) within the 'partner' government. The projects carried out by NGOs and PMUs are continually monitored through various meetings, reports, and donor visits.

The global anti-corruption scene is thus a transnational one, with transnational players and local counterparts. These players cooperate *and* compete for resources. The resources are projects, contracts, catchy ideas, the attention of major donors, and the support of what are called 'stakeholders' and 'target groups'. At times, these competing actors will come together: NGO activists, the World Bank, private oil companies, European development agencies, and international advocacy groups cast aside their interests and agree upon, for example, an anti-corruption convention or a new regulation to recover stolen assets. This is anti-corruptionism as policy-making, and it takes place at the summit of our anti-corruption landscape. The landscape thus consists of metaphorical mountains, hills, plateaus, valleys, and enclaves. Moving through this landscape – sometimes unhindered, other times diverted – are anti-corruption discourses, policies, organizations, activists, and practices. Like every landscape, the landscape of anti-corruption appears differently depending on the vantage point of the observer. The summit of the landscape are the policy offices at the European Commission in Brussels, at the United States Agency for International Development's (USAID) Office of Democracy and Governance, at the World Bank's governance unit and its lending officers, in the offices implementing the UN Convention against Corruption, and in the Organisation for Economic Co-operation and Development's (OECD) anti-bribery convention-monitoring office. These are the sources from which emerge 'programme priorities' and 'country strategies' to which more peripheral anti-corruption actors must adapt. This is where the signals are sent, as they travel through the landscape.

Just below these elite, policy-making and agenda-setting institutions are other bilateral aid agencies and grant-giving foundations. These include the Department for International Development (DFID (UK), the German *Deutsche Gesellschaft für Technische Zusammenarbeit* (GTZ), and the Scandinavian aid donors (the Danish International Development Agency (DANIDA), the Swedish International Development Cooperation Agency (SIDA), the Norwegian Agency for Development Cooperation (NORAD)). As government units, they formulate policy, receive allocations from ministries, and contract implementing NGOs or firms, after which they monitor progress. Among foundations, the Soros (Open Society) foundations and National Endowment for Democracy can be mentioned. At regional levels are other players: in Southeast Europe, for example, are the Group of States against Corruption (GRECO), the EU/PHARE (Poland and Hungary: Assistance for Restructing their Economies) missions, the UN Missions in Bosnia and Kosovo, the Organization for Security and Co-operation in Europe (OSCE) democratization offices, and the Stability Pact Anti-corruption Initiative (SPAI). Similar constellations exist in Asia, Africa, and Latin America.

Further down the landscape, 'off the road' from these central policy actors and donors, are the various contracting NGOs and consulting companies. They search out signals or submit tender proposals for 'good governance' or 'public administration reform'. These groups commute between the summits where policies are formed and the local enclaves where anti-corruption projects are implemented. Finally, in the local enclaves are the ministries in the aid-receiving countries (now called 'partners'), the local counterpart organizations (NGOs, anti-corruption agencies). Partners and counterparts select suitable 'target groups' who are the subject of campaigns (e.g. police, judges, the business community, health institutions, the general public, youth, etc.).

In this landscape, relationships form between the central actors and the intermediaries, and between intermediaries and the local groups on the receiving end of anti-corruption projects. These relations can take the form of cooperation, complementarity, or competition where each actor pursues their own agenda. Cooperative/complementary relations exist when an international intervention adjusts itself to a local situation; competition/conflictual relations occur when the two interests collide, and we may also find the situation where the intervention is simply irrelevant to local interests because it brings in no resources.

The landscape metaphor, with its peaks and valleys, its flows and its Khyber passes controlled by intermediaries, provides us with an image of global anti-corruption policy in the making. As policies flow, the various actors are both objects of these policies and manipulators of the resources attached to these policies. Such manipulation could be at the level of flexible interpretations of policy guidelines, selective application of policy to political opponents, or outright diversion of funds for other agendas. The result is what we could call the politics of anti-corruption.

From policy-making landscapes to local sites

Once governments ratify conventions or make commitments, the anti-corruption policies must be implemented in the local space of cities, communities, and government offices. These implementations are supposed to affect the every-day behaviour of officials, citizens, and businessmen. In these local spaces also dwell the anti-corruption activists, who I previously termed 'integrity warriors' (Sampson 2005). Attuned to global trends, the activists seek out information about donor priorities, about anti-corruption strategies or tools, or about the latest international initiative. Activists search out grants for training, conference participation, for carrying out projects, for office space and printing, or they bid directly on contracts to implement donor pro-grammes. This activity runs parallel to other activities of a purely local nature: uncovering suspicious payments in a telecom bid, finding out which politician bought a new house, or monitoring bribes to police or doctors. Anti-corruption practice links together the high peaks and the narrow val-leys of corruption. This practice includes anti-corruption campaigns and the local corruption scandals. Local gatekeepers translate the global discourses from Brussels or Washington into fundable projects in Bucharest or Prish-tina. To understand anti-corruptionism, we need to understand how these global flows are launched, how they move along hills and plateaus, and how they are blocked or diverted. The study of anti-corruptionism involves understanding which key actors are manipulating what kind of resources for what kinds of ends.

Along this anti-corruption landscape there is a flow of five basic types of resources: money, knowledge, ideas, people, and technologies. Money takes the form of grants or projects. The flow of knowledge includes conventional wisdom about the causes, consequences, and remedies for corruption. The flow of ideas and values focuses on the importance of fighting corruption, and these ideas and values are disseminated by a flow of people – donors, officials, consultants – who implement anti-corruption projects. The flow of technologies involve the so-called 'tools' for measuring and preventing corruption (regulations, training programmes, auditing routines). These resources are launched at the anti-corruption policy-making level in a transnational, or supranational, context. Project implementation occurs at specific sites. Anti-corruption is thus a 'world of projects' (Sampson 1996). These flows are affected by the strategies and resources of relevant actors. Hence, they are blocked, diverted, or manipulated by intermediaries and by local actors in specific sites. One of the key intermediaries is Transparency International.

Fighting corruption with Transparency International

The history and development of TI is described by Luís de Sousa in this volume. Although TI refers to itself as a 'movement', it is in fact a complex organization. TI consists of a secretariat in Berlin and 91 affiliated national chapters, but with only one chapter in any one country.[6] The TI secretariat, which both coordinates and serves the chapters, covers the global anti-corruption scene, organizes advocacy campaigns, publishes research and documentation about corruption (such as the Corruption Perception Index and Global Corruption Report) and liaises with its chapters about projects and activities.

TI was founded in 1993 by ex-World Bank staffer Peter Eigen and several colleagues with experience in international law, commerce, and development. Its breakthrough can be said to have occurred with World Bank president James Wolfensohn's 'cancer of corruption' speech in 1996, which placed anti-corruption on the aid agenda. Today, TI has a budget of €6–7 million per year, financed mostly by West European government donors, USAID part-nerships, and some foundations. Eigen is a German citizen and is now retired in Germany, and it is largely due to his role that TI is based in Berlin.

Life at the TI Secretariat is like life in any office. TI staff come into the office each day around 8.30 a.m., sit down at their computers, and peruse their incoming emails. Those with the same geographic responsibility – Latin America, Africa, or Europe, for example – share offices. During the day, staff examine their messages or review documents sent from outside, from their co-workers and superiors, or communicate with relevant national chapters. An inordinate number of these messages and documents have nothing to do with what informants call 'the anti-corruption movement' as might be envi-sioned. Rather they have to do with project management: reports, budgets, applications, grant proposals, lists, agendas, meetings, etc.

Besides document processing and cooperation with national chapters, the other activity during the day is occasional meetings. Secretariat staff take a meeting, usually in one of the larger offices or meeting rooms, in order to make a decision about a policy move, document, or project, arranging a conference, or deciding to undertake an international mission. Meetings would last 10–30 minutes, and people would then go back to their computer again.

Much of the meeting activity concerns planning and reporting on inter-national trips. These trips include monitoring visits to national chapters, participation at international conferences, or fundraising trips to meet with donors.

Every Wednesday, the entire staff eats lunch together for the weekly staff meeting. The meeting consists of a series of brief announcements about who is going on what mission, who has been where, which international meetings or events are on the agenda, which reports have been published, or practical matters about office routines or personnel changes. Most TI staff are non-Germans and therefore have career plans or family obligations that would cause them to leave Germany. Following the staff meeting, it is back to work until 5, 6, or 7 p.m. As one TI staffer explained to me when I asked her, around 6 p.m., when she would be going home: 'No, I just have to finish one more thing ... ' Around 6.30 p.m., most people have left while others stay on to finish up documents or perhaps catch up on private correspondence. Such is everyday life in an international NGO office filled with cosmopolitan NGO professionals.

The TI Secretariat's target group are international decision-makers, governments, and aid officials. In this situation, national chapters may feel overlooked. Indeed, nearly every encounter between representatives of the TI secretariat and those from national chapters – at the annual meetings of TI chapters, for instance – includes complaints from the chapters that Berlin does not inform them about major decisions, new procedures or funding opportunities. Berlin counters that the chapters do not respond to their queries or read their memos.

TI considers itself part of an international movement. Being hired by TI is called 'joining the movement'. A movement is usually considered to be a loose collection of volunteers who carry out actions to affect society. Movements have strategy discussions, ideological wrangling, factional disputes; they have their purists and pragmatists; movements have believers. Movements have a basic doctrine which is subject to periodic reinterpretation or even exegesis. Global movements these days go to mass gatherings such as the World Social Forum. They organize, they march, they protest, and they somehow find the funds or volunteers to carry out their activities. People in movements do not have CVs. They do not write grant proposals, and they do not take training courses in strategic planning or project-cycle management.

TI, as we can see, is not a movement. It is an organization. Those working at the TI Secretariat in Berlin are professionals. They are project officers, programme directors, legal specialists, financial officers, database specialists, webmasters, and interns. They are what we call 'staff'. The anti-corruption scene around TI has no virulent debates, no factional disputes, no struggles over dogma, no urge to go out and demonstrate, no urge to proselytize, no effort to link anti-corruption with even moderate anti-globalization movements. The only 'marching' in TI are the sojourns to international conferences and to donors' offices in European capitals and in Washington. These donors are the furthest thing from global social movements. Instead of manifestos, TI produces interminable project applications and evaluation reports. TI is a project organization. Life at TI, and at many local TI branches, resembles the life in any kind of modern office. The TI Secretariat in Berlin is a quiet place.

With TI well into its second decade, founder Peter Eigen has turned over the reigns to a new generation of middle-aged professionals with experience in international aid. On Eigen's retirement as chairman of TI's board (2006), announced at the annual meeting of all TI chapters, elections for a new chair

were held. The winning candidate was Huguette Labelle, university admin-
istrator and former director of the Canadian International Development
Agency (CIDA). Other board members are lawyers, business consultants,
and former aid officials. In Berlin, TI's former executive director had come
from the private sector and had served as financial officer for OXFAM; he
has now moved on to the World Wildlife Fund. The new executive director,
a South African sociologist originally recruited to head TI's global programmes department, has been an NGO activist, government staff member,
and worked in the private sector. TI's new director of global programmes is a
former World Bank officer. The communications director was formerly at the
White House Office of Management and Budget. TI senior staff manage a
well-established international advocacy organization, and they feel at ease in
even the most elite international gatherings. TI's staff are professionals. They
are not (if they ever were) grass-roots activists. They have jobs on contract,
and they have dynamic careers. While TI policy priorities may change –
more emphasis on fighting poverty or on private sector corruption – TI's
general strategy remains that of founder Peter Eigen: to 'build coalitions'
with the broadest range of international policy actors so as to stay on the
inside. As reiterated by Eigen and other TI activists, 'coalition-building' means
negotiation and cooperation. It excludes confrontation, a policy continually
stressed by Eigen in all his public statements.

From a landscape perspective, the TI Secretariat operates close to the
policy-making donor summit. To stay in close touch with these elites, TI is
the secretariat and organizer of the International Anti-corruption Conference which is held every second year. This gathering brings together over
a thousand governmental and non-governmental actors (the vast majority of
the latter being TI activists whose travel has been paid by the Secretariat).
However, the Secretariat also interacts with TI chapters in each country.

The national chapters reflect different blends of activism and professionalism. In Latin America and Africa, courageous anti-corruption activists risk
violence and imprisonment in their struggle to reform corrupt political systems. Anti-corruption in these countries is part of a political movement led
by high profile lawyers, journalists, and academics. Anti-corruption takes the
form of political activism.

In Western Europe, TI chapters consist of smaller groups of volunteers
who work in business, law, or as foreign aid consultants. There is often only
one paid staff member. These chapters usually have a small number of
members (20–50) and may meet only once or twice a year. The directors
make statements, often connected to local scandals, to the press, or perhaps
they lobby for whistle-blowing legislation or hold conferences; in some
cases they may partner with another TI group in a developing country.

In Eastern Europe and the Balkans, TI branches operate as both grass-
roots groups and as project units, financed by grants from various donors.
The chapters conduct projects such as legal counselling, citizen surveys,
information dissemination, and campaigns against corruption in sectors such

as procurement, health, media, and the customs service. In this project activity, Berlin may act as an intermediary for various donors, disbursing funds or monitoring projects, or Berlin may bring together several TI chapters into regional projects. All the Southeast European TI organizations subsist on foreign donor funding, support, and training. There are many types of donors – the European Union (EU), the United States Agency for International Development (USAID), European governments or embassies, the United Nations Development Programme (UNDP) and private foundations. Besides grants and donations, the local chapters may derive income from contracting tasks, such as conducting a survey or training civil servants. Hence, the portfolio of a local TI organization in the Balkans may be a complex mixture of project funds, training contracts, free rent, and seed money for operating costs, plus a foreign intern paid by a foreign donor such as USAID or the Soros Foundation. Were this foreign donor funding to cease – were donors to move elsewhere – these organizations would collapse completely. Donors, TI's local leaders, and especially staff are well aware of this.

Fighting corruption in Southeast Europe

Reviewing anti-corruption assistance in Southeastern Europe, Tisné and Smilov describe three phases of anti-corruption policy since the 1990s: first, awareness-raising, a second phase centred on international conventions, and 'a third and crucial phase: implementation' (2004: 64). Yet, despite campaigns to improve public sector management and enact new laws and regulations, measurable results have been limited. Efforts to establish civil society coalitions, for example, 'failed to attract the broad backing they were designed to bring together, and tangible results of their actions were few and far between' (Tisné and Smilov 2004: 66). Similarly, 'broad public awareness campaigns have reached saturation point', while 'governmental omnibus anti-corruption programs ... have failed conclusively [to] reduce corruption or to reassure the public and foreign investors' (Tisné and Smilov 2004: 67). Several studies cite a lack of political will as the key factor in explaining the failure of anti-corruption strategies to produce results.

Since this 2004 report, and many others with similar conclusions, anti-corruption assistance to Southeastern Europe has continued unabated. The number of citizens helped by complaint centres, or the number of training sessions carried out, or seminars held may be impressive, but we have little evidence of any significant reduction in the rate or extent of corruption. For example, a Council of Europe project to help Southeast European countries formulate anti-corruption strategies, 'did not reach its targets', and 'chances for success are not great.' (Institute of Public Management 2006: 25, 34). Swedish anti-corruption training programmes in Serbia and a German-backed hotline programme in Bosnia and US anti-corruption coalition-building in Albania all showed successful goal fulfilment, but without any effect on the extent of corruption in these countries (SIDA 2007; McCarthy 2005).[7]

Despite their lack of direct impact, such programmes succeed in integrating local sites into a much larger anti-corruption landscape. They become part of what the US State Department (1999) has called 'an anti-corruption regime'. How do such regimes become a part of the local site? How are they adapted to local conditions? In the development aid literature, this problem is usually articulated as the problem of 'ownership'. Without ownership, programmes and projects become money that is wasted; there is no fundamental change, no 'sustainability'. Instead, global resources are used in local political struggles. This is particularly the case in Southeast Europe with its focus on integration/membership of these countries into EU frameworks. Here I will use the example of Romania, where reticent political leaders were pushed and prodded to pursue anti-corruption platforms. Let me therefore provide a brief description of the anti-corruption site as I experienced it in Romania, mostly prior to its EU accession.

The anti-corruption landscape in Romania

In Romania, as elsewhere in Southeastern Europe, surveys of corruption have shown high levels of abuse within the state enterprises, in the privatization process, in the administration of Western aid, in tax assessments and collections, in public procurement, and in the customs service (World Bank 2001a, 2001b; Global Integrity 2006). For ordinary citizens, the health system and the courts are notorious for bribes and favouritism. Doctors and nurses, police and judges, teachers and professors, bureaucrats and customs officers all seem to be taking some sort of payment or are susceptible to nepotistic appeals. Public life is replete with accusations and exposés of corruption in politics, state-run enterprises, and EU aid.

Examining the Romanian anti-corruption site, we can identify six actors: the government, the opposition parties, the media, the national anti-corruption agency, the international donors, and that all-embracing category now called 'civil society'. The various actors try to point out the guilty, propose measures to fight corruption, and pronounce on the effectiveness of these measures as well. Each actor has their own resources at their disposal. They interact with each other, striking alliances or garnering rewards. In certain conjunctures, these alliances shift, as occurs when key international donors descend on Romania to carry out assessment missions and issue warnings. Let me briefly review these six actors on the local scene.[8]

The Government

Pressured by the conditions of EU accession, Romania has enacted a National Programme for Preventing Corruption, a National Action Plan to Prevent Corruption, and a National Anti-Corruption Strategy 2005–07. The government's programme, drafted with foreign expertise and clear foreign pressure, is a familiar package of measures culled from well-known World Bank and OECD strategies for fighting corruption. A new anti-corruption law compels public officials to declare their assets, and enacting this law was not without protest by parliamentarians (Stan 2004). The government's fight against corruption takes places on several fronts: enacting of new regulations, training of personnel, programmes for more transparent administration, efforts to make courts more honest, and public education about the dangers of corruption. The Romanian government participates in international forums on anti-corruption, such as the Stability Pact Anti-corruption Initiative (for Southeast Europe) and the country is monitored by the Council of Europe's Group of States against Corruption (GRECO). Government ministers and functionaries attend international anti-corruption meetings and training sessions, and submit to evaluations by the EU, by the World Bank, and by other outside consultants. In late 2002, the government established the Anti-corruption Prosecution Office (financed by the EU and USAID), and this office later became the National Anti-corruption Department (DNA).

In practice, an anti-corruption campaign might suddenly focus on a ministry or department, such as the fiscal office or the customs authority (reminiscent of the 'islands of integrity' campaigns once used by TI). Officials continue to attend training sessions in making government more open to citizens, and in how to hold press conferences or conduct public hearings. Up to and even after accession to the EU in 2007, the Romanian government has had to endure criticism by EU monitors commenting on the lack of sufficient efforts to fight corruption and threats to withdraw agricultural subsidies.

The opposition parties

The opposition parties can exploit media accusations against the government. The opposition can tip-off journalists to instances of favouritism in a ministry or in some piece of legislation. Some of the opposition are considered by civil society to be more NGO-friendly, so it is common for civil society activists to approach opposition politicians with information about corrupt practices or with complaints of abuse. Some opposition politicians sided with the EU in its criticism of Romania's inadequate anti-corruption efforts. Corruption accusations thus occur as a result of various political agendas, and we can speak of a genuine politics of anti-corruption in Romania.[9]

The media

Romania's print media and independent television, always looking for scandal, focus on prominent public officials who appear to be living too lavishly or promoting their friends or cronies. Week in and week out, the media highlight cases of abuse, bribery, special laws, nepotism, pay-offs, and suspicious connections between officials and business tycoons. A politician who acquires a cheap property or has a brush with the law can expect the scrutiny of the press. The media depict Romanian society as a never-ending series of corruption scandals, typified by the aforementioned envelope given to the agricultural minister. Corruption is interpreted as the hijacking of reform; its persistence is emblematic of weaknesses in the Romanian national character, and it is an international embarrassment.

The government, of course, periodically accuses the press of promoting false or sensational accusations, whereupon the press pressures for more access to data. Journalists can also be taken to court for obtaining data illegally or for libelling politicians. The media – subject to a complex system of licensing and regulation – is itself the object of corruption scandals, a process helped by the celebrity status of publishers, newspaper editors, and media moguls.

The Anti-corruption Agency

Operating between the government mandate, the opposition demands, and the media search for scandal is the National Anti-corruption Department (DNA), originally evolved from an Anti-corruption Prosecution Office. The DNA now has about 500 employees in Bucharest and in its district offices. Like anti-corruption offices elsewhere, the DNA can begin investigations or act on complaints. When this anti-corruption agency first began operating in 2002, there was scepticism as to whether it would prosecute senior officials. Under the leadership of former minister Monica Macoviei, they have. In 2006 alone, the DNA had solved 1,092 cases, indicting 360 defendants; these defendants included seven MPs, one minister, two state secretaries, and two mayors.[10] Several cases involved embezzlement of EU funds as well, thus drawing the attention of foreign donors. The DNA has continually endeavoured to refurbish its image as impartial, but its staff can not operate effectively under the stigma of a cynical society, and it is subject to political pressures. In April 2007, Ms Macovei was discharged, partly due to her active prosecution of high level corruption. In late 2007, several investigations of high officials remained delayed.

The international donors

Overshadowing these local political actors are the various international actors, chiefly the EU, World Bank, the International Monetary Fund (IMF), and the United States embassy, all of whom are making demands on Romania to meet international standards, pursue more transparent policies, promote good governance, promulgate a culture of accountability, and improve the climate for foreign investment. Pressure on Romania was greater during the period prior to EU accession, but Brussels still threatens to withhold key disbursements. Criticisms by foreign diplomats do not go unnoticed by government leaders who invariably reply that the foreigners have exaggerated or misunderstood the situation or overlooked the country's progress. When the US ambassador, in April 2003, made well-publicized remarks about Romanian corruption and the government's inability to do anything about it, several Romanian politicians discussed whether his remarks were made in sympathy or not, and whether his critique was directed to 'the entire Romanian political class' or the current governing coalition.[11] The current controversy about the Romanian branch of Freedom House and its role in the '15,000 euro envelope', is an example of Romania's ambivalence about foreign pressure.

Civil society

The final actor in the Romanian anti-corruption scene is the NGO sector, and especially those organizations advocating civil liberties, human rights, honesty in government, and anti-corruption. This includes, for example, the Romanian chapter of Transparency International, first established in 2000. TI-Romania's projects include a programme for legal advice to citizens, translation of anti-corruption documents into Romanian, monitoring of local government procurement practices, investigation of corruption in the media, and awareness-raising with youth about corruption. TI Romania originally had hostile relations with the Anti-corruption Prosecution Office, but it has now become an integral part of government initiatives. TI is joined by a number of supporting NGOs representing media, human rights, civic education, and youth. Many of the staff of these NGOs have acquired sufficient skills or have social networks enabling them to be invited into government service. In this sense, Romanian NGOs function as a training venue, with people moving along different sites in the landscape.

Summary and conclusions: Local sites in a global landscape

Romania is just one site in the global anti-corruption landscape. These sites bring together political formations, government institutions, and the disgruntled citizens, each with their own interests. Meanwhile, the media focus on uncovering scandal, exposing the guilty, and drawing conclusions as to Romania's fate in the EU. In Romania, as elsewhere, corrupt practices and anti-corruption initiatives are tied to *accusations* of corruption, and of course, counter-accusations. In this site, the anti-corruption agency must continually deal with the forces that are pushing and pulling it in different directions: expectations of the government, demands from the opposition, and the scrutiny of foreign donors. The agency is itself a field of contestation about resources, claims, and legitimacy.

Actors on the Romanian anti-corruption scene, like other local sites, have their own theories of what corruption is, how it operates, why it is sustained, and how it should be combated. These ideas move transnationally, but take special form in the local context. A similar flow occurs with the various anti-corruption rituals that are sponsored by both government and society. These would include the press conferences, the statistical presentations of successful anti-corruption campaigns, the public events such as the opening of anti-corruption units, the expressions of support for harassed corruption fighters, the individual appeals of frustrated citizens in the press, and the interminable televised debates between politicians, journalists, and experts.

In this context, corruption arrests and indictments are not just 'law enforcement'. They are 'signals' by the authorities that they are doing something about corrupt behaviour. Through the sensation-hungry media, the signals are sent to the political opposition, to the public, and to the international actors who can decide on aid priorities and can raise or lower Romania's international credit rating. The Romanian world of anti-corruption is thus a complex intersection of government claims that morality is being safeguarded, citizen demands for justice, and political jockeying for power.

This local scene operates as a node in the global landscape of anti-corruption. Along this landscape flow decisions about strategy and funding and the newest capacity-building tools for achieving good governance and administrative effectiveness. As new discourses emerge from the summit of the landscape (the major donor meetings), the surrounding international NGOs, smaller bilateral agencies, and consulting companies 'wait for a signal', passing down the news to their local counterparts, resident representatives, and so-called 'partners' in the various Balkan capitals. Outdated concepts are now retooled into newer, more fashionable techniques: awareness-raising and civil society coalitions are replaced by public servant codes of ethics. Corruption is now linked to other projects such as human rights, poverty alleviation, or trafficking. In the local anti-corruption field, the various actors attempt to gain access to the resources that flow through the anti-corruption landscape: they compete for ideas, knowledge, funds, and for the attention of those people who have access to these resources.

This panorama of the anti-corruption scene in Romania could certainly be extended to other Balkan countries. Some of the actors would change (due to weaker NGOs, more political will, or the degree of donor influence). The leitmotifs of corruption discourse – 'declining trust', 'everyone is doing it', 'we need to crack down', 'outsiders are watching us', etc. might change as well. Yet there is in fact an uncanny resemblance between the local anti-corruption sites across Southeast Europe, especially in the way in which anti-corruption enters through outside projects and interacts with local understandings about political life and the everyday struggle over public goods and private projects. I would therefore postulate that it is through corruption and anti-corruption practices that we might identify similarities in how the people of Southeast Europe relate to their formal institutions, on the one hand trying to get around them, and on the other insisting that these institutions function properly so as to prevent unchecked personal aggrandizement by those in power. In this sense, anti-corruption landscapes and the local site are a window for understanding how people deal with profound transformation and the accompanying uncertainties such transformations bring.

With so many international actors, and so much traffic in resources channelled through transnational vectors, what sense is it to speak of a 'national anti-corruption programme'? USAID in Albania, the European Commission in Romania, TI and the Soros Foundation in Bosnia, the OSCE in Kosovo, and Swedish aid in Serbia all are part of this global anti-corruption landscape. Local anti-corruption movements are thus drawn into well-trodden, protected pathways along the anti-corruption landscape, pathways of money, knowledge, networks, and power. As these resources travel the landscape, they become – to exploit a standard political science concept – literally 'path dependent'. What might have been incipient, autonomous movements, with their own dynamic and social support, become locked into the rhetoric of good governance projects, integrity pacts, project management, and the search for a donor. What might have been anti-corruption movements become anti-corruption budget lines. What might have been anti-corruption activists become anti-corruption project staff. What might have been social change becomes the reproduction of projects.

In this context, our understanding of corruption also changes. We need to understand corruption in the shadow of the global 'anti-corruption industry'. Any national anti-corruption programme is but a site in a global anti-corruption landscape that measures, assesses, and organizes against corruption. The global vectors of anti-corruption are the international anti-corruption gatherings, the lobbying activities of organizations like Transparency International in Brussels, New York, Washington, and London, the fundraising trips to foreign donors, and the apparatus of international anti-corruption conventions and monitoring mechanisms. All these take place in cosmopolitan venues. These practices affect how anti-corruptionism unfolds at the local level, where real people are struggling against bureaucratic abuse, criminal politicians, unchecked bribery, and political cronyism. Viewing anti-corruptionism in terms of global landscapes and local sites is a means of unlocking a riddle. The riddle is to figure out how local anti-corruption movements are transformed into anti-corruption budget lines, and how local activists become project 'staff'. And finally, how these staff get locked into anti-corruption projects of questionable impact.

Notes

1 Acknowledgement: The author wishes to thank participants at the 2006 European Consortium for Political Research (ECPR) panel on anti-corruption in Nicosia for helpful comments on earlier versions of this chapter. Special thanks to editors Luís de Sousa and Peter Larmour for their supreme patience in waiting for the final version.
2 Available at HTTP: <http://english.hotnews.ro/Public-television-broadcasts-images-of-Agriculture-minister-Remes-taking-bribe-from-ex-minister-VIDEO-articol_46129. htm> accessed 11 October 2007. See also <http//www.realitatea.net100186_Scandalul-spagii-Ciorbea-Muresan-Remes>.

3 Research during this period was partially funded by the Swedish National Research Council (*Vetenskapsrådet*) whose support I gratefully acknowledge. I have conducted fieldwork in several sites: TI headquarters in Berlin, local TI offices in Bosnia and Romania, anti-corruption and democracy offices in Albania and Kosovo, various conferences and training sessions in these four countries, as well as international anti-corruption expert gatherings in Berlin, Passau, Prague, Nairobi, Seoul, Guatemala City, Stockholm, and in my own hometown of Copenhagen. The fieldwork included following typical anti-corruption activities included assessment missions, implementation projects, grant monitoring, training sessions, evaluation missions, courses, meetings, and seminars. I have reviewed documents such as consulting proposals, policy statements, minutes of meetings, and online forums. And I have interviewed anti-corruption practitioners in government aid units, intergovernmental organizations, private consulting companies, and NGOs, including staff and former staff of Transparency International in Berlin and at several TI member gatherings. As a member of the Danish branch of Transparency International, I also participated in various Scandinavian anti-corruption meetings and events, several of which were relevant to Southeast Europe due to the Scandinavian countries' interest in democracy-building in both the Baltic countries and the Balkans.

4 Bryane Michael (2004c) has used the figure of US$100 million and 2,000 specialists, but these estimates are certainly undervalued. USAID, for example, has as much as US$700 million available for anti-corruption initiatives. See also an interview with Michael on the 'flourishing anti-corruption industry' applied to Romania at <http://users.ox.ac.uk/~scat1663/anticorruption_good.doc> (Romanian version 'Industria anticorupție', *Jurnalul National*, 29 June 2007, <http://www.jurnalul.ro/articole/96022/industria-anticoruptie>) accessed 13 October 2007.

5 The emergence of a private anti-corruption consulting branch deserves a study in itself. US-based firms in this area include Casals, Chemonix, Management Systems International (MSI), and DPK Consulting. In Europe, most of these firms originally specialized in improving public sector management and then went over to governance and anti-corruption.

6 Approximate because some are full-fledged chapters, others, 'chapters in formation', and still others, 'contact points' or 'partners'.

7 In Albania, the USAID-financed project, implemented by the private firm MSI, set up an anti-corruption coalition and helped established a citizens' advisory office. After some years of negotiation, the Citizens Advisory Office is now a TI chapter in formation.

8 This section updates a discussion in an earlier article (Sampson 2005).

9 The function of these accusations can be usefully compared to the anthropological study of African witchcraft accusations, or the use of accusations of secret police complicity. Regardless of the phenomenon, the accusations take on a life of their own.

10 See the DNA's annual reports at <www.pna.ro> (accessed 10 October 2007), summarized, and *Southeast European Times*, 9 April 2007, 'Nivelul corupției din România a scăzut, dar reprezintă încă o problemă'. Online. Available at HTTP: <http://www.setimes.com/cocoon/setimes/xhtml/ro/features/setimes/features/2007/04/09/feature-03> (accessed 10 October 2007).

11 See *Curiel National*, 17 April 2003, <http://www.curierulnational.ro/Politic/2003-04-17/Ion+Iliescu:+Afirmatiile+sunt+facute+cu+%E2%80%9Csimpatie%E2%80%9D+pentru+eforturile+Guvernului> (accessed 13 October 2007).

12 TI in search of a constituency

The institutionalization and franchising of the global anti-corruption doctrine

Luís de Sousa

Introduction

Three features of the post-Cold War political map deserve close attention: the global expansion of democracy; the growth of non-governmental organizations (NGOs); and the evolution of corruption into a global concern at all levels of decision-making. Linking all these three developments is the birth of a new anti-corruption actor, Transparency International (TI), an international non-governmental organization (INGO) based in Berlin whose primary mission was recently defined as 'to work to create change towards a world free of corruption'.[1] TI has gained an indisputable reputation as the most prominent civil society 'corruption-fighter' at the global level for several reasons. It was the first to give attention to a transnational issue that had only been sporadically and vaguely addressed by other NGOs.[2] It has framed the issue in a non-dichotomous way. Everybody is called upon the fight against 'the evil of corruption' through a coalition involving all sectors of society: government, private sector, and civil society. No concrete 'enemies' were individualized. This all-inclusive strategy in the pursuit of their holistic mission ('a world free of corruption') gave the organization considerable political leverage, both at the national and international level. TI has played an active role in pressing for the adoption of two international conventions against corruption (by the the Organisation for Economic Co-operation and Development (OECD) and the United Nations (UN)) and some of its National Chapters (NCs)[3] have created corruption-monitoring mechanisms and pressed for the adoption or review of national legal frameworks. It displays wide international representation of local arrangements. In short, TI has played a major role in bringing corruption and anti-corruption onto the agenda of multilateral organizations and national governments.

Though some of its founders refer to TI as 'the global anti-corruption movement', TI is only part of that wider process. TI is better defined as an INGO whose franchising process has, on some occasions, been entangled with local dynamics and movements. At most, we can refer to it as a confederation of anti-corruption NGOs since it does not qualify on many criteria[4] as a social movement or transnational activist network. It was founded in May 1993 by a group of high profile people, 'grey suits', such as two former World Bank executives, lawyers, aid and development officials, chief executive officers (CEOs), and retired political leaders, with the ultimate and limited goal of promoting transparency and curbing corruption in international business transactions. The founders of TI had never envisaged that their organization would catch fire in quite the way it did, and certainly its governance was never designed for that of a global institution. Rather, they had envisaged TI as being a 'ginger group', to shake the corruption issue out into the open (Galtung and Pope 1999: 257–60).

TI has moved from being a tiny INGO to become a global franchised organization in less than a decade. It has enlarged – it currently comprises more than 90 locally established NCs and chapters-in-formation of a variable size and nature – and it has deepened its mission. It is no longer concerned solely with bribery of foreign officials and corruption in international business transactions, but with corruption as 'the abuse of entrusted power for private gain' (Transparency International (2007c) operational definition of corruption available at: <http://www.transparency.org/about_us> (access date 19 August 2008)). Thus it has taken on issues such as political corruption and corporate crime at the national, regional, and global levels.

Whilst traditional anti-corruption national actors look outwards to international fora and higher levels of decision-making to compensate for the insufficiency of domestic instruments in addressing cross-border corruption, TI had to look downwards in search of national partners and constituencies where most of anti-instruments need to be ratified, implemented, and, hopefully, evaluated. Despite its apparently cohesive outlook, NCs have differing concerns in spite of a global agenda to which they are required to adhere as constituents. This inevitably gives rise to tension between the NCs and the Secretariat in Berlin TI-S; NCs have gradually looked at the Secretariat in Berlin (TI-S) as a head office trying to dictate approaches to them.[5]

The purpose of this chapter is to assess the process of institutionalization of TI and how it has helped to spread the anti-corruption doctrine worldwide.[6] The remainder of the chapter is divided into three parts. The first deals with TI's franchising process and its legal, financial, and organizational implications. The second part explores the variable nature and quality of NCs by focusing on sensitive aspects of their governance: their political neutrality; their financial independence; and the extent to which they are autonomous from TI-S in setting their priorities and strategies of engagement. Finally, some concluding remarks about TI's role as a global anti-corruption civil society actor are presented.

The franchising of TI and its implications

TI's institutionalization, can be tentatively divided into four phases (see Table 12.1):

Table 12.1 The formation of TI NCs: waves of franchising and membership status*

Existence as local NGO prior to TI	1st wave 1993–1995 (the foundation phase)†	2nd wave 1995–1999 (the institutionalization phase)	3rd wave 1999–2003 (the consolidation phase)	4th wave 2003… (the redefinition phase)
Argentina (1989), Ecuador (1990), Estonia (1991), Senegal (1993)…	Argentina, Bangladesh, Ecuador, Germany, Kenya, UK, USA, Denmark, France	Australia, Belgium, Benin, Bolivia, Bulgaria, Canada, Chile, Colombia, Czech Republic, Egypt, Gambia, Greece, India, Israel, Italy, Jamaica, Latvia, Lebanon, Malawi, Malaysia, Mauritius, Morocco, Nepal, Nigeria; Pakistan, Panama, PNG, Paraguay, Philippines, Poland, Slovak Republic, Spain, South Africa, Switzerland, Tanzania, Thailand, Trinidad and Tobago, Turkey, Uganda, Uruguay, Zimbabwe	Armenia, Azerbaijan, Bosnia & Herzegovina, Botswana, Brazil, Estonia, Fiji, Georgia, Ghana, Indonesia, Kazakhstan, Korea (South), Lebanon, Lithuania, Madagascar, Mexico, Moldova, New Zealand, Norway, Pakistan, Peru, Romania, Russia, Senegal, Serbia, Sri Lanka, Trinidad & Tobago, Vanuatu, Zambia	Croatia, Haiti, Ireland, Japan, Niger, Palestine Authority, Sweden, Venezuela

Notes: * Some of the early Chapters, incorporated prior to the accreditation system being put into practice, have been replaced by new local entities, this was the case for the NCs of Brazil, Hungary, Uruguay, Ukraine, Venezuela and Costa Rica which has recently been revoked of its title of Chapter in Formation. The table refers only to the date of adhesion of the local entities which constitute today's NCs. Some Chapters are still in formation, and others have decided not to become full accredited NCs, but still collaborate with TI on a regular basis. *Latest information on potential new NCs (TI 2006 Report)*: Albania (CH-IF); Algeria (CH-IF); Austria (CH-IF); Bahrain (CH-IF); Burundi (Nat'l Ct); Cameroon (CH-IF); China (Nat'l Ct); Côte d'Ivoire (Nat'l Ct); Dominican Republic (Nat'l Ct); Ethiopia (Nat'l Ct); Finland (CH-IF); Guatemala (CH-IF); Guinea (Nat'l Ct); Haiti (CH-IF); Hungary (Nat'l Ct); Kuwait (Nat'l Ct); Kyrgyzstan (CH-IF); Mongolia (CH-IF); Netherlands (The) (CH-IF); Nicaragua (CH-IF); Solomon Islands (CH-IF); Spain (CH-IF); Taiwan (CH-IF); Uruguay (CH-IF); Ukraine (Nat'l Ct); Yemen (CH-IF). Membership status abbreviations: Chapter in Formation (CH-IF) and National Contact (Nat'l Ct).

† As previously mentioned, the initial five accredited national Chapters were: Denmark, Ecuador, Germany, the UK and the USA.

Source: TI Annual Reports, memorandum provided Andrea Figari (TI-S staff) and NCs websites.

- The brief foundation period from 1993 to 1995, during which TI formally accredited an initial network of five NCs: Denmark, Ecuador, Germany, the UK, and the US. These founding constituents would prove important within TI's internal governance structure and process in years to come. The franchising of TI started formally at the 1994 Annual General Meeting (AGM) in Quito, but at that stage its goals and activities were yet too narrow and there was no clear idea in which direction the organization would be heading.
- The post-1994 AGM period, which lasts until the entry into force of the OECD Convention in 1999. In this period, TI institutionalized and expanded rapidly thanks to the success of highly mediatized initiatives, of which the Corruption Perceptions Index (CPI) was the most relevant. The creation of TI's official website at this stage also proved crucial to give visibility to the organization's activities and instruments.
- From 1999 to 2003, TI was at its peak. It displayed a consolidated organization and a reputable brand in the domain of anti-corruption. Following the October 2002 Casablanca Meeting, TI redefined its mission and introduced new accreditation rules for membership to control the scope and quality of the franchising process.
- And the post-2003 period, when TI's future (from a financial and functional point of view) looked uncertain, its capacity to deliver innovative and highly mediatized products was less striking (thus wearing out some of the glamour of the brand), and the internal governance problems and power contests between the NCs at the bottom and the network core or establishment at the top started to mount. The products were wearing thin and even its charismatic Chairman, Peter Eigen, admitted that the TI's Corruption Index had 'certain weakness ... '[7] The organization appeared to be facing a mounting crisis as the tasks it faced demanded a degree of professionalism which, after the enforced departures of Fredrik Galtung and Jeremy Pope, TI-S appeared unable to meet. Eigen himself retired in 2005, to be replaced by Huguette Labelle.[8]

These four stages in TI's institutionalization can be explained through two main dynamics of franchising. At an early stage, and following the unexpected success[9] of the first CPI, TI expanded fast into a global organization. The *centrifugal* drive for franchising was dictated both by the need to search for a constituency (legitimization and representation factors) and the need to consolidate the brand (the marketing factor). Once the organization became relatively solid (in terms of its membership, structure, governance, and funding) and its brand became well known worldwide – particularly through the CPI and the passing of the OECD anti-bribery convention – the franchising became inevitably *centripetal* as TI tried to maintain the reputation of its brand.

Most of the first NCs started from informal contacts developed by the two TI founding fathers, Peter Eigen and Jeremy Pope, drawing from their previous careers as a World Bank official and in the Commonwealth Secretariat respectively. The recruitment of Jeremy Pope as TI's founding Managing Director on 1 January 1994 was particularly crucial. Right from the start, he promoted the creation of NCs, something that would give him considerable leverage within the organization. If TI was to operate as a global NGO it had to enlarge its membership and franchise its organization, since most anti-corruption work had to be carried out at the national level.[10] The adoption of international anti-bribery conventions or the simple translation of TI's Source Book into various languages as a mobilization tool highlighted the need for a constituency. Pope's National Integrity System (NIS) project was evidence of his view that after successfully mobilizing global concern towards corruption, TI had to search for a constituency through which to carry out its anti-corruption work (Galtung and Pope 1999: 268–72).

According to TI's official history,[11] at the beginning only 15 NCs were envisaged. Incrementalism would soon give place to unleashed membership as TI profited from the initial mobilization impact of the CPI. TI rushed into franchising. Catch-all membership preceded the organization's consolidation and what it had to offer in terms of initiatives against corruption. Moreover, Peter Eigen's insistence that TI chapters be 'new' NGOs, and not signed-up existing NGOs, dictated that these new chapters began at the bottom of a steep learning curve. Most of these new TI-S-'sponsored' entities had no grass-roots support or experience in corruption control issues. These NCs would nevertheless play a decisive role in supporting TI-S policies at a later consolidation stage.[12]

The first round of NCs included developing and OECD countries, transition and consolidated democracies, with a fair geographical spread: Kenya, Bangladesh, US, UK, Denmark, France, Germany, and Ecuador (where the Ecuadorian Vice President Alberto Dahik was serving as the first Chair of TI's Advisory Council until his enforced resignation[13]).

In spite of the apparently diverse initial franchising and its juridical existence under the German Law of Associations,[14] early TI was essentially a Western organization and mainly of Anglo-American origin, a situation which has since gradually changed. At the beginning, only one out of the ten initial Charter signatory members was from the developing world (Bangladesh). The first nine Board members had a Western majority, even if it was more balanced (five members from developed countries against four from developing countries); and out of the 24 initial Advisory Council members, 14 were from the Western developed world, out of which half were Anglo-American. Today, the Board is composed of 12 members of whom only three are from Anglo-American countries[15] and nine from developing and transition democracies.

One membership trump for TI was the adhesion of *Poder Ciudadano* in 1994, a prestigious Argentinean civil rights NGO created in 1989 and whose founder, Luis Moreno Ocampo, had been appointed General Prosecutor at the International Criminal Court at The Hague. The reputation of *Poder Ciudadano* and its well-established networks with other Latin American civil society organizations (CSOs) and national contacts paved the way for TI's expansion in the region. By 2000, all major Latin American countries (LAC) were covered, with Mexico joining in 1999 and Brazil some months later.[16]

In 2003, TI put in place an accreditation system and committee[17] to control a process that was no longer easily controllable. TI insisted on a key number of normative and organizational requisites which future members must adhere to (*membership acquis*[18]) and designed graded statuses for local constituents in relation to the organization: National Chapter (full member); Chapter in Formation (in view of short-term full membership); National Contact (regular contact without membership); and Ally (informal contact). Although these different statuses may imply a kind of evolutionary path to full membership, not all NCs have followed it. Some Chapters in Formation have now applied for NC status (such as the case with *Acción Ciudadana* in Guatemala). Others have opted to remain local anti-corruption NGOs allied to TI's mission (e.g. the Algerian National Contact[19] (*Association Algérienne de Lutte contre la corruption*)) or to cooperate with TI or some of its NCs from time to time (e.g. the case of Bolivia[20] and El Salvador[21]).

During the 2004 Nairobi Annual Membership Meeting,[22] TI's global network included: 72 accredited NCs; two new accredited NCs (Peru and Norway, which had just been the object of a major scandal relating to one of its major donors and founding member, Statoil[23]); three NCs in formation (Haiti, Mongolia, and Sweden); three National Contacts (Austria, Togo, and China); and a new National Contact from Ireland, which is currently an NC.

The process of enlarging TI's membership had three major implications, which I will address next: financial, organizational, and legal.

Adjusting to a changing international donor panorama

The move towards franchising (and TI's insistence on being labelled a movement) was not just a strategy of institutionalization, but was partly a response to the changing international donors' agenda. If, during the 1970s and 1980s, collaboration between world financial institutions, development agencies, and NGOs was mainly directed towards INGOs headquartered in developed countries and carrying out operations in more than one developing country, in recent years this trend seems to have been reversed. With globalization comes localism. NGO collaborations funded by these entities were now geared towards local, community-based organizations (CBOs), in other words, grass-root organizations. According to World Bank figures, in 1994, when TI started to consider its franchising at the AGM in Ecuador, among projects involving NGO collaboration 40 per cent involved CBOs, 70 per cent involved traditional national NGOs, and 10 per cent involved

INGOs. These CBOs are substantially different from TI: they are individual membership organizations, based on voluntary action, and display a flexible organization. They tend to be the recipient of project goods and services rather than the deliverers, designers, or implementers of those projects. TI was not a grass-roots organization and had to search for some sort of constituency to respond to this changing financial panorama. It would still have been able to carry on its mobilization and advocacy work as a tiny NGO, but in order to frame large-scale projects for funding it needed to constitute local branches. The consolidation of TI's finances went hand in hand with its franchising and the development of high media impact products (such as the CPI). Yet its innovative capacity to attract project-based funding has gradually declined.[24]

The putting in place of a confederal[25] style of organization was not purely driven by the need to boost participation from below, to increase critical mass and knowledge about local problems, or to broaden its territorial representation. There were also important financial implications on both sides of the fence. For TI, franchising can translate both into an opportunity to apply for large-scale funding and a burden in the sense that demands will increase as some NCs start looking at TI as a 'headquarter' with redistributive and funding obligations towards its branches. These NCs may even question its costly and resource-draining existence. For those joining the organization from below, there is a clear financial strategy upon which rests their survival. First, TI can provide a safety net for new or weak local branches, either through its donor networks or because it has the adequate size, structure, and credibility to obtain the necessary funds from multilateral organizations, national aid agencies, the corporate sector, and even other civil society organizations (such as foundations). Second, those local NGOs that are well implanted (some of which are older than TI itself, such as the Argentinean[26] and Ecuadorian[27] National Chapters), and have solid and sustainable funding negotiate their membership – joining the brand without loosing their autonomy – as a sound strategy to ensure a better access to international resources.

The organizational challenge from below

Once enlarged membership and franchising were set on track, there was little TI-S could do to stop increasing demands from below for greater internal transparency, accountability, and democratization. This organizational change, which would raise internal governance questions between TI-S and the NCs, became evident right from the outset during TI's first Annual General Meeting in Quito, Ecuador, in 1994. There, a young Ecuadorian lawyer Valéria Merino Dirani[28] would epitomize this evolution when, after hearing the Ecuadorian Vice President (and first Chair of TI's advisory council) Alberto Dahik, questioned him on the nature and composition of the Ecuadorian National Chapter:

When he [Dahik] listed the members, recalls Pope, she responded: 'That's not a National Chapter, that's a collection of your friends! That's not Ecuadorian civil society.' In response, the Ecuador chapter was disbanded and pledges made to reconstitute it with wider representation.

(Lundberg 2002: 8)

Diriani's intervention was more far reaching than might be thought in the first place. Her protest against the nepotistic and closed membership of TI Ecuador had alerted listeners to the dangers of having politicians closely involved in the organization or its NCs, something that TI would learn as a bitter lesson following a series of unfortunate events involving Mr Dahik.[29] Moreover, she also made clear during that meeting that TI would lack credibility and capacity to deliver if it confined itself to corruption in international business transactions and disregarded the real corruption faced by ordinary citizens at the national level.[30]

The legal/statutory conundrum

The inclusion of NCs in the internal governance of TI was not legally impossible, but it raised an important problem: 'under German law, it was nearly impossible to get rid of a *Verein* member' (Lundberg 2002: 7). The law requires at least seven voting members – permanent active members (PAMs) – and a few other statutory bodies in place to constitute an *eingetragener Verein* (a not-for profit non-governmental organization with tax exemption status). The incorporation of foreign NCs into a *Verein* was not foreseen under the German law of associations, hence not easily adjusted in legal terms. A PAM was there for life, unless there were strong grounds for expelling him/her.[31] After considerable legal advice, NCs were granted conditional membership, which would allow the Chairperson or its legal representative (Official Chapter Representative[32]) to be a PAM of TI with voting rights, despite that the person holding that position might change according to the internal statutes of the NC in question (and under the national regulations in which NCs are incorporated as legal entities). In this way, compromise between German law and the different national regulations and between TI and NCs was finally reached. The legal mechanism for franchising was now in place[33] and TI's institutionalization would assume a whole new meaning. The NCs would become the most important feature of TI's organizational structure and functioning to the extent that they are now perceived as 'the "owners" of the TI movement' (TI Sourcebook 2000: Ch. 15).

The resolution to extend membership to NCs was not simply a complex juridical puzzle with regard to entry, but also with regard to exit. Entry to an association, movement, or party, which imposes upon its members both organizational and, above all, normative membership conditions (e.g. allegiance to organization's *acquis*, goals, and mission) is often an easier process than exit. NCs can voluntarily exit from TI, but what price will they pay if they wished to remain in the anti-corruption business? The advantages of being part of such a wide network would probably be hampered: communication, exchange of ideas, transfer of knowledge, increased credibility of domestic claims, and development of fundraising capacities (given that TI is now a consolidated brand in the 'industry' of anti-corruption). A more complex situation is that relating to disaccreditation or forced exit by misconduct, lack of loyalty to the organization, or violation of TI's Statement of Vision, Values and Guiding Principles (the Umbrella Statement). In such a case, the room for discretion is considerable.

The decision not to grant membership to a candidate for NC or to expel an existing NC has important legal implications for TI, as well as political ones. The Membership Accreditation Committee's[34] role is not so much about minimizing legal ordeals that can arise from granting active membership status, but about controlling enlargement, which has institutional and power implications for TI's internal governance. It is more a screening mechanism for future members than a continuous process of quality certification. With regards to entry, if TI were to be considered a movement, as it often claims, no conditionality other than allegiance to a basic set of principles and lines of action could be put in place. As Della Porta and Diani put it succinctly, 'social movements do not have members, but participants' (2006: 26). The system of accreditation is a threat to the autonomy of NCs. Likewise, whatever the criteria used, the disaccreditation system will intensify the already evident tension between the two contending bodies within TI's internal system of governance: on the one side, the growing number of NCs that are trying to gain status and leverage within the organization, on the other, the establishment (i.e. the Board and the permanent active members (PAMs)) which is trying to hold on to power amidst the profound transformations in the organization's composition. Visible conflict is not the only evidence of a continuing power struggle. So far, TI-S has been able to accommodate demands without losing too much of its power within the organization.[35]

The nature and quality of NCs

NCs are very different in nature and quality, something that is not intrinsic to TI's franchising process, but common to other INGOs. Some NCs preceded TI as well-established local NGOs of high public standing and 'have amended their constitutions to adopt the TI approaches and then become their country's national chapter' (TI Sourcebook 2000, Ch. 15). These NCs enjoy a greater degree of respect and autonomy within TI. Those created during the foundation years, such as TI-UK, TI-USA, or TI-Kenya are the bastions of TI, so to speak. They are the most pro-Board, pro-TI-S, and pro-leader. However, longevity in the organization is not the only way to ensure strong loyalty to the international organizational bodies of TI and its leadership. NCs whose existence is strictly linked to TI membership and who lack financial sustainability are equally faithful supporters. One special case was the creation of TI-Germany, founded by TI's establishment people[36] as a means to overcome the problem of identifying TI 'headquarters' as Germany's chapter.

Some NCs were created by design others by default (Lundberg 2002: 17). Some have overcome the initial dependence on the ideas, interests, and vision of TI's founders and have become institutionalized. Others remain a few-men band. Some are financially autonomous; others are unable to guarantee their subsistence without a little help from their big brother TI. Some have clear agendas in response to specific needs and problems in their respective countries; others have simply adjusted TI global priorities to their own set-tings with little applicability or impact. Some are extremely active and appear to be effective; others seem to be active only about the time of an AGM when the prospect of foreign travel looms.

Two elements contributed to this multi-faceted constellation of NCs: the various national laws of associations and taxation (which force NCs to assume a particular model of organization), and Berlin's initial incapacity to define a 'model NC'[37] and later resolution not to do so.[38] The decision not to do so was justified by both the juridical/cultural diversity of the countries concerned and the unwillingness to interfere in what should be a sponta-neous initiative. But TI has not been fully coherent in its non-interventionist approach to the formation of NCs.

TI claims that one of its top priorities is to build capacity to deliver at the grass-roots level, where most problems are felt and action is needed, without forgetting membership in a global network an adhesion to an overarching mission. In order to achieve this priority, it seeks to engage 'groups that are expressly non-partisan and non-confrontational. Consultations draw in other relevant segments of civil society – typically business leaders, journalists, religious figures, academics, existing NGOs with shared aims, members of chambers of commerce and other professional bodies – to test the interests and feasibility of forming a national chapter' (TI Sourcebook 2000, Ch. 15). Thanks to the formation of local NCs, run by local individuals and aimed at local concerns, TI thought it could finally claim the label of 'global anti-corruption movement'. But TI was not fully consistent in its grass-root approach. It suffices to read TI's Guidelines for the formation of National Chapters to have an idea of the understanding of what a movement should look like: under the grass-root façade lies a more centralized, organic, and instrumental reality. TI's own definition of 'movement' is a centralized and hierarchical organization: 'The TI movement comprises the TI interna-tional organs'.[39] It is not about ideas and people, but organs and, it goes without saying, rules and power. Moreover, 'Whenever TI is invited by a government to develop a programme in its country, a national chapter will be organized'.[40] In other words, TI has an instrumentalist view of how civil society should mobilize to promote social change: the government wishes, TI provides approach to the formation of NCs not only undermines any attempt to identify TI as a grass-root movement (Wang and Rosenau 2001: 39), it also casts serious doubts on the political impartiality and neutrality of some of these national entities.

The (political) impartiality and neutrality of NCs: The dangers of instrumentalization

Despite the Guidelines' recommendation that NCs be 'non-partisan and non-political', the predominance of the coalition-building strategy over all other traditional forms of civil society engagement – such as confrontation, protest, watchdog – opens the way to a series of comfortable compromises and conflicts of interest which put at risk TI's credibility and serious aims.

For example, the move of senior personnel of TI-Kenya to the government, and the government's definition of an anti-corruption strategy which targets primarily the outgoing incumbents and remains at the level of cosmetic measures, damages the credibility and independence of the NC as a civil society actor by making it look like a useful electoral ramp with a clearly defined political agenda. The resignation of the head of the presidential anti-corruption office, John Githongo, a leading figure of TI-Kenya, in protest against President Mwai Kibaki's alleged inertia and lack of commitment to fight corruption did not fully clarify the chapter's involvement in the whole process.[41]

The promiscuous relationship between NCs and domestic politics is also true for OECD countries. TI-Italy is run by sympathizers of the populist party *Lega Nord*, that has, on various occasions, muffled news about the current centre–right government coalition (of which *Lega* is a member), including Mr Berlusconi's successive corruption scandals. Members of TI-Italy have consistently claimed that legal reforms to soften anti-corruption laws have been 'misreported' in, for example, *The Economist*.

In the US, the matter is not so much proximity to the government, but to large American corporate interests. TI-USA has virtually said or done nothing about corruption in the US or in its business corporations abroad, but this does not come as a surprise. The chapter is largely a creation of the US corporate community. TI-USA's members are drawn almost exclusively from corporate lawyers, and its prime interest was to extend anti-corruption provisions similar to those of 1977 US Foreign Corrupt Practices Act to companies from the rest of the developed world by the adoption of the 1997 OECD Convention. Even less surprising is TI's passivity to the chapter's short-sighted view, since the latter is crucial to the financial sustainability of the former.

The financial sustainability and independence of NCs

Funding is crucial to any organization in order to carry out their activities. The capacity to raise the appropriate funds and to ensure the organization's independence vis-à-vis their donors/contributors are two important dimensions of the nature of NCs. Other relevant issues concern the transparency and independent auditing of accounts and the integrity of an NC's officers and members in relation to sources and amounts of donations.

NCs vary in the amount and sustainability of their funding. The financial needs of NCs are something that cannot be interpreted simply in 'wealthy North' and 'poor South' terms. Contrary to what one might expect, some NCs in developing countries are often better resourced than their counterparts in the northern hemisphere (for instance, Western European NCs), thanks to funding from the international donor community.

As mentioned before, the formation and franchising of new NCs is closely associated to TI's need to adjust to a changing donor panorama. The need to constitute local constituencies in order to secure continuous support of TI activities from aid and development agencies applies to the creation of NCs in developing parts of the world, as well as to some OECD countries. According to the Chairperson of TI-Canada, continuing support from the Canadian International Development Agency (CIDA) to TI was closely associated to the constitution of a local chapter.

In some cases, TI-S direct involvement and interest in NC formation was financially crucial. This was particularly the case with the inclusion of a US chapter from the start. The Chairman of the Board of TI-USA was a lawyer in the legal department of General Electric. He was a full-time TI staffer, seconded by the company to TI during the first years. This senior corporate lawyer was very active at various levels. He developed very close relationships between TI-USA and a series of national and international institutions: the US State Department (USAID),[42] the World Bank, US foundations (such as the Ford Foundation, which has made a large grant to TI), and the US business community (some members of which were known worldwide for their involvement in major corruption and fraud scandals).[43] TI-USA has played an important role in attracting funding for TI, which has granted it considerable leverage within the organization. From the standpoint of TI's moral crusade, TI-USA funding connections are probably more a problem than a solution.

Finding a sustainable funding strategy is not an easy task for most NCs and there is little help they can hope to obtain from TI-S, except managerial advice from an entity whose finances have been less than sound. In some cases, NCs have benefited from a lump sum to start business, but have been unable to design a membership and fee strategy capable of ensuring diversity of sources and regularity of funding. US money, whether from corporations, state agencies, or foundations is not welcomed in some Arab countries where there is an understanding that such aid has hidden political intentions.[44] The risk of dependence on one source of funding is also a fact for NCs in OECD countries. TI-UK and TI-Australia, for instance, have difficulties in attracting private funding and are mainly sponsored by aid agencies or national governments. In other cases, such imbalance between sources of funding is created by the view that banning certain forms of funding, namely corporate donations will guarantee the chapter's indepen-dence (TI Lebanon). The bottom line is that most NCs are in similar finan-cial straits as TI-S and have been unable to attract regular funding. Most survive on an annual income that is less than the annual salary-cum-benefits of one senior official of TI-S. This creates considerable tension between NCs and TI-S. The *raison d'être* of the latter has been measured against its decreasing capacity to attract funding for its local partners, thus leading NCs to question one of the major advantages of being part of such a network. Fixed running costs (rent and personnel) take much of TI's budget,[45] whereas money spent in actual research and the amount of money being transferred to NCs is minimal.[46] A large number of NCs in developing countries rely on international donations, primarily from Western founda-tions and aid agencies, which account for more than half of their annual income.

Financial reporting and auditing procedures are also a source of concern. The need to strengthen internal auditing systems to prevent any wrongdoing at TI-S or at NCs was raised again during the 2004 Nairobi AGM, which showed the morally charged context in which TI discusses internal govern-ance issues. Few NCs have put in place a clear accounting system compre-hensible to everyone, especially donors and the public at large. Although NCs are registered as local NGOs and subject to different national accounting regimes and auditing standards, this is not a sufficient justifica-tion for not making their annual accounts and financial statements available for public scrutiny. TI feels uneasy about the likelihood of financial impro-priety resulting from business contributions. For instance, if a donor cor-poration has bribed anyone or any organization, should TI or any NC financed by that company refuse to take their money? If a company bribes in one country, does that mean that an NC from another country, and also financed by the same corporation, must return the contribution? TI's unea-siness about these issues results from the moral high ground that it has stood on throughout the years and cannot now coherently sustain.

The financial dealings between TI and the corporate world are based on a moral paradox: whilst some NC and TI leaders are publicly in favour of the introduction of anti-corruption instruments such as 'corporate black lists' – thus raising the moral stakes against corporate misconduct – they are also too willing to build coalitions with the business sector and open their hands to attractive corporate contributions. For a corporation or politician sus-pected of corruption or facing a court prosecution to join TI or simply make a large donation to a local chapter might be quite convenient. Although TI's philosophy is sometimes stated as being to take corporations at their word, and then insist that they stick by it, there is a high price to be paid when things go wrong. TI's avowed strategy to achieve support from the private sector has brought some unpleasant experiences and bad press coverage that has damaged the organization's image.[47]

The spreading of the global anti-corruption doctrine: between ownership and replication

Although there is some variation in the areas of concern across NCs, not all have been able to define their priority areas by drawing on local contexts and issues of concern. NCs' agendas are often unrepresentative of the major corruption scandals and issues of concern in their respective countries and do not offer a holistic approach to control. Most NCs have adopted TI's global priorities as a sign of allegiance to its transnational agenda, but only a few have been active in contributing to its implementation. There are also a number of additional issues, such as securing access to information, combating money-laundering, supporting recovery of illicit assets, and creating ethics education programmes, which some NCs have started on their own initiative and which TI-S has picked up as 'good practice' to be exported to the whole network. Table 12.2 shows a comparative overview highlighting the variation of the volume and type of activities developed by NCs and their degree of autonomy in agenda setting.

Most NCs share a domestic and international interest in corruption, though priority seems to be given to the domestic interest, with very few exceptions, such as TI-UK and TI-USA who have said very little about corruption in their own countries. The NCs' autonomy in setting their own agendas is largely dependent upon their capacity to attract critical mass (for instance, through internship programmes or by establishing close relationships with academia) and financial resources. Unsustainable NCs tend to go along with TI's global priorities, which in practical terms means carrying out symbolic initiatives, such as awareness-raising ('corruption is bad'), workshops, media coverage of the latest Corruption Perceptions Index, signing of protocols and integrity pledges, and awarding public figures for their anti-corruption role.

The majority of NCs accept TI's definition of corruption and have not sat down to discuss it in detail with their peers or with TI-S. It is simply not an issue. There is a general lack of understanding of conflicting values and undemocratic effects of some anti-corruption measures when devising, recommending, or supporting governmental initiatives. At this level, different civic and democratic traditions across NCs come into play, but part of the problem also resides in TI's populist approach to corruption. TI's obsession in curbing corruption at all costs ignores both the negative implications that some anti-corruption measures have upon transition or consolidating democracies and the fact that the 'pursuit of absolute integrity' often results in dysfunctional government. In an attempt to overcome this paradox, TI has gradually developed two menus or strategies for new NCs, which are adjustable to the institutional and political contexts of the hosting country. There is what we might call a 'full menu', in which anti-corruption is understood as part of a greater social and political change (i.e. democracy promotion and consolidation). Then there is a 'light menu', in which anti-corruption is simply a

Table 12.2 Global priorities and domestic concerns (by region)

	Middle East		Europe		Africa		Latin America		Oceania & Pacific		Asia		North America	
	TI Lebanon (NC)	TI Palestine (NC)	TI UK (NC)	TI Switzerland (NC)	TI Tanzania (NC)	TI South Africa (NC)	TI Brazil (NC)	TI Argentina (NC)	TI Australia (NC)	TI PNG (NC)	TI Pakistan (NC)	TI Thailand (NC)	TI Canada (NC)	TI USA (NC)
Waves of membership	II	IV	I	II	-	II	III	I	II	-	II	II	II	I
Global priorities														
Political corruption	●												○	
Public procurement corruption	●		●		○		●	●	●	●	●			●
Corporate crime/ethics	●		●	●	●		●	●	●	●	●	●	●	●
Anti-corruption conventions			●	●	●		●	○	●		●		●	●
Additional global priorities														
Securing access to information	●						●	●	●	●	●	●	●	
Measuring corruption		●			●		●				●		●	○
Combating money laundering and supporting recovery of assets			●	●	●		●		●		●	●	●	●
Fostering anti-corruption education and ethics	●	●				●		●	●	●	●	●		
Accountability of CSOs and preventing corruption in development cooperation			●						●		●		○	
Tackling corruption in specific industries and sectors	●	●	●	○			●		●			●	●	
Domestic concerns														
Democratization and citizenship		●	●	●	●	●		●		●				
Access to and performance of justice apparatus		●						●			●			

(continued on next page)

Table 12.2 (continued)

	Middle East		Europe		Africa		Latin America		Oceania & Pacific		Asia		North America	
	TI Lebanon (NC)	TI Palestine (NC)	TI UK (NC)	TI Switzerland (NC)	TI Tanzania (NC)	TI South Africa (NC)	TI Brazil (NC)	TI Argentina (NC)	TI Australia (NC)	TI PNG (NC)	TI Pakistan (NC)	TI Thailand (NC)	TI Canada (NC)	TI USA (NC)
Complaint systems	●	●									●			
Attitude surveys											●		●	
E-governance			●				●				●		●	
Good governance		●	●	●		●	●	●			○			
Depoliticizing public service							●							
Post-war reconstruction	●													
Empowering Youth	●●											●		
Institutional, legislative and constitutional anti-corruption reform (NIS diagnosis)		●	●				●		●	●	●		●	
Privatization processes											○			
Local government		●	●								●			
Nepotism and favouritism public service		●	●											
Depoliticizing public service														
Corruption and Poverty	●	●	●			●			●	●			●●	
Regional / international scope		●	●					●	●	●	●		●	
Security	●								●	●	●			●
Whistleblowing			●	●○										
Conditionality in aid and debt relief		●	●											
Bank secrecy laws				●										

Legend: ● active/engaged; ○ interested/newly engaged
Source: Andrea Figari (TI-S staff) and NCs websites.

means to risk-free and effective development (regardless of the strengthening of civic and democratic rights in the country concerned). TI and NCs in some developing countries are more inclined towards the latter version which avoids lengthy and unpleasant debates on Western-dominated formats of anti-corruption reforms and allows for cultural relativism; whereas other NCs, especially those in Europe and Latin America, tend to prefer a more systemic approach to corruption control which cannot be disassociated from the performance of democratic institutions.

Concerns about corporate crime and political corruption are, generally speaking, regarded by NCs as secondary to public sector misconduct. Private sector anti-corruption initiatives do not go much further than the adoption of international conventions while political corruption is something that a large number of NCs find hard to address, often due to the incapacity of their senior officials to keep at arm's length from the business and political sectors. These two TI priorities have witnessed little progress, partly due to the coalition-building strategy recommended by TI and adopted by all NCs. In most cases, coalition-building has not been translated into effective and independent partnerships, but into rather instrumental or symbolic gatherings with the political and business sectors. Where some results have been obtained, it has been through a watchdog approach and by assessing, analysing, and diagnosing risk areas and collecting, publicizing, and supplying information to stakeholders.

The strategies of engagement are largely standardized. Most NCs do not see themselves as engaged in protest and street mobilizing, but rather as opinion-forming organizations. In line with TI's position, their major strategies of engagement are about informing and raising awareness and, to some extent, lobbying and pressing decision-makers to adopt certain corruption control instruments. The coalition-building strategy is in itself evidence of TI's lack of a grass-roots composition. To compare TI with another sector, trade unions have also developed partnership strategies of negotiation vis-à-vis decision-makers, because (un)employment, similar to corruption, is a policy issue that raises an ultimate common interest between the parties involved. However, common interest does not mean uniform interest. It is not unusual that trade unions decide to abandon negotiations and return to strikes and street protests. In fact, they do not use the word 'coalition-building', preferring 'negotiation'. In other words, they are not coalition partners, but social partners. A coalition presumes a strategic bond between the partners that regularly leads to a real or perceived compromise and amalgamation of positions and interests, and hence a shared responsibility in the decisions or actions taken. Such promiscuity of roles and interests inevitably hampers the free judgement and independent action of NCs. Working close to governments raises the possibility that some politicians might use TI as a political ramp and makes TI co-responsible for the (lack of) success with regard to government anti-corruption policies.

Conclusion

Today TI is represented in more than 90 countries from tiny Pacific Islands to colossal Russia, from developed to developing countries, from north, south, east, and west, consolidated democracies and very imperfect ones, countries with high perceived levels of corruption, such as Nigeria, and countries with low perceived levels of corruption, such as Sweden. In terms of countries, TI represents 40 per cent of the political world as we know it today. Numbers are still growing, but the fourth wave of franchising takes place in a less favourable context – TI has lost much of its initial flair and shine – and under a more scrutinized, closed accession/membership process its democratic deficits have become apparent.

The mode of franchising adopted by TI is quite puzzling for an organization that claims to be an embodiment of civil society. Its constituency looks more like the UN General Assembly than a people's movement. The decision to constitute single national units (thus excluding the possibility of having subnational units or more than one unit per country) has had its pluses and minuses. On the one hand, TI has been able to acquire a hegemonic position in the industry of anti-corruption and to launch well-synchronized and global awareness-raising actions thanks to its strategy of franchising. On the other hand, it has converted the self-proclaimed movement into a bureaucratic, conservative, and resource-draining organization, excluding along the way many valuable contributions.

TI's actions, priorities, and strategies are replicated to a greater or lesser extent at the local level. Most NCs have not been able to define their priority areas and, with some conspicuous exceptions, their high-profile activities are reduced to engaging in the synchronized symbolic initiatives put in place by TI-S every year, such as the launching of the CPI or the Global Corruption Report. The coalition-building strategy which TI induces NCs to adopt vis-à-vis the political and business actors in their own countries can be more of a liability than a success. By not ensuring the arm's length distance from decision-makers and the corporate world, TI and its NCs compromise their independence, mission, and objectives. Although some chapters have put in place a balanced and sustainable system of financing, most depend on one source of donations which leaves their independence and integrity in peril, and with considerable risk to TI's image and reputation.

TI's decision to franchise was not purely driven by the need to boost participation, to increase critical mass and knowledge about local problems, or to broaden its territorial representation. It was also a strategy of adjustment to a changing donor panorama. The reverse side of the coin is that as soon as enlarged membership and franchising were set on track, there was little TI could do to stop the increasing demands from NCs for greater internal transparency, accountability, and democratization. We could argue that the recent dismissal of TI's CEO and the extinction of the CEO position (with executive powers) and its replacement with a managing director (with coordinating competences only) was a victory of the periphery against the core. However, the inevitable recentralization of power in the new Chair, Mrs Huguette Labelle, may raise interesting power dynamics for the internal governance of TI in the near future. TI certainly faces important governance challenges ahead as numbers of NCs grow and its capacity to raise funds to NCs and deliver innovate products is less convincing.

TI stands today as the world's best-known anti-corruption actor. It has been able to both institutionalize the anti-corruption norm and spread its doctrine at the global level via the action of its local constituencies. Its role in the global anti-corruption scene is neither marginal nor expendable.

Notes

1 <http://www.transparency.org/about_us> accessed 19 August 2008.
2 There are plenty of NGOs at the national level from which TI can chose to develop partnerships or propose for NC membership, but TI has no real competitors in the global arena. Once TI captured the issue of anti-corruption and consolidated its brand, it would have been difficult for a new INGO to emerge and try to leapfrog TI's monopoly in this domain. TI seized effectively an opportunity structure which emerged as a result of various conjunctural factors (Mény and de Sousa 1999; Krastev 2000), but this does not mean that it is the only INGO with an interest in corruption-related issues. Global Witness and George Soros' Open Society Institute, which were founded about the same time (1993) and with whom TI has collaborated regularly, also have an interest in and, to an extent, a different understanding of corruption and anti-corruption. Not surprisingly, TI has generally avoided creating close partnerships with other, more established INGOs with whom it has much in common, such as Amnesty International, Friends of the Earth, and Doctors Without Borders as part of a strategy of territorial demarcation. Having said this, some collaboration between TI and other INGOs has taken place, but only after careful consideration of the expected costs and benefits involved. Strategic cooperation has taken place when the partners facilitate TI's access to power circles and potential sources of funding. These criteria have equally been used to refuse certain partnerships (Cisar 2003: 47).
3 In order to simplify the designation of NCs, the expression 'TI-country' (e.g. TI-Brazil) will often be used as a substitute for the chapter's real name (e.g. *Transparência Brasil*). By no means is it intended to give a subsidiary role to the NCs, since, formally speaking, these locally registered NGOs do not depend upon TI to exist as legal entities.
4 According to Wang and Rosenau there are 'two reasons why TI is neither a social movement nor transnational activist network closely linked with grassroots organizations. First, ... activist networks that base their campaigns on "short and clear" causal chains and that can galvanize support by images of bodily damage, especially to the vulnerable members of the population, are likely to succeed. But neither of these is easily done regarding corruption. ... Second, the covert and dispersed nature of corruption ... indicates that it is hard for potential participants to know that they have made a difference; and yet this knowledge is the lifeblood of any social movement' (2001: 39). In the same vein, Cisar argues that TI has never sought confrontational action as an anti-corruption strategy (2003: 46). Protest is central to the definition of social movements (Della Porta and Diani 2006: 20–29), whereas building coalitions with all power actors has been TI's strategy throughout its existence (See 'TI Approach', <http://www.

transparency.org/about_us/approach> accessed 2 November 2007). This explains why TI prefers to sit at the 'high table' with World Economic Forum (WEF) institutions instead of being 'out on the streets' standing in opposition to the promoters of neo-liberalism and globalization (world governing and financial institutions, corporations, governments of powerful/developed countries). This is also evidence that, intentionally or inadvertently, TI's anti-corruption discourse has conveniently married the neo-liberal discourse promoted by those international agencies whose action TI claims to have contested (Hindess 2005, 2004c, Börzel and Risse 2002).

5 It is precisely in those countries where TI's franchising process has followed local civil society mobilizations that the relationships with TI-S have been particularly difficult. This was particularly the case with The Philippines and Brazil, whose NCs have always rejected the idea of 'incorporation' and a top-down approach to agenda setting. *Transparência Brasil* has recently renounced its NC status and opted to maintain a non-institutionalized cooperative relationship with TI without statutory obligations of any sort, treating TI as one amongst several potential partners in the field of anti-corruption.

6 The research material used to produce this chapter comprises both interviews with representatives of NCs and TI-S officials, as well as the examination of their websites and other relevant documentation. Interviews were open-ended and focused on regional and national differences in conceptualizing corruption; the structure and functioning of the National Chapter, its actions, strategies and programmes; the role of research in the organization's activities; funding issues; and the relationship with partners. Most interviews took place during TI's Annual Membership Meeting (AMM) in Nairobi, 6–12 October 2004.

7 *Vanguard* newspaper, Nigeria, 30 November 2004.

8 Huguette Labelle is a powerful figure in Canada. She served in several state department offices before she was appointed President of the Canadian International Development Agency (CIDA) where she worked for almost seven years, during which she was active in over 100 countries. Her election as Chairperson of TI was very important in a period during which TI was facing important financial difficulties. CIDA is currently one of the major donors to TI.

9 Initially, the founders had more humble expectations of TI's franchising process: they thought that the organization would only reach approximately 15 NCs in a decade or so.

10 The fight against corruption is still mainly, if not mostly, a national-based and national-oriented effort. Democracy is a territorial-based concept and if the fight against corruption is meant to improve its quality or ensure its normal functioning, it will have to be implemented at the domestic level, responding to the exceptions of its citizens, and coping with national leaders' predisposition to do something about it. People show only limited concern about what has been done and how successful the fight against corruption has been in neighbouring countries. People may resort to stereotyped visions of foreign societies and political systems, which CPI has probably reinforced, but remain largely indifferent to corruption and anti-corruption efforts elsewhere.

11 *TI History*, from the TI website <http://www.transparency.org/about_ti/history.html> accessed 10 May 2007 (webpage no longer available).

12 It was Fredrik Galtung who succeeded in breaking this mould when he persuaded Eigen to accept an exiting Argentinean NGO, *Poder Ciudadano*, as a national chapter, on the grounds that it had already filled the space there might otherwise have been for a national chapter.

13 Dahik had been at the World Bank and was a personal friend of Peter Eigen. His relationship with TI ended in 1995 when he was accused of corruption and he fled the country to live in Costa Rica where he was granted political asylum.

14 The fact that TI was founded under the German Law of Associations is in great measure a practical decision related to Eigen's central role in setting up the organization. It would have been politically unwise to set up TI 'headquarters' in the US, as it would immediately be regarded as an instrument of those US corporations pressing for a level playing field, that is an anti-bribery convention. There is no clear explanation, however, as to why it was not founded in Britain, which has both a strong NGO tradition (Oxfam, Amnesty International) and one of the world's major business centres (TI's initial target), which leaves us only with the 'officialized' version of making things easier for Eigen to start his vision of some kind of organization to mobilize global concern against corruption. Moreover, an offer had been made by the government of The Netherlands to fund TI in accordance with other Dutch NGOs – i.e. by providing 50 per cent of its budget as a grant and respecting its full independence and autonomy. No explanation is available as to why this offer (which would have given the organization a firm financial basis) was rejected.

15 The new Chair from Canada, the President of TI-US, and one of the initial PAMs, Frank Vogl President of the Vogl Communications.

16 There was a previous failed attempt at constituting a NC in Brazil by an organization *Transparência, Consciência e Cidadania*. In 2000, another Brazilian NGO *Transparência Brazil* became an accredited NC of TI.

17 Although we can talk of accreditation previously, the rules and principles underpinning this process were only defined in 2003, when a new Membership Accreditation Committee was put in place.

18 TI NCs are free to organize themselves in the way they see fit and to define their own mandates and work programmes, but 'they must follow two important rules of conduct: 1) they will not investigate and expose individual cases of corruption as such activity would undermine efforts to build coalitions which promote professional and technical improvements of anti-corruption systems; and 2) they must avoid party politics as partisan activity would damage TI's credibility' (TI Sourcebook 2000, Ch. 15). These two principles were agreed to by the initial NCs at the first AGM, in Quito, Ecuador, in May 1994 and still constitute the baseline of TI's membership *acquis*. During the Annual Membership Meeting held in Prague on 6 October 2001, TI defined these standards and policies in greater detail in the Statement of Vision, Values and Guiding Principles of Transparency International (called the Umbrella Statement).

19 National Contact is an embryonic membership status, based on loose forms of association, attributed to certain domestic NGOs, which may or not may become full TI members – i.e. National Chapters – in the future.

20 *Fundacíon Ética y Democracia*.

21 *Probidad*.

22 Creating change together towards a world free of corruption and TI's Annual Membership Meeting, 9–10 October 2004, Nairobi, Kenya. The author of this chapter attended the meeting as an observer.

23 Along with two other companies, Hydro and Telenor, Statoil helped to set up the Norwegian chapter of Transparency International with a NOK 250,000 (approximately US$39,960). In June 2004, the Norwegian oil company Statoil was found guilty of attempted corruption in Iran relating to a business contract and agreed to pay a 20-million kroner (US$2.97 million) fine imposed by the Norwegian Economic Crime Unit, *Økokrim*. Following these events, Statoil's top three CEOs resigned and Jannik Lindbæk, previously chairman of the Board in the bank DnB, and chairman of the board of TI-Norway was appointed as the new Chairman of Statoil. His role as chairman of the Norwegian NC gave him the greatest leverage to mend Statoil's torn image.

24 After starting with an income of around US$591,581 in 1994, by 2000, when TI had become a reputable 'brand' in anti-corruption, the organization was cashing

in US$3,769,000. Ten years later, TI was running a budget of US$8,820,853. However, it should be underlined that as TI consolidated its organization and finances, its innovative capacity to attract project-based funding gradually declined: from US$213,207 in 1994 to nearly US$4,075,824 in 2000–01, and down to around US$346,402 in 2006, as shown in TI financial statements published in the Annual Reports.

25 Some NCs reject the term headquarters to define TI-S. They see no hierarchical structure or binding bottom-up responsiveness. In their view, TI ought to operate as a horizontal accountability organization and TI-S's *raison d'être* is to serve NCs by aggregating critical mass, fostering the organization's capability to apply for funding, and enabling intra-communication and coordination of activities.

26 *Poder Ciudadano.*

27 *Corporación Latinoamericana para el Desarrollo* (CLD).

28 The current Managing Director of CLD.

29 See n 13.

30 *TI History*, from the TI website <http://www.transparency.org/about_ti/history.html> accessed 10 May 2008 (webpage no longer available).

31 As a result, TI has a number of PAMs that have not attended AGMs for a number of years and that appear to have lost interest in the organization. There have been suggestions made to the effect that their membership generates proxy votes at AGMs to enable an inner clique to control membership of the Board. This was one of the sensitive governance issues dealt in Galtung's letter of resignation.

32 The Official Chapter Representatives are appointed by their national executive committees.

33 NCs are regulated by their own national laws and regulations, whilst their chairpersons or legal representatives have legal status under German law as permanent (yet conditional) voting members of TI.

34 Three seats in the Membership Accreditation Committee are held by non-voting members of TI.

35 At the time of the 2004 Nairobi meeting, TI-Brazil was 'at war' with TI concerning a membership contractual clause which would compel NCs to follow the guidelines of the Board, a conditionality that the chapter was not prepared to accept. The issue was conveniently ignored during the general meeting. Meanwhile, TI-Brazil refused to sign the contract and, as a consequence, it was threatened with disaccreditation. At that stage, *Transparência Brasil* decided to bring the matter to the knowledge of the other NCs. A year later, TI was forced to review its position as contestation started to mount. The episode is both an example of TI's unsuccessful attempt to impose its will upon NCs as well as an example of the fact that, even in a crisis situation, accommodation can be sought with success. Whether TI's withdrawal of the contractual clause represents a political loss to the organization, it is a disputable question. By ceding to the contractual demand, which had only agenda-setting implications, TI was able to maintain the network's cohesiveness and move the chapters' attention away from more serious governance matters such as the recent recentralization of powers in TI's chairperson.

36 Hansjörg Elshorst, one of the most influential founders and individual members of TI, was a major supporter of the idea of a separate German National Chapter and would later serve as the first Chair of TI-Deutschland.

37 In the early days of TI, hardly any of the founding fathers, including Eigen himself, had a clear idea of what an NGO looked like. TI's second Managing Director, Hansjorg Elshorst, formerly an official with GTZ (the German Development Agency), openly boasted that 'None of us have any experience of civil society'.

38 'There are no hard and fast rules about the structure or status of a non-governmental organisation in a country which wishes to work in support of TI's objectives' *TI*

Guidelines for the formation of National Chapters, from the TI website <http:// www.transparency.org/contacting_ti/chapters/guidelines-overview.html> (webpage no longer available). *The Guidelines for National Chapters of Transparency International* is now available at <http://www.transparency.org/about_us/organisation/ accreditation/guidelines> (accessed 19 August 2008).

39 *Guidelines for National Chapters of Transparency International*, from the TI website <http://www.transparency.org/about_us/organisation/accreditation/guidelines> (accessed 19 August 2008).

40 Ibid.

41 *BBC World*, Tuesday 8 February 2005.

42 From the beginning of TI, USAID has funded several TI annual meetings and sponsored the participation of National Chapter representatives in the International Anti Corruption Conference (IACC). The support has made an enormous difference to the institutionalization and projection of TI. The impact of Eigen and TI at the international level has largely been dependent on that.

43 To mention two: General Electrics and Lockheed Martin. For further information on the business community that supports TI-USA, see <http://www.transparency-usa. org/intro.html> accessed 19 August 2008.

44 For the Palestine NC, US funding would be intolerable to the majority of Palestinians and would discredit the organization's work. However, the chapter is largely funded by other Western donors. Foreign money comes from UNDP for Palestine, Scandinavian aid agencies, the British Council (for the resource centre, books, and website), and German foundations, such as *Konrad Adenauer*.

45 The three major fixed costs are: (1) rent of TI-S in Berlin; (2) rent of TI-UK; and (3) TI-S staff.

46 The figures presented at the 2004 AGM were: US$6,000 per region with one quarter of this amount being retained by TI-S for the development of common projects.

47 On April 2000, *Le Monde Diplomatique* published an article criticizing the dubious relationship between TI and the US corporate world (an English translation is available online at <http://mondediplo.com/2000/04/05debrie> (accessed 19 August 2008)): 'En témoigne le succès rencontré auprès des médias par la publication d'un indice annuel de cotation des pays corrupteurs et corrompus établi par Transparency International, association de lobbying, correspondante de la CIA et financée par des gouvernements et des entreprises, surtout américaines, expertes en la matière, telles Lockheed, Boeing, IBM, General Motors, Exxon, General Electric ou Texaco. Les campagnes anti-corruption, relayées par les organisations internationales (Banque mondiale, FMI, OCDE), n'ont d'autre objectif que la « bonne gouvernance » d'une criminalité financière désormais intégrée à la mondialisation des marchés, sous la houlette de la démocratie américaine, la plus corrompue de la planète. […]' (Christian de Brie, 'Dans l'archipel planétaire de la criminalité financière: Etats, mafias et transnationales comme larrons en foire', *Le Monde Diplomatique*, Avril 2000: 4–5).

13 Conclusion

Luís de Sousa, Peter Larmour and Barry Hindess

Here we return to some of the issues raised in our Introduction. The other chapters in this collection help answer, or reframe, several of the questions that originally concerned us, particularly:

- the reasons for the explosion of international interest in corruption;
- the balance between moralistic and professional approaches;
- the relationships between NGOs and official anti-corruption agencies;
- the types of policy transfer involved; and
- the role of Transparency International (TI), and its Corruption Perceptions Index (CPI).

We go on to suggest two issues for further research: the impact of the new international interest on levels of corruption itself; and the relationship between democracy and (anti-)corruption.

Why the international interest?

We saw the end of the Cold War as dividing the earlier period of national anti-corruption campaigns, particularly in Europe, from the more global interest in corruption since. Certainly the collapse of the Soviet Union released the successor states that later sought accession to the EU. The chapters by Smilov, Dahl, and Sampson each analyse the process whereby formerly socialist applicants to join the EU adopted, in form at least, the measures that the EU required (even if these were more than the Union required of its longer standing members, such as France, Italy, and Germany). The chapter by Andersson and Heywood shows how the end of the Cold War resonated through Asia. Vietnam, losing its Soviet patron, turned to the West and had to accept its conditions. The end of the Cold War also hastened the processes of democratization in South Korea and Taiwan, as described in Göbel's chapter. In both countries there was widespread popular discontent with corruption, though Göbel found that 'democratization did not obliterate but even increased the intensity and scope of corruption'. Schmidt-Pfister's chapter describes how Russia itself became more open to the foreign funding of domestic NGOs, though the government sought to outflank them by appeals to nationalism, and took on the role of campaigner against corruption in its own ranks.

As these examples show, the more proximate cause is the increasing influence of international organizations, including the EU, rather than the end of the Cold War itself. Even as far away as the Pacific, the EU was critical in international sanctions against the Fiji coup, in spite of the coup leader's anti-corruption rhetoric. Fiji depended on preferential access for its sugar into Europe, and the EU believed that democracy was more important, when it came to the crunch, than anti-corruption. Heywood and Andersson emphasize the influence of the World Bank in their discussion of governance. As Sampson and de Sousa's chapters suggest, TI itself may be best seen as a new form of international organization, and in some ways is a creature of the World Bank. It was formed by Bank dissidents, particularly Peter Eigen, a former staffer, and his anti-corruption message was at first rejected and later embraced when Wolfensohn took charge of the Bank.

Moralism and professionalism

In the introduction we contrasted an earlier, pragmatic approach to controlling corruption with a new moralism associated with social movements. Our contributors tell a more complicated story. Anechiarico points to a long history of moralistic opposition to corruption in the US, particularly from the late nineteenth century Progressive movement, and notes that the latter also promoted ideas of public service professionalism. The Progressives compared their campaigns against corruption to the campaign against slavery. Progressive assumptions about the contamination of 'good government' by 'politics' underlie much of the global anti-corruption rhetoric in general, and US international anti-corruption policy since the 1970s in particular. Several chapters point out the dangers and difficulties that anti-corruption campaigns cause for the practice of democratic politics. Moralism enters through the media as the scandals and *affaires* referred to in Mény's Foreword. Larmour's chapter on Fiji shows links between the coup leaders' rhetoric and Catholic religious morality, and the old Moral Rearmament Campaign that began in the 1930s.

Sampson distinguishes the moralism of activists, with their doctrinal disputes, from the professionalism of the anti-corruption industry, represented by the office workers in TI Berlin. Dahl neatly brings it to the micro-level through her descriptions of the way TI followers in the Baltic treat the ideal types in the TI Source Book as a 'bible', and through her idea of 'glorification', in which activists sanctify each other and their tasks.

The relationships between NGOs and official anti-corruption agencies

The chapters show that the key relationships for NGOs are with their funders rather than their official counterparts at national level. At the international level, TI has no strong links with intergovernmental organizations dealing with crime or justice. de Sousa's and Dahl's chapters show some national TI groups engaging with official anti-corruption agencies (ACAs) – for example, in drawing up a 'corruption map' in Lithuania. Smilov describes how at a certain point in the development of anti-corruption politics in Eastern Europe, governments reached out to the NGOs as a way of controlling the discourse on corruption. TI's coalitional ideology would certainly encourage such relationships. In the cases of Kenya and Fiji, however, the chapters show the dangers of getting too close. de Sousa mentions how leading lights of TI-Kenya joined the Kibaki government (though not all stayed on board). Larmour's chapter describes how the 2006 coup in Fiji split the national TI chapter three ways: one member of the Board becoming Attorney General in an interim government led by the military commander; another resigning in protest; while the rest of the Board and management tried to continue to act as an autonomous pressure group, promoting their anti-corruption agenda without compromising on their commitment to democracy.

Policy transfer and copying

The conventional model of policy transfer suggests a movement from the First World to the Second or Third. This is too simple, as Larmour (2005) has shown. Smilov's chapter in this volume points out that, in the case of corruption, the EU accession criteria did not involve the transfer of European models, as there were none available.

The typical anti-corruption export model was devised in the Third World circumstances of late colonial Hong Kong, and later transferred to the different circumstances of three Australian states, South Korea, and Fiji (as Göbel's and Larmour's chapter describe). The processes of transfer were partly mimetic – a search for 'international best practice', even if it was only loosely relevant to local circumstances – and partly coercive, insisted upon as a condition for membership of a valued club. As Mény's foreword proposed, 'Democracy and good governance are desirable objectives but they are also straitjackets imposed by powerful actors from outside.'

Doig's chapter deals particularly with the difficulties of exporting generic ACAs, and emphasizes the managerial and implementation issues. High expectations combined with low resources and capacity meant that they were almost bound to fail. Schmidt-Pfister's chapter on Russia shows the way a government can delegitimate NGOs with foreign ties and funding. Göbel's chapter spells out the political difficulties of introducing an ACA, and the importance of understanding the broader social forces at work. Different social and political structures explained why Korea introduced an ACA after democratization but Taiwan didn't. The transfer seems to have been easier in parts of Eastern Europe, with Smilov's chapter describing how investigative and prosecutorial agencies were being created after the first wave of comprehensive but shallow 'omnibus' anti-corruption programmes. In Fiji the democratic government was moving slowly to introduce the Independent Commission Against Corruption (ICAC) that the coup established within months. The conclusions about transfer are thus somewhat contradictory. In some ways the process seems very difficult, an effect of the resistance posed by local conditions, or the absence of local champions. In other ways the process seems too easy – a facile adoption of best practice that is at best formalistic or symbolic.

The role of TI and its Corruption Perceptions Index (CPI)

The last few chapters deal particularly with TI, the original anti-corruption NGO, and still the main player in what Sampson calls, rather sourly, the anti-corruption industry. Both Sampson and de Sousa dispute its self-description as a movement, pointing to its character as an organization. Sampson notices the absence of doctrinal disputes and dissent – the characteristics of a movement – in the quiet, corporate style of TI-S. The academics are often irritated by the way that TI eschews discussion of what counts as corruption, in favour of getting on with the job of fighting it. And, not surprisingly, TI gets irritated by carping criticism from academics, particularly political scientists. (It gets more professional sympathy from economists, who can use its CPI.) A quiet professionalism also seems to pervade the Baltic branches of TI, and, in spite of the complications brought about by the coup, the branch in Fiji. De Sousa characterizes TI's structure as a franchising operation – bestowing its brand on particular local organizations, and ensuring that they meet standards of behaviour that do not besmirch it. He also describes the painful problems of governance that it encountered in its rapid growth from a small group of insiders – friends of Peter Eigen, its founder – to a global international organization, faced with demands for equity, democracy, and inclusion. On the way it lost founding members like Jeremy Pope and Fredrik Galtung who set up their own breakaway Tiri.[1]

Schmidt-Pfister steps back and locates TI in an alphabet soup of national and regional NGOs in Russia, some looking for overseas funding, others eschewing it. She sees it engaged in a form of information politics through the annual announcement of the CPI, and the eddying debates about reliability and validity that it generates. The CPI remains TI's signature product, although it has since produced other indices that try to take the point of view of the victim of bribery (the Bribe Payers Index (BPI)) or the ordinary citizen (the Global Corruption Barometer). Its difficulty is that the CPI does not register change particularly well and therefore contributes to the sense that all this new anti-corruption activity has generated a great deal of talk, training, and networking, but with very little perceptible impact on the level of corruption itself.

Issues for further research

There has been no end in sight to the numerous corruption scandals that have shaken most countries' public institutions, as well as some of the high-profile international organizations that have adopted an anti-corruption agenda, such as the UN, the EU, and the World Bank. This persistence brings us back to Hindess' original question: why are all these activists and agencies so busily engaged in an enterprise that seems to have so little impact on corruption itself? Schmidt-Pfister's chapter argues for setting aside the questions of success and effectiveness until we have a clearer understanding of the processes of coalition-building in particular national contexts. Doig's chapter, by contrast, is more practically focused on effectiveness, citing the United Nations Development Programme's (UNDP) finding that there are very few successful independent anti-corruption agencies (ACAs) (UNDP 2005b: 5). He looks for answers in ACAs' internal management processes. Whichever way the authors approach the problem, the chapters tend to describe (or quote other authorities to the effect that) the results of recent anti-corruption activity have been meagre, limited or mixed. Smilov is more positive, arguing while 'no reliable performance measurement device' has yet been discovered there is 'no doubt' that ACAs could, in the right circumstances, produce 'positive results'. Both Singapore and Hong Kong have gained a reputation for clean business markets in the East thanks to the 'cleaning' action of their anti-corruption agencies (Corrupt Practices Investigation Bureau (CPIB) and Independent Commission Against Corruption (ICAC) respectively). Anechiarico suggests that, in the New York case, the new Independent Private Sector Inspector Generals (IPSIGs) are likely to increase levels of integrity. Impact is clearly one issue for further research.

A second area for further research is the difficult relationship between democracy, democratization, and corruption, dealt with most directly in Heywood and Andersson's chapter. The moral tone and econometric way in which corruption is now discussed in multilateral and academic circles have pushed aside the older tradition of research about the sociology and role of corruption in modernizing societies represented here in Göbel's chapter. Hindess has argued elsewhere (2000) that democracy, at least until the early twentieth century, was often regarded with some suspicions as a source of corrupt government. Now the international doctrine of good governance assumes democracy and anti-corruption march in step. Anti-corruption is expected to improve the quality of democracy's core institutions, safeguard the principles underpinning its functioning, and reinforce citizens' support to its cause.

The chapters show a more complicated picture. Heywood and Andersson draw particularly on the pioneering scepticism of Ivan Krastev and his colleagues who noticed the way that donor-sponsored anti-corruption campaigns in Eastern Europe seemed to be undermining democratic politics, or at least emptying it of policy content. Schmidt-Pfister's chapter describes

Russian politics in the period after its *kompromat* phase of mutual accusations of corruption. Russia has become more nationalist and popular under Putin but perhaps less democratic. Anechiarico traces the history of anti-corruption in the oldest democracy. He tells us how the spoils system was seen by Andrew Jackson, at least, as a democratic alternative to the elitism of America's immediate post-colonial government. The subsequent Progressive movement sought to draw a bright line between the dirty business of democratic politics and the professional business of administration, but the subsequent growth of government obscured it.

The influential model of an ICAC was devised in the undemocratic circumstances of late colonial Hong Kong, and the ICAC has survived elections in Hong Kong and the reunification with China. Göbel's chapter shows how democratization in Taiwan and South Korea created new opportunities for corruption even if popular opinion was opposed to it. The later Fiji case shows a military government unleashing a popular cleanup campaign that its democratically elected predecessors had failed to achieve.

Finally, by highlighting the problems TI itself has had with internal democracy, de Sousa's chapter also shows the old truism about moralizing public life: public virtues, private vices. Leaders and their organizations can rarely live up to the anti-corruption rhetoric they direct at the abstract 'system' or onto concrete adversaries. TI's public intransigence towards corruption contrasts with its managerial willingness to engage with corporate sponsorship. But a similar dilemma is faced by populist and even opposition political parties whose internal processes do not necessarily live up to the high standards they insist of governments. The fight against corruption, the deployment of populist tactics, and the struggle for improved democracy represent an unresolved dilemma of modern governance.

Notes

1 Tiri is a Maori word, not an acronym, though it mischievously invokes TI. Tiri's website tells us 'its meanings include the protection of society by the removal of no-go areas (taboos) and the lifting of prohibitions or obstructions', see <www.tiri.org>.

Bibliography

ABC News, 8 June 2007.

Abramo, C.W. (2005) 'How Far Go Perceptions', *Working Paper Transparência Brasil*, Online. Available HTTP: <http://www.transparencia.org.br/docs/HowFar.pdf> (accessed 17 May 2006).

Adams, G.B. and Balfour, D.L. (2004) *Unmasking Administrative Evil*, Rev. edn., Armonk, NY: M.E. Sharpe.

Agence France Presse (2004), 'US cracking down on corrupt Latin Americans: Bush envoy', 22 January.

Altheide, D. and Snow, R.P. (1979) *Media Logic*, Beverly Hills: Sage.

American Bar Association (2007) "About the ABA". Online. Available HTTP: <http://www.abanet.org> (accessed 2 October 2007).

American Institute of Certified Public Accountants (2007) 'Professional Resources'. Online. Available HTTP: <https://www.aicpa.org> (accessed 2 October 2007).

Amnesty International (2005a) 'Report 2005. China'. Online. Available HTTP: < http://web.amnesty.org/report2005/chn-summary-eng> (accessed 21 March 2006)

—— (2005b) 'Report 2005. Vietnam'. Online. Available HTTP: <http://web.amnesty. org/report2005/vnm-summary-eng> (accessed 2006-03-21).

Amsterdam, A. and Bruner, J. (2000) *Minding the Law*, Cambridge, Mass.: Harvard University Press.

Andvig, J.C. and Fjeldstad, O.-H. (2001) 'Corruption: a review of contemporary research', *Report R 2001*:7, Chr. Michelsen Institute, Development Studies and Human Rights.

Anechiarico, F. (2005) 'The Cure for a Public Disease: The Foibles and Future of Corruption Control' in H.G. Frederickson and R. Ghere, *Ethics in Public Management*. Armonk, NY: M.E. Sharpe.

Anechiarico, F. and Jacobs, J. (1996) *The Pursuit of Absolute Integrity: How Corruption Control Makes Government Ineffective*, Chicago and London: The University of Chicago Press.

Argyiades, D. (2001) 'The International Anticorruption Campaigns: Whose Ethics?' in Gerald Caiden *et al.* (eds), *Where Corruption Lives*, Bloomfield, KY: Kumarian Press, 217–26.

Associated Press (2002) 'Businesswoman sentenced to death for embezzlement in southern Vietnam', November 30, 2002.

—— (2004) 'U.S. makes concessions at Summit of the Americas in effort to smooth relations', 13 January, 2004.

Audit Commission (UK) (1995). *Paying the Piper ... Calling the Tune.* London: HMSO.

Bajolle, J. (2006) 'The Origins and Motivations of the Current Emphasis on Corruption: The Case of Transparency International' paper presented at the *Workshop 2: The International Anti-Corruption Movement*, European Consortium for Political Research Joint Sessions of Workshops, Nicosia, Cyprus, 25–30 April (unpublished).

Barry, D. (2000) 'Courthouse That Tweed Built Seeks to Shed Notorious Past', *New York Times*, December 12, Sec.B: 1.

BBC World, 'Kenya's anti-graft czar resigns' BBC News / Africa, Tuesday, 8 February, 2005, 14:26 GMT. Online. Available HTTP: <http://news.bbc.co.uk/2/hi/africa/4245767.stm> (accessed 19 August 2008).

Bertucci, G. and Yi Armstrong, E. (2000) 'Why anti-corruption crusades often fail to win lasting victories', *The Anti-corruption Summit 2000*, 21–23 September 2000, Arlington, Virginia, USA. Online. Available HTTP: <http://www.respondanet.com/english/anti_corruption/reports/presentation_materials/Bertucci-Speech.doc> (accessed 7 February 2006).

Bicchieri, C. and Duffy, J. (1997) 'Corruption Cycles' in Heywood (ed.) *Political Corruption*, Oxford: Blackwell/PSA, 61–79.

Blechinger, V. (2000) *Report on Recent Bribery Scandals, 1996–2000*. Online, Available HTTP: <http://unpan1.un.org/intradoc/groups/public/documents/APCITY/UNPAN013119.pdf> (accessed 30 October 2007).

Bloomberg, W. (2005) 'Anti-corruption campaigns becoming crucial for Asian leaders', *Taipei Times* Friday, 5 August. Online. Available HTTP: <www.taipeitimes.com/News/editorials/archives/2005/08/05/2003266523> (accessed 21 March 2006).

Blustein, P. (2001) The Chastening. Inside the crisis that rocked the global financial system and humbled the IMF, Cambridge, MA: Public Affairs/Perseus Books.

Booth, S. (1993) *Crisis Management Strategy*, London: Routledge.

Börzel, T.A. and Risse, T. (2002) 'Public-Private Partnerships: Effective and Legitimate Tools of International Governance?' in E. Grande and L.W. Pauly (eds) *Complex Sovereignty: On the Reconstitution of Political Authority in the 21st Century*, Toronto: University of Toronto Press, 195–216.

Bosco, J. (1994) 'Taiwan Factions. Guanxi, Patronage, and the State in Local Politics' in M.A. Rubinstein (ed.) *The Other Taiwan. 1945 to the Present*, Armonk, NY: M.E. Sharpe, 114–44.

Brademas, J. and Heimann, F. (1998) 'Tackling International Corruption: No longer Taboo', *Foreign affairs*, 77 (5): 17.

Brint, S. (1996) *In an Age of Experts*, Princeton, NJ: Princeton University Press.

Brown, A.J. (2003) 'The Leaning Tower of NISA: towards a framework methodology for National Integrity Systems Assessments', *Working paper, Griffith University Key Centre for Ethics, Law, Justice and Governance*.

Brown, E. and Cloke, J. (2004) 'Neoliberal Reform, Governance and Corruption in the South: Assessing the International Anti-Corruption Crusade', *Antipode,* 36 (2): 272–94.

Brunsson, N. and Jacobsson, B. (2000) *A world of standards*, Oxford: Oxford University Press.

Burnes, B. (1992) *Managing Change*, London: Pitman Publishing.

Caiden, G. et al. (eds) (2001) *Where Corruption Lives*, Bloomfield, CT: Kumarian Press.

Carothers, T. (2006) *Confronting the Weakest Link: Aiding Political Parties in New Democracies*, Washington, DC: Carnegie Endowment for International Peace.

—— (2000) *Aiding Democracy Abroad: The Learning Curve,* Washington, DC: Carnegie Endowment for International Peace.

Carothers, T. and Ottaway, M. (2005) *Uncharted Journey: Promoting Democracy in the Middle East,* Washington, DC: Carnegie Endowment for International Peace.

Carter J. et al. (1990) *Korea Old and New. A History,* Cambridge, MA: Harvard University Press.

Case, W. (2003) *Politics in Southeast Asia. Democracy or Less,* London: Routledge.

Caulfield, C. (1997) *Masters of Illusion: The World Bank and the Poverty of Nations,* New York: Henry Holt.

Chan, P. (1999) *Confession of Vote-Buying* (in Chinese), Taipei: Shangzhou.

Chang, H.-J., G. Palma *et al.* (1998) 'The Asian Crisis: Introduction', *Cambridge Journal of Economics* 22 (6): 649–52.

Chao, K. (2000) 'Honest Government Bureau Two Track System, An Opportunity for Impeachment and the Fight Against Corruption' (in Chinese), *China Times,* May 29.

Chen, M. (1995) *Factional Politics and Taiwan's Political Development* (in Chinese), Taipei: Yuedan.

Chen, M. and Chu, Y. (1992) 'Regional Oligopolistic Economy, Local Factions, and Provincial Assembly Elections: An Analysis of the Socio-economic Background of Candidates, 1950–86' (in Chinese), *Proceedings of the National Science Council Part C: Social Sciences and Humanities,* 2 (1): 89–90.

Chin, K. (2003) *Heijin: Organized Crime, Business, and Politics in Taiwan,* Armonk, NY: M.E. Sharpe.

China Post (2001) 'Phones tapped to catch vote-buyers', 21 October. Online. Available HTTP: <http://www.chinapost.com.tw/taiwan/2001/10/25/18612/Phones-tapped.htm> (accessed August 2008).

Chirkova, E. and Bowser, D. (2004) 'Corruption in Russian regions' in Transparency International (ed.) *Global Corruption Report 2004,* London and Sterling, VA: Transparency International, 295–97.

Chon, S. (2000) 'The Election Process and Informal Politics in South Korea' in L. Dittmer, H. Fukui and P. Lee (eds) *Informal Politics in East Asia,* Cambridge: Cambridge University Press, 66–82.

Cirtautas, A.M. (2001) 'Corruption and the New Ethical Infrastructure of Capitalism', *East European Constitutional Review,* 10 (2/3). Online. Available HTTP: <http://www.law.nyu.edu/eecr/vol10num2_3/special/cirtautas.html> (accessed 8 February 2006).

Cisar, O. (2003) 'Strategies for Using Information Technologies for Curbing Public-Sector Corruption: The Case of the Czech Republic (CR)', International Policy Fellowship 2002, *Final Research Report,* Released in March, Budapest: Open Society Institute 2003. Online. Available HTTP: <http://www.policy.hu/cisar/IPF_final.pdf> (accessed 19 August 2008).

Coalition 2000 (2005) *Anti-Corruption Reforms in Bulgaria,* Sofia: Coalition 2000.

Collier, R., (2001) 'Populism' in N. Smelser and P. Baltes (eds) *International Encyclopedia of the Social and Behavioral Sciences,* Vol. 17, Oxford: Elsevier, 11813–16.

Communist Party of Vietnam (2005) 'Report on the Findings of the Diagnostic Study on Corruption in Vietnam', Hanoi, December.

—— (2002) 'Corruption and anti-corruption solutions in Vietnam today', project report, Hanoi, 22 July.

Côté-Freeman, S. (1999) 'What NGOs Can Do Against Corruption', *TI Working Papers.* March 1999.

Cottrell, J. and Ghai, Y. (2007) 'Constitutionalising Affirmative Action in the Fiji Islands' *The International Journal of Human Rights*, 11 (1–2): 227–57.

Coulloudon, V. (2002) 'Russia's Distorted Anticorruption Campaigns' in S. Kotkin and A. Sajó (eds) *Political Corruption in Transition. A Sceptic's Handbook*, Budapest/ New York: CEU Press, 187–206.

Curierul National, 17 April 2003. Online. Available at HTTP: <http://www.curierulnational.ro/Politic/2003-04-17/Ion+Iliescu:+Afirmatiile+sunt+facute+cu+%E2%80%9Csimpatie%E2%80%9D+pentru+eforturile+Guvernului> (accessed 13 October 2007).

'Current Developments: City Contracts' (1995), *City Law*, 3: 1.

Czarniawska, B. (2002) *A tale of three cities, or the glocalization of city management*, Oxford: Oxford University Press.

—— (2000) 'Identity lost or identity found? Celebration and lamentation over the postmodern view of identity in social science and fiction' in M. Schultz, M.J. Hatch, and M.H. Larsen (eds) *The expressive organization. Linking identity, reputation and the corporate brand*, Oxford: Oxford University Press, 271–83.

—— (1996) 'Changing times and accounts: Tales from an organization field' in R. Munro and J. Mouritsen (eds) *Accountability: Power, ethos and the techniques of managing*, London: Thomson International Business Press, 307–28.

de Brie, C. (2004) 'Dans l'archipel planétaire de la criminalité financière: Etats, mafias et transnationales comme larrons en foire', *Le Monde Diplomatique*, Avril 2000: 4–5. Online. Available HTTP: <http://www.monde-diplomatique.fr/2000/04/DE_BRIE/13634> (accessed 19 August 2008).

Della Porta, D. and Vannucci, A. (1999) Corrupt Exchanges: Actors, Resources, and Mechanisms of Political Corruption, New York: Aldine de Gruyter.

Della Porta, D. and Mény, Y. (1997) *Democracy and Corruption in Europe*, London: Pinter.

Della Porta, D. and Diani, M. (2006) *Social Movements: An Introduction*. Oxford: Blackwell Publishing.

de Sousa, L. (2002) 'Corruption: Assessing Ethical Standards in Political Life through Control Policies', unpublished PhD thesis, European University Institute.

DeWeaver, M. (2005) 'Hidden motives in anti-corruption campaign', *Asia Times Online*, China Business, October 29, Online. Available HTTP: <http://www.atimes.com/atimes/China_Business/GJ29Cb05.html> (accessed 8 February 2006).

Diamond, L., Plattner, M., Chu, Y. and Tien, H. (eds) (1997) *Consolidating the Third Wave Democracies*, New York: Johns Hopkins University Press.

DiFranceisco, W. and Gitelman, Z. (1984) 'Soviet Culture and "Covert Participation" in Policy Implementation', *The American Political Science Review*, 78 (3): 603–21.

Dininio, P. and Orttung, R. (2005) 'Explaining Patterns of Corruption in the Russian Regions', *World Politics*, 57 (4): 500–29.

Doig, A. (1999). 'In the State we Trust? Democratisation, Corruption and Development', *Journal of Commonwealth and Comparative Politics*, 37 (3): 13–36.

Doig, A. and Marquette, H. (2004) 'Corruption and democratisation: the litmus test of international donor agency intentions?', *Futures*, 37: 199–213.

Doig, A. and McIvor, S. (2003) 'The National Integrity System: Assessing Corruption and Reform', *Public Administration and Development*, 23: 317–32.

Doig, A., McIvor, S. and Theobald, R. (2006) 'Numbers, Nuances and Moving Targets: Converging the Use of Corruption Indicators or Descriptors in Assessing State Development', *International Review of Administrative Sciences*, 72 (2): 239–52.

Doig, A. and Theobald, R. (1999) 'Introduction: Why Corruption?', *Journal of Commonwealth and Comparative Politics*, 37 (3): 1–12.

Doig, A., Moran, J. and Watt, D. (2001) 'Managing Anti-corruption Agencies', *Forum on Crime and Society*, 1 (1): 69–87.

Doig, A., Watt, D. and Williams, R. (2007) 'Why Developing Country Anticorruption Agencies Fail To Develop: Understanding The Dilemmas Of Organisational Development, Performance Expectation, And Donor And Government Cycles In African Anticorruption Agencies', *Public Administration and Development*. 27 (3): 251–59.

—— (2006) 'Hands-On Or Hands-Off? Anti-Corruption Agencies In Action, Donor Expectations, And A Good Enough Reality', *Public Administration and Development*, 26 (2): 163–72.

Eckert, C.J., Ki-baik, L., Lew, Y. I, Robinson, M and Wagner, E. W. (1990) *Korea Old and New: A History*, Seoul: Ilchokak Publishers.

Elliot, K.A. (2002) 'Corruption as an International Policy Problem' in A.J. Heidenheimer and M. Johnston (eds) *Political Corruption. Concepts and Contexts*, New Brunswick, NJ: Transaction, 925–41.

Embassy of Sweden (2002) 'Project: Corruption and anti-corruption solutions in Vietnam today', Assessment memo on proposed Swedish support for anti-corruption in Vietnam, Hanoi, 17 September.

EurActiv (2003) 'Good governance and corruption', 25 September 2003, Online. Available HTTP: <www.euractiv.com/en/corruption> (accessed 2006-01-23).

Eurobarometer 2005 <http://ec.europa.eu/public_opinion/archives/eb/eb63/eb63.4_en_first.pdf>, p. 41.

European Commission (2001, 2000, 1999, 1998) Regular Report from the Commission on Estonia's progress towards accession, Brussels: EC.

—— (2001, 2000, 1999, 1998) Regular Report from the Commission on Latvia's progress towards accession, Brussels: EC.

—— (2001, 2000, 1999, 1998) Regular Report from the Commission on Lithuania's progress towards accession, Brussels: EC.

—— (2000) 'Report on progress towards accession by each of the candidate countries', *Enlargement Strategy Paper*, Brussels: European Commission.

European Bank for Reconstruction and Development (2004) *Strategy for the Russian Federation*, London: EBRD.

—— (2002) *Strategy for the Russian Federation*, London: EBRD.

—— (1998) *Transition Report 1998*. London: EBRD.

Feng, J. (2005) 'Anti-Corruption Crusade', Beijing Review 2005, Online. Available HTTP: <www.bjreview.com.cn/05–08-e/Nation-2005-8(A).htm> (accessed 21 March 2006).

Fidler, D. P. (2000). 'A Kinder, Gentler System of Capitulations? International Law, Structural Adjustment Policies, and the Standard of Liberal, Globalized Civilization', *Texas International Law Journal*, 35: 387–413.

Fiji Government (2007a) 'Provisional Results – 2007 Population and Housing Census' Press release No 1747 November 1 2007. Online. Available HTTP: <www.fiji.gov.fj> (accessed 9 November 2007).

—— (2007b) 'Interim Government challenged to bring about prosperity' Press Release 27 June 2007 Online. Available HTTP: <www.fiji.gov.fj> (accessed 7 December 2007).

—— (2006) 'Fiji to host initiatives of change conference' Press Release 12 October 2006. Online. Available HTTP: <www.fiji.gov.fj> (accessed 24 October 2007).

Fiji Law Reform Commission (2004) 'Building an Anti Corruption Culture: Final Report', *Parliamentary Paper*, 85. Online. Available HTTP: <www.lawreform.gov.fj> (accessed 7 December 2007).

Fijilive.com, 16 November 2007.

Fiji Times, 4 December 2006, 11 December 2006, 15 December 2006, 18 December 2006, 19 December 2006, 29 December 2006, 1 January 2007, 8 January 2007, 9 January 2007, 15 January 2007, 25 January 2007, 29 January 2007, 1 February 2007, 2 February 2007, 3 February 2007, 13 February 2007, 18 February 2007, 19 February 2007, 25 February 2007, 26 February 2007, 21 March 2007, 24 March 2007, 27 March 2007, 29 March 2007, 30 March 2007, 17 June 2007, 31 August 2007, 30 September 2007, 31 October 2007, 14 November 2007, 16 December 2007, 27 December 2007.

Finel, B. and Lord, K. (2000) *Power and conflict in the age of transparency*, New York: Palgrave.

Fish, S. (2005) *Democracy Derailed in Russia. The Failure of Open Politics*, Cambridge and New York: Cambridge University Press.

Florini, A. (ed.) (2007) *The Right to Know Transparency for an Open World*, New York: Columbia University Press.

Florini, A. (2005) The coming democracy: new rules for running a new world, Washington, DC: Island Press.

—— (2000) *The Third Force: The Rise of Transnational Civil Society*, Washington, DC: Carnegie Endowment for International Peace.

Fowler, B. (2002) 'Legitimacy and Accountability in the EU enlargement: Political perspectives from the candidate states' in A. Arnull and D. Wincott (eds) *Accountability and Legitimacy in the European Union*, Oxford: Oxford University Press, 419–36.

Fraenkel, J. (2007) 'The Fiji Coup of December 2006: who, what, where and why?' in J. Fraenkel and S. Firth (eds) *From election to Coup in Fiji: the 2006 Campaign and its Aftermath*, Canberra: ANU E-Press, 420–49.

Fraud Review (2006) *Final Report of the Fraud Review Team*, London: Secretariat to the Law Officers. Online. Available HTTP: <http://www.attorneygeneral.gov.uk/Fraud%20Review/Fraud%20Review%20Final%20Report%20July%202006.pdf> (accessed 3 December 2007).

Frederickson, H.G. (ed.) (1993) *Ethics and Public Administration*, NY: M.E. Sharpe.

Freedom House (2005) Freedom in the World 2005: The Annual Survey of Political Rights and Civil Liberties, Lanham, MD: Rowman and Littlefield.

Fukuyama, F. (2004) *State-Building: Governance and World Order in the 21st Century*, Ithaca, NY: Cornell University Press.

G8 Centre (2006) *Fighting High-Level Corruption*, St. Petersburg Summit Documents, 16 July. Online. Available HTTP: <http://www.g7.utoronto.ca/summit/2006stpetersburg/corruption.html> (accessed 7 August 2006).

Galtung, F. (2006) 'Measuring the Immeasurable: Boundaries and Functions of (Macro) Corruption Indices' in C. Sampford *et al.* (eds) *Measuring Corruption*, Aldershot and Burlington: Ashgate, 101–30.

—— (2001) 'Transparency International's Network to Curb Global Corruption' in Gerald Caiden *et al.* (eds) *Where Corruption Lives*. Bloomfield, CT: Kumarian Press, 189–206.

—— (2000) 'A Global Network to Curb Corruption: The Experience of Transparency International' in A. Florini (ed.) *The Third Force: The Rise of Transnational*

Civil Society, Tokyo/Washington DC: Japan Center for International Exchange – Carnegie Endowment for International Peace, 17–47.

Galtung, F. and Pope, J. (1999) 'The Global Coalition Against Corruption: Evaluating Transparency International' in Andreas Schedler *et al.* (eds) *The Self-Restraining State: Power and Accountability in New Democracies.* London: Lynne Rienner Publishers, 257–82.

Getnick, N.V. and Getnick, M.E. (2007) 'Internal Investigations and Private Monitoring', *Getnick and Getnick.* Online. Available HTTP: <www.getnicklaw.com/practice/internal.html> (accessed 5 November 2007).

Gilbert, C.L. and Vines, D. (eds) (2000) *The World Bank: structure and policies.* Cambridge: Cambridge University Press.

Gill, S. (1995) 'Globalization, Market Civilization, and Disciplinary Neoliberalism' *Millennium*, 24: 399–423.

Gillespie, K. and Okruhlik, G. (1991) 'The Political Dimensions of Corruption Cleanups: A Framework for Analysis' *Comparative Politics*, 24(1): 77–95.

Global Integrity (2006) *Country Report: Romania.* Online. Available HTTP <http://www.globalintegrity.org/reports/2006/pdfs/romania.pdf> (accessed 14 October 2007).

Glynn, P., Kobrin, S., Naím, M. (1997) 'The globalization of Corruption' in K.A. Elliot (ed.) *Corruption and the global economy,* Washington, DC: Institute for international economics, 7–30.

Göbel, C. (2006a) 'The Long Arm of Authoritarianism: Elections and Governance in Taiwan and South Korea' (in German) in C. Derichs and T. Heberer (eds) *Wahlsysteme und Wahltypen. Politische Systeme und regionale Kontexte im Vergleich,* Wiesbaden: VS Verlag für Sozialwissenschaften, 217–39.

—— (2006b) 'Beheading the Hydra: Combating Corruption and Organized Crime in the KMT and DPP Eras' in D. Fell, H. Klöter, and B. Chang (eds) *What has Changed? Taiwan Before and After the Change in Ruling Parties,* Wiesbaden: Harrassowitz, 61–82.

—— (2001) 'Towards a Consolidated Democracy? Informal and Formal Institutions in Taiwan's Political Process', paper presented at the Annual Meeting of the American Political Science Association, San Francisco, September 2001 (unpublished).

Green, M. (ed.) (1991) *Government Ethics Reform for the 1990s: Collected Reports of the New York State Commission on Government Integrity,* New York: Fordham University Press.

Greenlees, D. (2006) 'Anticorruption drive: Bark or bite?', *International Herald Tribune,* 6 April 2006. Online. Available HTTP: <http://www.iht.com/articles/2006/04/05/business/corrupt.php> (accessed 06 April 2006).

Grødeland, A.B., Koshechkina, T.Y. and Miller, W.L. (1988) '"Foolish to Give and Yet More Foolish Not to Take" – In-depth Interviews with Post-Communist Citizens on Their Everyday Use of Bribes and Contacts', *Europe-Asia Studies,* 50 (4): 651–77.

Grynberg, R., Munro, D. and White, M. (2002) *Crisis: Collapse of the National Bank of Fiji* (Second Impression). Suva: USP Book Centre.

Hallstrom, K.T. (2004) *Organizing International Standardization : ISO and the IASC in Quest of Authority,* Cheltenham: Edward Elgar Publishing Limited.

Harper, R.H.R. (1998) *Inside the IMF,* San Diego: Academic Press.

Heidenheimer, A., Johnston, M. and LeVine, V. (eds) (1989) *Political Corruption,* New Brunswick, NJ: Transaction Publishers.

Heidenheimer, J. (1989) 'Perspectives on the Perception of Corruption' in Heidenheimer *et al.* (eds) *Political Corruption: A Handbook*, New Brunswick, NJ: Transaction Publishers, 149–71.

Heilbrunn, J.R. (2004) *Anti-Corruption Agencies: Panacea or Real Medicine to Fight Corruption*, Washington, DC: International Bank for Reconstruction and Development/ World Bank.

Hellman, J. and Kaufman, D. (2001) 'Confronting the Challenge of State Capture in Transition Economies', *Finance & Development*, 38 (3): 1–8.

Hellman, J., Jones, G. and Kaufman, D. (2000) '"Seize the State, Seize the Day": State Capture, corruption, and Influence in Transition', *Policy Research Working Paper*, 2444, The World Bank.

Henderson, K. (2000) 'The challenges of EU eastward enlargement' *International Politics*, 34 (1): 1–17.

Henderson, S.L. (2003) *Building Democracy in Contemporary Russia. Western Support for Grassroots Organisations*, Ithaca, NY and London: Cornell University Press.

Henderson, T. (1976) *Tammany Hall and the New Immigrants: The Progressive Years*, New York: Arno Press.

Henry, L. (2002) 'Two paths to a greener future: environmentalism and civil society development in Russia', *Demokratizatsiya* 10 (2): 184–206.

Heywood, P. and Krastev, I. (2006) 'Political Scandals and Corruption' in P. Heywood, E. Jones, M. Rhodes, and U. Sedelmeier (eds) *Developments in European Politics*, Basingstoke: Palgrave Macmillan, 157–78.

Hiatt, F. (1999) 'Corruption is finally getting the attention it needs', *International Herald Tribune*, 25 February: 9.

Hindess, B. (2005) 'Investigating International Anti-Corruption', *Third World Quarterly*, 26 (8): 1389–98.

—— (2004a) *Corruption and Democracy in Austrália*, Canberra: Democratic Audit of Australia, Australian National University.

—— (2004b) 'Liberalism: what's in a name?' in W. Larner and W. Walters (eds) *Global Governmentality*, London: Routledge, 23–39.

—— (2004c) 'International anti-corruption as a program of normalisation', paper presented at the ISA Conference, Montreal, March. 2004 (unpublished).

Holmes, L. (2003) 'Political Corruption in Central and Eastern Europe', in M.J. Bull and J.L. Newell (eds) *Corruption in Contemporary Politics*, Basingstoke: Palgrave Macmillan, 193–206.

—— (1993) *The End of Communist Power. Anti Corruption Campaigns and Legitimation Crisis*, Cambridge: Polity.

Hopwood, A.G. and Miller, P. (1994) *Accounting as Social and Institutional Practice*, Cambridge: Cambridge University Press.

Human Rights Watch (2004) *Joint NGO Statement on the Beslan Hostage Tragedy*. New York: HRW. Online. Available HTTP: <http://hrw.org/english/docs/2004/09/08/russia9336_txt.htm> (accessed 25/02/2005).

Hsia, C. (1997) 'Illegal guns spread far and wide. Enough to equip at least three divisions' (in Chinese), *Zhongguo Shibao,* May 25.

Huntington, S. (1968) *Political Order in Changing Societies*, London and New Haven, CT: Yale University Press.

Hutchcroft, P. (1998) *Booty Capitalism. The Politics of Banking in the Phillippines*, Ithaca, NY: Cornell University Press.

Huther, J. and Shah, A. (2000) 'Anti-corruption Policies and Programs: A Framework for Evaluation', *World Bank Policy Research Working Paper*, 2501.

Information Science for Democracy (2005) *Vo skol'ko raz uvelichilas' korruptsia za 4 goda:resul'taty novogo issledovaniia Fonda INDEM*, Moskva. Online. Available

HTTP: <http://www.anti-corr.ru/indem/2005diagnost/2005diag_press.doc> (accessed 28 September 2005).

—— (2001) *Diagnostics of Corruption in Russia. Sociological Analysis*, Survey Commissioned by the World Bank, Moscow: INDEM Foundation.

Institute of Public Management (2006) 'Evaluation of Evaluation of the Swedish Support in the Area of Anti-corruption in South Eastern Europe- PACO Impact 2004 – 2006, Final report'. Online. Available HTTP <http://www.coe.int/t/e/legal_ affairs/legal_co-operation/combating_economic_crime/3_technical_cooperation/paco/ paco-impact/PACO%20Impact%20Evaluation%20Final%20report.PDF> (accessed 14 October 2007).

Interim Government of the Fiji Islands (2007a) 'Fiji Independent Commission Against Corruption (Promulgation No 11 of 2007)', *Republic of the Fiji Islands Government Gazette*, 7 (29): 1083–92.

International Herald Tribune (2004) 'Cheney's trip is just 2nd appearance overseas', 23 January.

—— (2007b) 'Prevention of Bribery (Promulgation No 12 of 2007)', *Republic of the Fiji Islands Government Gazette*, 7 (29): 1093–1118.

International Monetary Fund (2003) 'The IMF and Good Governance. A Factsheet – April 2003'. Online. Available HTTP: <http://www.imf.org/external/np/exr/ facts/gov.htm> (accessed 22 March 2006).

ISSP – International Social Survey Programme (2004) *'Citizenship' - ZA No. 3950*, Cologne: Zentralarchiv fuer empirische sozialforschung.

Jacobsson B. (2000) 'Standardization and expert knowledge' in B. Jacobsson (eds) *A World of Standards,* Oxford: Oxford University Press, 40–49.

—— (2005) 'Scripted states', paper presented at SCORE conference *Organizing the World*, Stockholm October 13–15 (unpublished).

Jacobsson, B. and Mörth, U. (1998) 'Europeiseringen och den svenska staten' in G. Ahrne (eds) *Stater som organisationer*, Nerenius och Santerus Förlag Change: Stockholm: Nerenius & Santérus, 179–202.

Jacobsson, B., Sahlin-Andersson, K. (2002) 'The dynamics of transnational regulations', paper prepared for EGOS 18th Colloquium July 2002 in Barcelona, (unpublished).

Jayasuriya, K (2002) 'Governance, Post-Washington Consensus and the new anti-politics' in T. Lindsey and H. Dick (eds) *Corruption in East Asia: rethinking the governance paradigm*, Sydney: Federation Press, 24–36.

Jayawickrama, N. (2006) 'Fighting Corruption Requires Good Government'. Online. Available HTTP: <www.thecommonwealth.org/Templates/InternalChogm. asp?NodeID = 33549> (accessed 22 March 2006).

—— (2001) 'Transparency International: combating corruption through institutional reform' in A. Lee-Chai and J. Bargh (eds) *The use and abuse of power: multiple perspectives on the causes of corruption*, Philadelphia, PA: Psychology Press, 281–98.

Johnson, G. and Scholes, K. (1997) *Exploring Corporate Strategy*, Hemel Hempstead: Prentice-Hall.

Johnson's Russia List (2005) *Press Conference with INDEM Fund President Georgy Satarov on Corruption Index Studies in Russia*, AIF Press Center, 13:00, July 20, 2005. Online Posting. Available JRL #9211, 28 July 2005, www.cdi.org.

Jos, P. (1993) 'Empirical Corruption Research: Beside the (Moral) Point?', *Journal of Public Administration Research and Theory*, J-Part, 3 (3): 359–75.

Jowell, R. and the Central Co-ordinating Team (2005) *European Social Survey Round 2 2004/2005* (Rotative Module on Economic Morality – section E), London: Centre for Comparative Social Surveys, City University.

Kang, D. (2002) 'Bad Loans to Good Friends. Money Politics and the Developmental State in South Korea', *International Organization,* 56 (1): 177–207.

—— (2001) 'The Institutional Foundations of Korean Politics' in S. Kil and C. Moon (eds) *Understanding Korean Politics. An Introduction,* Albany, NY: State University of New York Press, 71–106.

Kang, T. (1999) 'Inside, the Gambling Regulation Is Attacked and Defended, Outside Black Shadows Are Moving About' (in Chinese), *Shangye Zhoukan,* 605.

Kaufmann, D. (2005) 'Myths and Realities of Governance and Corruption', in World Economic Forum (2005) *The global competitiveness report 2005–2006: policies underpinning rising prosperity,* Augusto Lopez-Claros, director; Klaus Schwab, Michael E. Porter, co-directors, New York: Palgrave Macmillan.

—— (2003). Rethinking Governance: Empirical Lessons Challenge Orthodoxy, Discussion Draft March 11th. Online. Available HTTP: <www.worldbank.org/wbi/governance/wp-governance.html> (accessed 23 January 2006).

—— (1997) 'Corruption: The Facts.', *Foreign Policy,* 107: 114–31.

Keck, M.E. and Sikkink, K. (1998) *Activists Beyond Borders. Advocacy Networks in International Politics,* Ithaca, NY and London: Cornell University Press.

Kennedy, D. (1999) 'The international anti-corruption campaign' *Connecticut Journal of International Law,* 14 (2): 455–64.

Keuleers, P. (2005) 'Corruption, poverty and development', Background paper (Plenary 2), ADB/OECD Anti-corruption initiative for Asia and the Pacific, 5th regional anti-corruption conference, 28–30 September 2005, Beijing, PR China. Online. Available HTTP: <http://www1.oecd.org/daf/ASIAcom/pdf/5conf_ps2-keuleers2.pdf> (accessed 21 March 2006).

Khan, M.H. (2005) 'Patron-Client Networks and the Economic Effects of Corruption in Asia' in A. Heidenheimer and M. Johnston (eds) *Political Corruption: Concepts & Contexts,* 3rd edn, New Brunswick: Transaction Publishers, 467–88.

Korea Independent Commission Against Corruption (2005) *KICAC Annual Report 2004.* Online. Available HTTP: <http://www.kicac.go.kr/english/Download.jsp?filepath=/app/port_files/PO_XBBS_FILES_1/8208&filename=KICACAnnualReport2004-final.doc> (accessed 30 October 2007).

—— (2004) *KICAC Annual Report 2003.* Online. Available HTTP: <http://www.kicac.go.kr/english/Download.jsp?filepath=/app/port_files/PO_XBBS_FILES_1/1691&filename=AnnualReport2003.doc> (accessed 30 October 2007).

—— (2003) *KICAC Annual Report 2002.* Online. Available HTTP: <http://www.kicac.go.kr/open_content/download/2002AnnualReport.pdf> (accessed 30 October 2007).

Kim, B. and Im, H. (2001) 'Crony Capitalism in South Korea, Thailand and Taiwan: Myth and Reality', *Journal of East Asian Studies,* 1 (2): 5–52.

Kim, G. (2006) 'South Korea' in Transparency International (ed.) *Global Corruption Report 2006,* London: Pluto Press, 246–50.

Kim, T. (2003) 'Comparative Study of Anti-Corruption Systems, Efforts and Strategies in Asian Countries: Focussing on Hong Kong, Singapore, Malaysia, and Korea' in J. Kidd and F. Richter (eds) *Fighting Corruption in Asia. Causes, Effects, and Remedies,* New Jersey: World Scientific, 349–76.

Klitgaard, R. (1988) *Controlling Corruption,* Berkeley, CA: University of California Press.

Kotkin, S and Sajó, A. (eds) (2002) *Political Corruption in Transition: A Skeptic's Handbook*. Budapest: Central European University Press.

Krastev, I. (2007) 'The Strange Death of the Liberal Consensus', *Journal of Democracy*, 18 (4): 189–90.

—— (2004) *Shifting Obsessions. Three Essays on the Politics of Anticorruption*, Budapest and New York: CEU Press.

—— (2003) 'When "should" does not imply "can": the making of the Washington consensus on corruption'. Online. Available HTTP: <http://www.colbud.hu/honesty-trust/krastev/pub01.PDF> (accessed 27 February 2005).

—— (2002) 'The Balkans: Democracy without Choices', *Journal of Democracy*, 13 (3): 39–53.

—— (2000) 'The Strange (Re)Discovery of Corruption' in Dahrendorf et al. (eds) *The Paradoxes of Unintended Consequences*, Budapest: CEU Press, 23–42.

Lal, B. (2007) '"Anxiety, Uncertainty and Fear in Our Land" Fiji's Road to Military Coup' *The Round Table* 96 (389): 135–53

Lambsdorff, J. (2005) *The Methodology of the 2005 Corruption Perceptions Index*, Transparency International (TI) and University of Passau. Online. Available HTTP: <http://www.transparency.org/cpi/2005/dnld/methodology.pdf> (accessed 12 November 2005).

—— (2003) *Framework Document: Background paper to the 2003 Corruption Perception Index*, Transparency International and University of Passau. Online. Available HTTP: <http://www.transparency.org/policy_research/surveys_indices/cpi/2003> (accessed 11 December 2007).

Landfried, C. (1994) 'Political Finance in West Germany' in H.E. Alexander and R. Shiratori (eds) *Comparative Political Financing among the Democracies*, Boulder, CO: Westview Press, 133–44.

Lane, J-E. and Ersson, S (2000) *The New Institutional Politics: Performance and Outcomes*, London: Routledge.

Larmour, P. (2007) 'International Action Against Corruption in the Pacific Islands: Policy Transfer, Coercion and Effectiveness' *Asian Journal of Political Science*, 15 (1): 1–16.

—— (2006) 'Civilizing Techniques: Transparency International and the Spread of anti corruption' in B. Bowden and L. Seabrooke (eds) *Global Standards of Market Civilization*, London: Routledge, 95–106.

—— (2005) *Foreign Flowers: Institutional Transfer and Good Governance in the Pacific Islands*, Honolulu, HI: University of Hawaii Press.

Larmour, P. and Barcham, M. (2006) 'National Integrity Systems in Small Island States' *Public Administration and Development*, 26: 173–84.

Latour, B. (1986) *Laboratory life: the construction of scientific facts*, Princeton NJ: Princeton University Press.

Law Association for Asia and the Pacific (2007) *Report of Visit to Fiji by LAWASIA Observer Mission 25–28 March 2007*, Brisbane: LAWASIA Secretariat.

Ledeneva, A.V. (1998) *Russia's Economy of Favours. Blat, Networking and Informal Exchange*, (Cambridge Russia, Soviet and Post-Soviet Studies), Cambridge: Cambridge University Press.

Li, M. (2000) 'Grip for Money and Power: The Chaotic Lifayuan' (in Chinese), *Tianxia Zazhi*, 235: 70–78.

Liao, C. (1997) *Origins, Development and Qualitative Change of Taiwan's Local Factions* (in Chinese), Taipei: Yunchen.

Lindsey, T. and Dick, H. (eds) (2002) *Corruption in Asia: Rethinking the Governance Paradigm*, Sydney: The Federation Press.

Linn, J.F. (2001) 'Good Governance and Transparency in the Transition Countries', speech by the Vice President, Europe and Central Asia Region, the World Bank; OCSE conference on Good Governance and Transparency in the Transition Countries, Prague, May 15, 2001 Online. Available HTTP: <http://lnweb18.worldbank.org/eca/eca.nsf/0/d315c32906509bd685256a4f004fac9f?OpenDocument> (accessed 28 February 2006).

Lu, X. (2003) 'East Asia' in Transparency International (ed.) *Global Corruption Report 2003*, Berlin: TI, 128–39.

Lundberg, K. (2002) 'High Road or Low? Transparency International and the Corruption Perceptions Index', *Kennedy School of Government Case Program*, C15-02-1658.0 (Harvard University).

March, J. and Olsen, J.P. (1989) *Rediscovering Institutions: the Organizational Basis of Politics*, New York: Free Press.

Marquette, H. (2004) 'The creeping politicisation of the World Bank: the case of corruption', *Political Studies*, 52: 413–30.

Martirossian, J. (2004) 'Russia and Her Ghosts of the Past' in R.A. Johnson (ed.) *The Struggle Against Corruption: A Comparative Study*, New York and Houndmills: Palgrave Macmillan, 81–108.

Mason, D.S. (2004) 'Fairness Matters: Equity and the Transition to Democracy', *World Policy Journal*, XX (4). Online. Available HTTP: <http://www.worldpolicy.org/journal/articles/wpj03–04/mason.html> (accessed 2006-03-01).

Mbaku, J. (2007) 'Bureaucratic Corruption in Africa: the Futility of Cleanups' *The Cato Journal* 16 (1): 99–118.

McCarthy, P. (2005) 'Drivers of Change: An Evaluation of the Advocacy and Legal Advice Centers Project'. Online. Available HTTP: <http://www.ti-bih.org/documents/24-5-2005/ALAC%20Final%20Evaluation%20Report%202005.pdf> (accessed 14 October 2007).

McCauley, M. (2001) *Bandits, Gangsters and the Mafia. Russia, the Baltics States and the CIS*, Harlow and London: Longman/Pearson Education.

McComb, M.E. and Shaw, D.L. (1972) 'The agenda setting function of the Mass Media', *Public Opinion Quarterly*, 36: 176–87.

McCoy, J.L. and Heather, H. (2001) 'The Emergence of a Global Anti-Corruption Norm' *International Politics*, 38: 65–90.

Meagher, P. (2004) 'Anti-Corruption Agencies: A Review of Experience', *The IRIS Discussion Papers on Institutions and Development*, Paper No. 04/02 March 2004.

Mény, Y., (1998) 'The People, the Elites and the Populist Challenge', *Jean Monnet Chair Paper RSC*, 98/47. Florence: European University Institute.

—— (1993) 'La décennie de la corruption', *Le Débat*, 77: 15–25.

Mény, Y. and De Sousa, L. (1999) 'Corruption' in Association d'Economie Financière (eds), *Rapport Moral sur l'Argent dans le Monde 1999*, Paris: Montchrestien, 137–44.

Merton, R. (1940) 'Bureaucratic structure and personality', *Social Forces*, 18: 560–68.

Meyer, J. (1996) 'The promulgation and transmission of ideas in the modern organizational environment' in C. Sevon (eds) *Translating organizational change*, Berlin: de Gruyter, 241–52.

Meyer, J. and Rowan, B. (1977) 'Institutionalized organizations: Formal structure as myth and ceremony', *American Journal of Sociology*, 83: 340–63.

Meyer, J., Boli, J., Thomas, G. and Ramirez, R. (1997) 'World Society and the Nation-State', *American Journal of Sociology*, 103 (1): pp 144–81.

Michael, B. (2004a) 'The rapid rise of the anticorruption industry', *Local Governance Brief*, (Spring): 17–25.

—— (2004b) 'The Globalization of Anticorruption Policies: the Diffusion of Best Practices and the role of Knowledge Management' in D. Levi-Faur and E Vigoda-Gadot (eds) *International Public Policy and Management: Policy Learning Beyond Cultural and Political Boundaries*, New York: Marcel Dekker, 325–49.

—— (2004c) *The Rise and Fall of the Anti-Corruption Industry. Toward Second Generation Anti-corruption Reforms in Central and Eastern Europe*. Online. Available online: http://users.ox.ac.uk/~scat1663/Publications/Papers/Soros%20Article.pdf (accessed 14 October 2007).

Miller, W.L., Grodeland, A.B. and Koshechkina T.Y. (2001) *A Culture of Corruption: Coping with Government in Post-Communist Europe*, Budapest: CEU Press.

Ministry of Justice (2000) *Report Table of State of Implementation and Effects of the Ministry of Justice's Action Program to Sweep Out Black Gold* (in Chinese). Online. Available HTTP: <http://www.moj.gov.tw/ct.asp?xItem = 26443&ctNode = 11636> (accessed 30 October 2007).

—— (2003) *Follow-up Program to the Action Program to Sweep Out Black Gold* (in Chinese). Online. Available HTTP: <http://www.moj.gov.tw/ct.asp?xItem = 26802&ctNode = 11636> (accessed 30 October 2007).

—— (2004) *Periodic Statistical Table of Anti-Black Gold, Serious Corruption, and Investigation into Vote-Buying Cases Handled By The Local Courts' Prosecutor's Offices Subordinate to The Ministry of Justice* (in Chinese). Online. Available HTTP: <http://www.moj.gov.tw/public/Attachment/512251521285.jpg> (accessed 30 October 2007).

Moon, C. (1994) 'Changing Patterns of Business-Government Relations in South Korea' in MacIntyre, A. (ed.): *Business and Government in Industrializing Asia*, St. Leonards, Australia: Allen & Unwin Pty Ltd., 142–66.

Moore, B. (1966). *The Social Origins of Dictatorship and Democracy. Lord and Peasant in the Making of The Modern World*, Boston: Beacon Press.

Mungiu-Pippidi, A. (2007) 'EU Accession Is No "End of History"', *Journal of Democracy*, 18 (4): 189–90.

Myrdal, G. (1968) *Asian Drama: An Inquiry into the Poverty of Nations*, New York: Atheneum.

Nelson, William E. (1982) *The Roots of Amerian Bureaucracy: 1830–1900*, Cambridge, MA: Harvard University Press.

New Internationalist (2004) 'Life After Communism: The Facts'. Online. Available HTTP: <http://www.newint.org/issue366/facts.htm> (accessed 1 March 2006).

New York City Department of Information Technology and Telecommunications (2006) 'The 311 Plan'. Online. Available HTTP: <http://www.nyc.gov/html/doitt/html/about/about_311.shtml> (accessed 4 December 2007).

New York State Organized Crime Task Force (1991) *Corruption and Racketeering in the New York City Construction Industry*, New York: New York University Press.

OECD (2006) *Specialised Anti-Corruption Institutions: Review Of Models (Profiles)*. Final Draft report, Anti-Corruption Network for Eastern Europe and Central Asia, unpublished.

—— Sigma Paper no 7. The Audit of Secret and politically sensitive subjects: comparative audit practices. Online. Available HTTP: <http://www.oecd.org/dataoecd/21/54/36951937.pdf> (accessed August 2008).

Oh, J. (1999) *Korean Politics. The Quest for Democratization and Development*, Ithaca: Cornell University Press.

Olaks Consulting (2001) *National Integrity System Country Study Report, Fiji*, Suva: Transparency International – Fiji Islands.

Open Society Institute (2002) *Monitoring the EU accession process: corruption and anti corruption*, Budapest: Open Society Institute.

Orenstein, M. (1998) 'Vaclav Klaus: Revolutionary and Parliamentarian', *East European Constitutional Review*, 7 (1): 46–55.

Osborne, D. and Gaebler T. (1992) *Reinventing Government: How the Entrepreneurial Spirit is Transforming the Public Sector*, Reading, MA: Addison-Wesley.

OSCE (2004) *Best Practices in Combating Corruption*, Vienna: Office of the Coordinator for Economic and Environmental Matters.

Ottaway, M. and Carothers, T. (2000) *Funding Virtue: Civil Society, Aid and Democracy Promotion*. Washington, DC: Carnegie Endowment for International Peace.

PACO (2006) *PACO Impact Evaluation 2004 – 2006, Final report*. Online. Available HTTP: <http://www.coe.int/t/e/legal_affairs/legal_co-operation/combating_economic_crime/3_technical_cooperation/paco/paco-impact/PACO%20Impact%20Evaluation%20Final%20report.PDF> (accessed 14 October 2007).

Pagden, A. (1998) 'The genesis of "governance" and Enlightenment conceptions of the Cosmopolitan World Order', *International Social Science Journal*, (155): 7–15.

Pentland, B. (1993) 'Getting Comfortable with the numbers: Auditing and the microproduction of macro-order' in *Accounting, Organizations and Society*, 18 (7–8): 605–20.

Philp, M. (1997) 'Defining Political Corruption' in Heywood (ed.) *Political Corruption*, Oxford: Blackwell/PSA, 20–46.

Pierre, J. and Peters, G. (2000) *Governance, Politics and the State*, New York: St Martin Press.

Polanyi, K. (1944) *The Great Transformation: The Political and Economic Origins of Our Time*, Boston, MA: Beacon Press.

Polzer, T. (2001) *Corruption: Deconstructing the World Bank Discourse*, London: Development Studies Institute, LSE.

Pope, J. (2000) *The Source Book: Confronting Corruption: The Elements of a National Integrity System*, Berlin: TI.

Porter, T. (1996) 'Making things quantitative' in Power (ed.) *Accounting and science*, Cambridge: Cambridge University Press, 36–56.

Powell, W. and DiMaggio, P. (1991) 'The Iron cage revisited, institutional isomorphism and collective rationality in organizational fields' in P. Dimaggio and W. Powell (eds) *New institutionalism in organizational analysis*, Chicago, IL: University of Chicago Press, 63–82.

Power, M. (1997) *The audit society: Rituals of verification*, Oxford: Oxford University Press.

—— (1996) 'Making things auditable', *Accounting organization and society*, 21 (2/3): 289–315.

—— (1994) *Accounting and science*, Cambridge: Cambridge University Press.

Prochazka, R. (2002) *Mission Accomplished: On Founding Constitutional Adjudication in Central Europe*, Budapest: CEU Press.

Protiv Korruptsii (2006a) 'Nuzhna li Rossii bor'ba s korruptsiei?' *Protiv Korruptsii*, (18.09.). Online. Available HTTP: <http://www.anticorr.ru/news/news0x91x1253. html> (accessed 23 November 2006).

—— (2006b) 'Skol'ko Vsiatok Platit Rossiia? Korruptsiia – slishkom ser'eznaia problema, chtoby iskat' ee preyvelicheniami ... ' *Protiv Korruptsii*, (18.05.). Online. Available HTTP: <http://www.anticorr.ru/news/news420.html> (accessed 13 August 2006).

Quah, J. S. T. (1989) 'Singapore's Experience in Curbing Corruption', in Arnold J. Heidenheimer *et al.* (eds), Political Corruption: A Handbook. New Brunswick, NJ: Transaction.

Radio New Zealand, 17 August 2007.

Record, R. (2005) 'Corruption, good governance and the economic development of Vietnam', paper submitted to the Vietnam Development Forum (VDF), Tokyo Conference on the Development of Vietnam, Tokyo, 18 June 2005.

Rhodes, R. (1997) *Understanding Governance: Policy Networks, Governance, Reflexivity and Accountability*, Buckingham: Open University Press.

Rigger, S. (1994) 'Machine Politics in the New Taiwan. Institutional Reform and Electoral Strategy in the Republic of China on Taiwan', unpublished thesis, Harvard University.

Riley. S. (1998) 'The Political Economy of Anti-Corruption Campaigns', *European Journal of Development Research*, 10(1): 129–59.

Risse, T. and Sikkink, K. (1999) 'The socialization of international human rights norms into domestic practices: introduction' in T. Risse, S.C. Ropp and K. Sikkink (eds) *The Power of Human Rights. International Norms and Domestic Change*, Cambridge: Cambridge University Press, 1–38.

Risse, T. *et al.* (eds) (1999) *The Power of Human Rights. International Norms and Domestic Change*, Cambridge Studies in International Relations, Cambridge: Cambridge University Press.

Rojas, C. (2004) 'Governing through the social; representation of poverty and global governmentality' in W. Larner and W. Walters (eds) *Global Governmentality*, London: Routledge, 97–115.

Rose, N. (1999) *Powers of Freedom: reframing political thought*, Cambridge: Cambridge University Press.

Rose-Ackerman, S. (1999) *Corruption and Government: Causes, Consequences and Reforms*, Cambridge: Cambridge University Press.

Rueschemeyer, D., Huber Stephens E. and Stephens, J. (1992) *Capitalist Development and Democracy*, Chicago, IL: University of Chicago Press.

Rupnik, J., Bútora, M., Greskovits, B., Krastev, I., Mungiu-Pippidi, A., Jasiewicz, K. and Tismaneanu, V. (2000) 'Is East-Central Europe Backsliding?', *Journal of Democracy*, (Special Issue) October 2000, 18 (4): 17–25.

Sajó, A. (2002). 'Clientalism and Extortion' in S. Kotkin and A. Sajó (eds) *Political Corruption in Transition: a sceptics handbook*, Budapest and New York: CEU Press: 1–22.

—— (1998) 'Corruption, Clientelism, and the Future of the Constitutional State in Eastern Europe', *East European Constitutional Review*, 7 (2): 37–42.

Sampford, C. et al. (eds) (forthcoming), *National Integrity Systems*, London: Ashgate.

Sampson, S. (2005) 'Integrity Warriors: Global Morality and the Anti-Corruption Movement in the Balkans' in D. Haller and C. Shore (eds) *Corruption. Anthropological Perspectives*, London and Ann Arbor, MI: Pluto Press, 103–30.

—— (1996) 'The social life of projects: importing civil society to Albania' in C.M. Hann and E. Dunn (eds) *Civil Society: Challenging Western Models*, London: Routledge, 121–42.

Sandholtz, W. and Koetzle, W. (1998) 'Accounting for corruption: Economic structure, democratic norms, and trade', *UC Irvine Research Papers*, Center for the study of democracy.

Satter, D. (2003) *Darkness at Dawn: The Rise of the Russian Criminal State*, New Haven, CT: Yale University Press.

Savintseva, M. and Stykow, P. (2005) 'Country report. Russia' in Transparency International (ed.) *Global Corruption Report 2005*, London and Ann Arbor, MI: Pluto Press/TI: 199–202.

Schmidt, D. (2006) 'Anti-Corruption Advocacy in Contemporary Russia: Local Civil Society Actors, Transnational Networks and the State', unpublished PhD thesis, Queen's University Belfast.

—— (2005) 'CPI, INDEM Studie, und andere: Korruption in Russland 2005', *Russlandanalysen* (78): 7–9, 17–18.

Schubert, G. (1994) *Taiwan, the Chinese Alternative. Democratization in an East Asian Industrializing Country* (in German), Hamburg: Institut für Asienkunde.

Sejong Institute/National Endowment for Democracy (2001) *Political Finance and Democracy in East Asia: The Use and Abuse of Money in Campaigns and Elections.* Online. Available HTTP: <www.sejong.org:10002/korea/data/EDF2001–01.pdf> (accessed 30 October 2007).

Shah, A. and Schacter, M. (2004) 'Combating Corruption: Look Before You Leap', *Finance & Development*, December: 40–43.

Shameem, S. (2007) Report to the UN Commissioner for Human Rights on alleged breaches of international law and the 1997 Constitution in the removal of the Prime Minister, Lisenia Qarase on December 5th 2006. Suva: Fiji Human Rights Commission.

Sida (2007) *Sida Country Report 2006, Serbia and Montenegro*, Stockholm: Sida. Online. Available HTTP: <http://www.sida.se/sida/jsp/sida.jsp?d = 118&a = 32548> (accessed 10 October 2007).

Siegel, F. (2005) P*rince of the City: Giuliani, New York, and the Genius of American Life*, San Francisco, CA: Encounter Books.

Smilov, D. (2002) 'Structural Corruption of Party-Funding Models: Governmental Favoritism in Bulgaria and Russia', in Stephen Kotkin and Andras Sajo, *Political Corruption in Transition: A Sceptic's Handbook*, Budapest and New York: CEU Press.

—— (2006) 'EU Enlargement and the Constitutional Principle of Judicial Independence', in Sadurski, Wojciech; Czarnota, Adam; Krygier, Martin (eds.), *Spreading Democracy and the Rule of Law? The Impact of EU Enlargement for the Rule of Law, Democracy and Constitutionalism in Post-Communist Legal Orders*, Springer.

Smilov, D. and Toplak, J. (eds) (2007) Political Finance and Corruption in Eastern Europe: The Transition Period, London: Ashgate.

Smilov, D. and Dorosiev, R. (2007) 'Perceptions of Corruption in Bulgaria – A Content Analysis of Documents from Politics, Judiciary, Police, Media, Civil Society and Economy', *Crime and Culture Discussion Paper Series*, No. 7. Online. Available HTTP. < www.uni-konstanz.de/crimeandculture/index.htm> (accessed on 1 December 2007)

Southeast European Times (2007) 'Corruption down in Romania, but still an issue', 9 April. Online. Available HTTP: <http://www.setimes.com/cocoon/setimes/xhtml/en_GB/features/setimes/features/2007/04/09/feature-03> (accessed 24 October 2007).

Sperling, V. (2006) 'Women's Organizations: Institutionalized Interest Groups or Vulnerable Dissidents?', *Russian Civil Society: A Critical Assessment*, Armonk, NY: M.E. Sharpe, 161–77.

Stan, L. (2004) 'The Romanian Anti-corruption Bill', *Studies in Post-Communism,* Occasional Paper 6 (January).

Steinberg, A. (1972) *The Bosses,* New York: Macmillan.

Steves, F. and Rousso, A. (2004) 'Anti-corruption programmes in post-communist transition countries and changes in the business environment, 1999–2002', *EBRD Working Paper,* 85, London: European Bank for Reconstruction and Development.

Sundstrom, L.M. (2006) Funding Civil Society. Foreign Assistance and NGO Development in Russia, Stanford: Stanford University Press.

Taipei Times (2001) "MJIB Switch Called 'Abrupt'", 5 August. Online. Available HTTP: <http://www.taipeitimes.com/News/local/archives/2001/08/05/97207> (accessed August 2008).

Tamesis, P. (1998) 'Different perspectives of international development organisations in the fight against corruption' in UNDP (ed.) *Corruption and Integrity Improvement Initiatives in Developing Countries,* New York: UNDP, 129–39.

—— (2001) 'The UNDP Integrity Improvement Initiatives' in Gerald Caiden *et al.* (eds) *Where Corruption Lives,* Bloomfield: Kumarian Press, 207–16.

Tamm-Hallström, K. (2004) *Organizing international standardization,* Cheltenham: Edward Elgar Publishing.

Tanzi, V. (1998) 'Corruption Around the World: Causes, Consequences, Scope, and Cures', *IMF Staff Papers,* 45 (4): 559–94.

Tarling, N. (2005) 'Keynote speech: Corruption' in N. Tarling (ed.) *Corruption and good governance in Asia, London,* New York: Routledge, 5–18.

Tebbutt Research (2006) *Corruption Survey,* Suva: Transparency International.

Thanh Nien News (2006) 'Former customs officer executed for corruption', Than Nien News. Online. Available HTTP: <www.thanhniennews.com/society/?catid=3& newsid=13721> (accessed 3 April 2006).

—— (2005a) 'WB privides $225 min for Vietnam's poverty reduction', 19 September. Online. Available HTTP: <www.thanhniennews.com/print.php?catid=1& newsid=9255> (accessed 21 March 2006).

—— (2005b) 'Vietnam needs to get serious in fighting corruption: donors', 7 December. Online. Available HTTP: <www.thanhniennews.com/print.php? catid=1&newsid=11071> (accessed 21 March 2006).

—— (2005c) 'New law gives PM central role in battle against corruption, 29 November. Online. Available HTTP: <www.thanhniennews.com/print.php? catid=1&newsid=10870> (accessed 21 March 2006).

—— (2005d) 'Anti-graft law needs to protect whistleblowers', 26 October. Online. Available HTTP: <www.thanhniennews.com/print.php?catid=1&newsid=10102> (accessed 21 March 2006).

—— (2005e) 'Anti-corruption bill still has loopholes: house members', 25 October. Online. Available HTTP: <www.thanhniennews.com/print.php?catid=1&newsid= 10078> (accessed 21 March 2006).

—— (2005f) 'Vietnam enacts anti-corruption law', 24 December. Online. Available HTTP: <www.thanhniennews.com/print.php?catid=1&newsid=11530> (accessed 21 March 2006).

—— (2005g) 'Vietnam officially unveils "portrait of corruption"', 30 November. Online. Available HTTP: <www.thanhniennews.com/print.php?eatid=3&newsid= 10893> (accessed 21 March 2006).

The Economist (2006) 'The World Bank. Just Saying No: Paul Wolfovitz takes on graft', *The Economist,* 378 (8467): 83.

Theobald, R. (1990) *Corruption, Development and Underdevelopment*, Basingstoke: Macmillan.

Thompson, D. F. (1995) Ethics in Congress: from individual to institutional corruption, Washington, DC: Brookings.

TI-Brussels (1999) *Working Paper: Fighting corruption, what remains to be done at the EU level.* Online. Available HTTP: <http://www.transparency.org/working_papers/country/brussels_memorandum.html#3> (accessed September 2003).

TI-Fiji Islands (2007) 'Chairman's Report presented to the 2006/7 Annual General Meeting on the 26th April 2007'. Suva: TI.

—— (2005) 'Press Release No 4/05'. Suva: Transparency International (Fiji) Ltd.

TI-Russia (2002a) *Corruption Indices for Russian Regions. Project Description*, Moscow: TI-Russia. Online. Available HTTP: <http://www.transparency.org.ru/DOC/ProjectDescriptionEng.doc> (accessed 30 March 2006).

—— (2002b) Center for Anti-corruption Research and Initiative "Transparency International – R" presents Regional Corruption Indices 2002 (in co-operation with INDEM Fund), Press release, Moscow. Online. Available HTTP: <http://www.transparency.org.ru/DOC/Presentation_index-englFinal.doc> (accessed 24 September 2003).

Time, 5 February 2007: 45.

Tisné, M. and Smilov, D. (2004) 'From the Ground Up: Assessing the Record of Anticorruption Assistance in Southeastern Europe', *Policy Studies Series*, Budapest: Center for European Policy Studies/Central European University. Online. Available HTTP: <http://www.soros.org.ba/docs_pravo/wp-anticorruption.a1.pdf> (accessed 10 October 2007).

Transparency International (2008) *Corruption Fighter's Toolkit*. Online. Available HTTP: <http://www.transparency.org/tools/e_toolkit> (accessed August 2008).

—— (2007a) 'TI's National Integrity System Approach'. Online. Available HTTP: <http://www.transparency.org/policy_research/nis> (accessed 4 December 2007).

—— (2007b) 'Corruption Perceptions Index 2007'. Online. Available HTTP: <http://www.transparency.org/policy_research/surveys_indices/cpi> (accessed 4 December 2007).

—— (2007c) Transparency International operational definition of corruptional available at HTTP: <http://www.transparency.org/about_us> (accessed 19 August 2008).

—— (2006a) *Report on the Global Corruption Barometer 2006*. Online. Available HTTP: <http://www.transparency.org/content/download/12169/115654/version/1/file/Global_Corruption_Barometer_2006_Report.pdf> (accessed 30 October 2007).

—— (2006b) *Guidelines for National Chapters of Transparency International*. Online. Available HTTP: <http://www.transparency.org/about_us/organisation/accreditation/guidelines> (accessed 19 August 2008).

—— (2005a) *Report on the Global Corruption Barometer 2005*. Online. Available HTTP: <http://www.transparency.org/content/download/2160/12762/file/Global_Corruption_Barometer_2005_(full_report).pdf> (accessed 30 October 2007).

—— (2005b) 'TI Corruption Perceptions Index 2005'. Online. Available HTTP: <www.transparency.org/policy_research/surveys_indices/cpi/2005> (accessed 21 March 2006).

—— (2004a) 'Report on the Global Corruption Barometer 2004'. Online. Available HTTP: <http://www.transparency.org/content/download/1558/8065/file/barometer_report_8_12_2004.pdf> (accessed 30 October 2007).

—— (2004b) *Global Corruption Report*, Berlin and London: Pluto Press/TI.

—— (2003a) *Transparency International Charter*. Online. Available HTTP: <http://www.transparency.org/about_us/organisation/charter> (accessed 11 December 2007).

—— (2003b) *Informe Annual 2003: La coalición contra la corrupción*, Sección Especial/ TILAC – TI en América Latina e Caribe.

—— (2003c) Transparency International Global Corruption Barometer, Berlin/ London: TI.

—— (2003d) *Global Corruption Report*, Berlin: TI. Online. Available HTTP: <http://www.transparency.org/publications/gcr> (accessed 11 December 2007).

—— (2002a) *Annual Report 2002*. Berlin: Transparency International.

—— (2002b) *Transparency International Bribe Payers Index 2002. Explanatory notes and comparative tables*. Online. Available HTTP: <http://www.transparency.org/content/download/2863/17759/file/bpi2002.en.pdf> (accessed 12 January 2005).

—— (2001) *Global Corruption Report*, Berlin: Medialis.

—— (2000) The TI Source Book: Confronting Corruption. The elements of a National Integrity System. Berlin and London: TI.

Treisman, D. (2000) 'The causes of corruption: a cross national study', *Journal of Public Economics*, 76 (3): 399–457.

Tsuboi, Y. (2005) 'Corruption in Vietnam'. Online. Available HTTP: <www.waseda-coe-cas.jp/paper/20050406_tsuboi_eng.pdf> (accessed 16 November 2005).

UK Government (2000) 'Eliminating World Poverty: Making globalisation Work for the Poor', *White Paper on International Development*. Online. Available HTTP: < http://www.dfid.gov.uk/pubs/files/whitepaper2000.pdf> (accessed 10 February 2006).

UN ESCAP (2006) 'What is Good Governance?', United Nations Economic and Social commissions for Asia and the Pacific. Online. Available HTTP: <www.unescap.org/huset/gg/governance.htm> (accessed 22 March 2006).

UNDP (2005a) 'Addressing Corruption Through Democratic Government', *UNDP Vietnam*. Online. Available HTTP: <www.undp.org.vn/undp/unews/features/05feat/03feat.htm> (accessed 12 May 2005).

—— (2005b). Institutional Arrangements to Combat Corruption: A Comparative Study. Thailand: UNDP.

—— (1997) 'Governance for sustainable human development: a UNDP policy document', *United Nations Development Programme (UNDP)*. Online. Available HTTP: <http://magnet.undp.org/policy/> (accessed 10 March 2006).

US State Department (1999) 'Globalizing the anti-corruption regime'. Online. Available HTTP: <http://www.state.gov/www/global/narcotics_law/global_forum/F340docr.pdf> (accessed 28 October 2007) *Reprinted in Trends in Organized Crime* 5 (1): 71–97, 1999.

US Administrative Procedure Act (2005), 5 USCS, Sec. 551.

US Department of Justice (2002) 'Morse Diesel Plea. Online. Available HTTP: <www.uscfc.uscourts.gov/Unpublished%20Decisions/07/BRADEN.MDI.pdf> (accessed 11 December 2007).

USAID (2003) *Strategic Plan. Fiscal years 2004–2009*. Online. Available HTTP: <http://www.usaid.gov/policy/budget/state_usaid_strat_plan.pdf> (accessed 10 February 2006).

Varese, F. (2001) The Russian Mafia. Private Protection in a New Market Economy, Oxford/NY: Oxford University Press.

Vasagar, J. and Wrong, M. (2006) Kenya gets $25m loan from World Bank despite corruption row, *The Guardian*, 26 January. Available HTTP: <http://www.guardian.co.uk/world/2006/jan/26/kenya.jeevanvasagar> (accessed August 2008).

Vasavakul, T. (2003) 'Mapping Vietnam's Legal Cultures: Reflections on Corruption, Organized Crime, and State Building in the Post-Socialist Era', manuscript.

VDR (2005) 'Vietnam Development Report 2005: Governance', Joint Donor report to the Vietnam Consultative Group Meeting, Hanoi, December 1–2, 2004.

Vestergaard, J. (2004) 'The Asian Crisis and the shaping of "Proper" economies', *Cambridge Journal of Economics*, (28): 809–27.

Vietnam News (2005) 'NA passes new laws on corruption, housing, taxes', Vietnam News 2005-11-29. Online. Available HTTP: <http://vietnamnews.vnagency.com.vn/showarticle.php?num=05POL291105> (accessed 3 April 2006).

Volkov, V. (2002) Violent Entrepreneurs. The Use of Force in the Making of Russian Capitalism, Ithaca/London: Cornell University Press.

Wade, R. (1998) 'The Asian Crisis: the high debt model versus the Wall Street-Treasury-IMF Complex', *New Left Review* 228 (March/April).

Wang, H. and Rosenau, J.N. (2001) 'Transparency International and Corruption as an Issue of Global Governance', *Global Governance*, 7: 25–49.

Waterson, S., (2007) 'Command Reformer' *Time Online*, 1 March 2007 (accessed 20 August 2008).

Wedeman, A. (1997) 'Looters, Rent-Scrapers, and Dividend Collectors: Corruption and Growth in Zaire, South Korea, and the Philippines', *The Journal of Developing Areas,* 31: 457–78.

—— (2005) 'Anticorruption Campaigns and the Intensification of Corruption in China', *Journal of Contemporary China,* 14 (42): 93–116.

Wei, S-J (2000) 'How Taxing is Corruption on International Investors', *Review of Economics and Statistics*, 82(1): 1–11.

Weick, K. (2000) *Making Sense of the Organization*, Oxford: Blackwell Business.

Williams, R. (ed.) (2000) *The Politics of Corruption*, Vol. 1, Explaining Corruption. Cheltenham: Edward Elgar.

Wilson, W. (1887) 'The Study of Administration', *Political Science Quarterly*, 2 (2): 197–222.

Woodiwiss, M. (2006) 'The American Anticorruption Experience and International Efforts against Drugs, Crime and Corruption', paper presented at the Workshop *The International Anticorruption Movement* organized by Luís de Sousa and Barry Hindess, ECPR Nicosia 25–29 April 2006 (unpublished).

World Bank (2007) 'Multi-pronged Strategies for Combating Corruption' Online. Available HTTP: <http://web.worldbank.org/WBSITE/EXTERNAL/TOPICS/EXTPUBLICSECTORANDGOVERNANCE/EXTANTICORRUPTION/0, contentMDK:20222157~menuPK:1165494~pagePK:148956~piPK:216618~theSitePK:384455,00.html> (accessed 4 December 2007).

—— (2006a) 'Anti-Corruption'. Online. Available HTTP: <http://web.worldbank.org/WBSITE/EXTERNAL/TOPICS/EXTPUBLICSECTORANDGOVERNANCE/EXTANTICORRUPTION/0,menuPK:384461~pagePK:149018~piPK:149093~theSitePK:384455,00.html> (accessed 28 February 2006).

—— (2006b) 'FAQs'. Online. Available HTTP: <http://web.worldbank.org/WBSITE/EXTERNAL/WBI/WBIPROGRAMS/PSGLP/0,menuPK:461645~pagePK:64156294~piPK:64156292~theSitePK:461606,00.html> (accessed 28 February 2006)

—— (2006c) 'Governance & Anti-Corruption', World Bank Institute homepage. Online. Available HTTP: <http://www.worldbank.org/wbi/governance/index.html> (accessed 10 February 2006).

—— (2001a) *Corruption in Romania, Annex E to Country Assistance Strategy.* Online. Available HTTP: <http://wbln0018.worldbank.org/ECC05/Unit_AR/SecDocLib.nsf/5e365d3cc97f5917852569680075c6de/B257FAAEC14192C685256A7D003665AE> (accessed 28 October 2007).

—— (2001b) *Diagnostic Surveys of Corruption in Romania.* Online. Available HTTP: <http://www1.worldbank.org/publicsector/anticorrupt/romenglish.pdf)> (accessed 24 October 2007).

—— (2000) Anti-Corruption in Transition. A contribution to the policy debate, Washington: The World Bank.

Yanitskii, O.N. (1998) 'Ekologicheskoe Dvizhenie v "Perekhodnom" Obshchestve: Problemy Teorii', *Sotsis,* 10: 22–33.

Yardley, J. (2006) 'Corruption Scandal at Top Tests Taiwan's Democracy', *New York Times,* November 25.

You, J. (2005) 'Embedded Autonomy or Crony Capitalism? Explaining Corruption in South Korea, Relative to Taiwan and the Philippines, Focussing on the Role of Land Reform and Industrial Policy', paper presented at the Annual Meeting of the Political Science Association, Washington, DC, September.

Index